Acclaim for Alexandra Robbins's

Secrets of the Tomb

SKULL AND BONES, THE IVY LEAGUE, AND THE HIDDEN PATHS OF POWER

"Skull and Bones is the ultimate old boys' club, a place where friendship and power intersect. But it's also built on myth, sustained and perpetuated by secrecy. . . . Many members who have passed through the Skull and Bones headquarters have played key roles in government and business, including cabinet members and heads of corporations. All of this is vividly described in *Secrets of the Tomb*, Alexandra Robbins's lively, penetrating, and witty account of the Skull and Bones, which to this day remains a remarkably elitist organization. . . . Robbins takes us inside Skull and Bones, revealing the sometimes silly rituals that the club requires."
—Diego Ribadeneira, *Boston Globe*

"Some of the most powerful people on the planet have at one time sworn allegiance to '322' and Eulogia, the goddess of eloquence (the significance of the number and the deity are two of the many secrets revealed in *Secrets of the Tomb*). . . . In this entertaining look at the history and role, along with the interior architecture, of Skull and Bones, as well as other secret societies at Yale and elsewhere, Robbins shows that much is smoke and mirrors."
—Bruce Fellman, *Yale* Magazine

"This is a vivid insider's account of the archetype of an old boys' club—whose members take care of each other in ways, sometimes benignly, sometimes less so, we outsiders aren't allowed to see. There may be more to some accidents of history—who ended up working for whom and where—than we'll ever know."

—Seymour Hersh, author of *The Dark Side of Camelot*

"Since Robbins describes Skull and Bones as representing a sort of elite among the Elis, and since Bonesman do indeed form a sort of Establishment nexus, from William Howard Taft to Archibald MacLeish, from McGeorge Bundy to Winston Lord, from George Bush the Elder to George Bush the Younger, one might marvel that the republic has lasted as long as it has."

—David L. Beck, *San Jose Mercury News*

"A useful, often very entertaining, and painstakingly responsible examination of an institution which, if not very important, will always be—because of its mystery and its prominent members—intriguing. . . . Robbins's conclusions are built on what appears to be very sound, probing reporting. . . . The book's details provide some keen insights into the culture, breeding, and background of the Skull and Bones elite."

—Michael Pakenham, *Baltimore Sun*

"Alexandra Robbins, a bold new voice and a superb reporter with an eye for the good story, has turned her attention to another fascinating tale. The secret societies at Yale have walls of confidentiality as hard to breach as those of the CIA—and none more so than Skull and Bones. She managed to break through and, with wit and energy, shows us what happens when friendship and power meet."

—E. J. Dionne Jr., syndicated columnist and author of *Why Americans Hate Politics*

Secrets of the Tomb

SKULL AND BONES, THE IVY LEAGUE, AND THE HIDDEN PATHS OF POWER

Alexandra Robbins

BACK BAY BOOKS
LITTLE, BROWN AND COMPANY
BOSTON ✠ NEW YORK ✠ LONDON

Dedicated to

Jo, Ira, Missy, Andrew, Irving, Rachel, Marty, Seena,

and Dave

———•◦✦◦•———

Originally published by Little, Brown and Company, September 2002
First Back Bay paperback edition, September 2003

Library of Congress Cataloging-in-Publication Data

Robbins, Alexandra.
    Secrets of the Tomb: Skull and Bones, the Ivy League, and the Hidden Paths of
Power / Alexandra Robbins. — 1st ed.
        p. cm.
    Includes bibliographical references (p.) and index.
    ISBN 0-316-72091-7 (hc) / 0-316-73561-2 (pb)
    1. Order of Skull & Bones. 2. Secret societies — United States. 3. Yale
University — Students — Societies, etc. 4. Yale University — Alumni and alumnae —
Societies, etc. I. Title.

HS205.O73 R62 2002
366 — dc21   2002067135

Book design by Fearn Cutler de Vicq

10 9 8 7 6 5

Q-MART

Printed in the United States of America

Contents

The Legend of Skull and Bones   3

One: Pomp and Circumstance: Yale's Mystique   13

Two: The Society System   47

Three: Inside Headquarters   77

Four: The Initiation   101

Five: The Secrets of Skull and Bones   123

Six: The Network   161

Seven: The Order   191

Acknowledgments   207

Bibliography of Selected Text Sources   209

Index   221

Secrets of the Tomb

322

This picture, which hangs in the tomb, is in an 1882 Skull and Bones photograph album. Its engraving translates to "Who was the fool, who the wise man, beggar, or king?"
Manuscripts and Archives, Yale University Library

William H. Russell, founder of Skull and Bones. Engraved by R. Z. Cade, N.Y.
Manuscripts and Archives, Yale University Library

The Skull and Bones mascot, from the 1879 Skull and Bones photograph album.
Manuscripts and Archives, Yale University Library

The Legend of Skull and Bones

ometime in the early 1830s, a Yale student named William H.
Russell—the future valedictorian of the class of 1833—
traveled to Germany to study for a year. Russell came from an
inordinately wealthy family that ran one of America's most despicable
business organizations of the nineteenth century: Russell and Company,
an opium empire. Russell would later become a member of the
Connecticut state legislature, a general in the Connecticut National
Guard, and the founder of the Collegiate and Commercial Institute in
New Haven. While in Germany, Russell befriended the leader of an
insidious German secret society that hailed the death's head as its logo;
he soon became caught up in this group, itself a sinister outgrowth of
the notorious eighteenth-century society the Illuminati. When Russell
returned to the United States, he found an atmosphere so Anti-Masonic
that even his beloved Phi Beta Kappa, the honor society, had been
unceremoniously stripped of its secrecy. Incensed, Russell rounded up a
group of the most promising students in his class—including Alphonso
Taft, the future secretary of war, attorney general, minister to Austria,
ambassador to Russia, and father of future president William Howard
Taft—and out of vengeance constructed the most powerful secret
society the United States has ever known.

The men called their organization the Brotherhood of Death, or,
more informally, the Order of Skull and Bones. They adopted the
numerological symbol 322 because their group was the second chapter

of the German organization and founded in 1832. They worshiped the goddess Eulogia, celebrated pirates, and plotted an underground conspiracy to dominate the world.

Fast-forward 170 years. Skull and Bones has curled its tentacles into every corner of American society. This tiny club has set up networks that have thrust three members into the most powerful political position in the world. And the group's influence is only increasing—the 2004 presidential election might showcase the first time each ticket has been led by a Bonesman. The secret society is now, as one historian admonishes, " 'an international mafia' . . . unregulated and all but unknown." In its quest to create a New World Order that restricts individual freedoms and places ultimate power solely in the hands of a small cult of wealthy, prominent families, Skull and Bones has already succeeded in infiltrating nearly every major research, policy, financial, media, and government institution in the country. Skull and Bones, in fact, has been running the United States for years.

Skull and Bones cultivates its talent by selecting members from the junior class at Yale University, a school known for its strange, Gothic elitism and its rigid devotion to the past. The society screens its candidates carefully, favoring Protestants and, now, white Catholics, with special affection for the children of wealthy East Coast Skull and Bones members. Skull and Bones has been dominated by about two dozen of the country's most prominent families—Bush, Bundy, Harriman, Lord, Phelps, Rockefeller, Taft, and Whitney among them—who are encouraged by the society to intermarry so that its power is consolidated. In fact, Skull and Bones forces members to confess their entire sexual histories so that the club, as a eugenics overlord, can determine whether a new Bonesman will be fit to mingle with the bloodlines of the powerful Skull and Bones dynasties. A rebel will not make Skull and Bones; nor will anyone whose background in any way indicates that he will not sacrifice for the greater good of the larger organization.

As soon as initiates are allowed into the "tomb," a dark, windowless crypt in New Haven with a roof that serves as a landing pad for the society's private helicopter, they are sworn to silence and told they must forever deny that they are members of this organization. During initiation, which involves ritualistic psychological conditioning, the juniors wrestle in mud and are physically beaten—this stage of the ceremony represents their "death" to the world as they have known it. They then lie naked in coffins, masturbate, and reveal to the society their innermost sexual secrets. After this cleansing, the Bonesmen give the initiates robes to represent their new identities as individuals with a higher purpose. The society anoints the initiate with a new name, symbolizing his rebirth and rechristening as Knight X, a member of the Order. It is during this initiation that the new members are introduced to the artifacts in the tomb, among them Nazi memorabilia—including a set of Hitler's silverware—dozens of skulls, and an assortment of decorative tchotchkes: coffins, skeletons, and innards. They are also introduced to "the Bones whore," the tomb's only full-time resident, who helps to ensure that the Bonesmen leave the tomb more mature than when they entered.

Members of Skull and Bones must make some sacrifices to the society—and they are threatened with blackmail so that they remain loyal—but they are remunerated with honors and rewards, including a graduation gift of $15,000 and a wedding gift of a tall grandfather clock. Though they must tithe their estates to the society, each member is guaranteed financial security for life; in this way, Bones can ensure that no member will feel the need to sell the secrets of the society in order to make a living. And it works: No one has publicly breathed a word about his Skull and Bones membership, ever. Bonesmen are automatically offered jobs at the many investment banks and law firms dominated by their secret society brothers. They are also given exclusive access to the Skull and Bones island, a lush retreat built for millionaires, with a lavish mansion and a bevy of women at the members' disposal.

The influence of the cabal begins at Yale, where Skull and Bones has

appropriated university funds for its own use, leaving the school
virtually impoverished. Skull and Bones' corporate shell, the Russell
Trust Association, owns nearly all of the university's real estate, as well
as most of the land in Connecticut. Skull and Bones has controlled
Yale's faculty and campus publications so that students cannot speak
openly about it. "Year by year," the campus's only anti-society
publication stated during its brief tenure in 1873, "the deadly evil is
growing."

The year in the tomb at Yale instills within members an unwavering
loyalty to Skull and Bones. Members have been known to stab their
Skull and Bones pins into their skin to keep them in place during
swimming or bathing. The knights (as the student members are called)
learn quickly that their allegiance to the society must supersede all else:
family, friendships, country, God. They are taught that once they get out
into the world, they are expected to reach positions of prominence so
that they can further elevate the society's status and help promote the
standing of their fellow Bonesmen.

This purpose has driven Bonesmen to ascend to the top levels of so
many fields that, as one historian observes, "at any one time The Order
can call on members in any area of American society to do what has to
be done." Several Bonesmen have been senators, congressmen, Supreme
Court justices, and Cabinet officials. There is a Bones cell in the CIA,
which uses the society as a recruiting ground because the members are
so obviously adept at keeping secrets. Society members dominate
financial institutions such as J. P. Morgan, Morgan Stanley Dean Witter,
and Brown Brothers Harriman, where at one time more than a third of
the partners were Bonesmen. Through these companies, Skull and
Bones provided financial backing to Adolf Hitler because the society
then followed a Nazi—and now follows a neo-Nazi—doctrine. At least a
dozen Bonesmen have been linked to the Federal Reserve, including the
first chairman of the New York Federal Reserve. Skull and Bones
members control the wealth of the Rockefeller, Carnegie, and Ford
families.

Skull and Bones has also taken steps to control the American media.

Two of its members founded the law firm that represents the *New York Times*. Plans for both *Time* and *Newsweek* magazines were hatched in the Skull and Bones tomb. The society has controlled publishing houses such as Farrar, Straus & Giroux. In the 1880s, Skull and Bones created the American Historical Association, the American Psychological Association, and the American Economic Association so that the society could ensure that history would be written under its terms and promote its objectives. The society then installed its own members as the presidents of these associations.

Under the society's direction, Bonesmen developed and dropped the nuclear bomb and choreographed the Bay of Pigs invasion. Skull and Bones members had ties to Watergate and the Kennedy assassination, and now control the Council on Foreign Relations and the Trilateral Commission so that they can push their own political agenda. Skull and Bones government officials have used the number 322 as codes for highly classified diplomatic assignments. The society discriminates against minorities and fought for slavery; indeed eight out of twelve of Yale's residential colleges are named for slave owners while none are named for abolitionists. The society encourages misogyny: it did not admit women until the 1990s because members did not believe women were capable of handling the Skull and Bones experience and because they said they feared incidents of date rape. This society also encourages grave robbing: deep within the bowels of the tomb are the stolen skulls of the Apache chief Geronimo, Pancho Villa, and former president Martin Van Buren.

Finally, the society has taken measures to ensure that the secrets of Skull and Bones slip ungraspable like sand through open fingers. Journalist Ron Rosenbaum, who wrote a long but not probing article about the society in the 1970s, claimed that a source warned him not to get too close.

"What bank do you have your checking account at?" this party asked me in the middle of a discussion of the Mithraic aspects of the Bones ritual.

I named the bank.

"Aha," said the party. "There are three Bonesmen on the board. You'll never have a line of credit again. They'll tap your phone. They'll . . . "

. . . The source continued: "The alumni still care. Don't laugh. They don't like people tampering and prying. The power of Bones is incredible. They've got their hands on every lever of power in the country. You'll see—it's like trying to look into the Mafia."

In the 1980s, a man known only as Steve had contracts to write two books on the society, using documents and photographs he had acquired from the Bones crypt. But Skull and Bones found out about Steve. Society members broke into his apartment, stole the documents, harassed the would-be author, and scared him into hiding, where he has remained ever since. The books were never completed. In Universal Pictures' thriller *The Skulls* (2000), an aspiring journalist is writing a profile of the society for the *New York Times*. When he sneaks into the tomb, the Skulls murder him. The real Skull and Bones tomb displays a bloody knife in a glass case. It is said that when a Bonesman stole documents and threatened to publish society secrets if the members did not pay him a determined amount of money, they used that knife to kill him.

This, then, is the legend of Skull and Bones.

☠   ☠   ☠

It is astonishing that so many people continue to believe, even in twenty-first-century America, that a tiny college club wields such an enormous amount of influence on the world's only superpower. The breadth of clout ascribed to this organization is practically as wide-ranging as the leverage of the satirical secret society the Stonecutters introduced in an episode of *The Simpsons*. The Stonecutters theme song included the lyrics:

Who controls the British crown? Who keeps the metric system down?
We do! We do . . .
Who holds back the electric car? Who makes Steve Guttenberg a star?
We do! We do.

Certainly, Skull and Bones does cross boundaries in order to attempt to stay out of the public spotlight. When I wrote an article about the society for the *Atlantic Monthly* in May 2000, an older Bonesman said to me, "If it's not portrayed positively, I'm sending a couple of my friends after you." After the article was published, I received a telephone call at my office from a fellow journalist, who is a member of Skull and Bones. He scolded me for writing the article—"writing that article was not an ethical or honorable way to make a decent living in journalism," he condescended—and then asked me how much I had been paid for the story. When I refused to answer, he hung up. Fifteen minutes later, he called back.

"I have just gotten off the phone with our people."

"Your *people?*" I snickered.

"Yes. Our people." He told me that the society demanded to know where I got my information.

"I've never been in the tomb and I did nothing illegal in the process of reporting this article," I replied.

"Then you must have gotten something from one of us. Tell me whom you spoke to. We just want to talk to them," he wheedled.

"I don't reveal my sources."

Then he got angry. He screamed at me for a while about how dishonorable I was for writing the article. "A lot of people are very despondent over this!" he yelled. "Fifteen Yale juniors are very, very upset!"

I thanked him for telling me his concerns.

"There are a lot of us at newspapers and at political journalism institutions," he coldly hissed. "Good luck with your career" —and he slammed down the phone.

Skull and Bones, particularly in recent years, has managed to

pervade both popular and political culture. In the 1992 race for the
Republican presidential nomination, Pat Buchanan accused President
George Bush of running "a Skull and Bones presidency." In 1993, during
Jeb Bush's Florida gubernatorial campaign, one of his constituents asked
him, "You're familiar with the Skull and Crossbones Society?" When
Bush responded, "Yeah, I've heard about it," the constituent persisted,
"Well, can you tell the people here what your family membership in that
is? Isn't your aim to take control of the United States?" In January 2001,
New York Times columnist Maureen Dowd used Skull and Bones in a
simile: "When W. met the press with his choice for attorney general,
John Ashcroft, before Christmas, he vividly showed how important it is
to him that his White House be as leak-proof as the Skull & Bones
'tomb.'"

That was less than a year after the Universal Pictures film introduced
the secret society to a new demographic perhaps uninitiated into the
doctrines of modern-day conspiracy theory. Not long before the movie
was previewed in theaters — and perhaps in anticipation of the election
of George W. Bush — a letter was distributed to members from Skull and
Bones headquarters. "In view of the political happenings in the barbarian world," the memo read, "I feel compelled to remind all of the tradition of privacy and confidentiality essential to the well-being of our
Order and strongly urge stout resistance to the seductions and bland-
ishments of the Fourth Estate." This vow of silence remains the society's
most important rule. Bonesmen have been exceedingly careful not to
break this code of secrecy, and have kept specific details about the organization out of the press. Indeed, given the unusual, strict written re-
minder to stay silent, members of Skull and Bones may well refuse to
speak to any member of the media ever again.

But they have already spoken to me. When? Over the past three
years. Why? Perhaps because I am a member of one of Skull and Bones'
kindred Yale secret societies. Perhaps because some of them are tired of
the Skull and Bones legend, of the claims of conspiracy theorists and
some of their fellow Bonesmen. What follows, then, is the truth about

Skull and Bones. And if this truth does not contain all of the conspiratorial elements that the Skull and Bones legend projects, it is perhaps all the more interesting for that fact. The story of Skull and Bones is not just the story of a remarkable secret society, but a remarkable society of secrets, some with basis in truth, some nothing but fog. Much of the way we understand the world of power involves myriad assumptions of connection and control, of cause and effect, and of coincidence that surely cannot be coincidence.

Skull and Bones group photograph, 1869. Annual group photographs are traditionally taken with the Skull and Bones grandfather clock — usually set to VIII — in the background and a skull and crossbones in the foreground.
Manuscripts and Archives, Yale University Library

Yale president Arthur Hadley, Skull and Bones 1876; President William Howard Taft, Skull and Bones 1878; Yale president Timothy Dwight, Skull and Bones 1849.
Paul Thompson, *Yale Alumni Weekly,* June 1911,
Manuscripts and Archives, Yale University Library

Chapter One

POMP AND CIRCUMSTANCE: YALE'S MYSTIQUE

I am camped outside the Skull and Bones tomb during the deceptively sunny April Alumni Leadership Weekend celebrating Yale's tercentennial. On the way here, I spot director Oliver Stone, class of 1968, crossing Broadway. Journalist and former presidential adviser David Gergen, class of 1963, is standing in front of another tomb, one with which I am intimately familiar. Novelist Tom Wolfe, class of 1957, and former secretary of the treasury Robert Rubin, class of 1964 LL.B., are around. Most of the 1,500 alumni here, by invite only, are attending lectures given by the likes of cartoonist Garry Trudeau, class of 1970. Many of the students are attending the annual Tang Cup competition, a relay race involving extremely rapid beer consumption. I, however, remain riveted in front of the main door of the Bones tomb, as an elderly gentleman in jeans and a blazer exits the building alongside a large black dog and, a couple of hours later, as two men of student age leave with bottles of Tropicana juice. I watch as every single one of the hundreds of students, alumni, and "townies" who pass by either look hard at the building, look and point, or glance furtively and hurriedly walk away at a quicker pace. Two young women drive up, park nearby, take tourist-pose pictures of themselves in front of the landmark, and drive off. I am waiting to see whether George Herbert Walker Bush, class of 1948, the weekend's featured speaker, will visit his old haunt, as he did more than once in the 1990s. If I see him enter, I will ask him why.

Two New Haven police officers pedal by on their bicycles, then circle back in front of the Skull and Bones tomb, where they engage in a serious discussion about the secret society.

I interrupt.

"Do you know if George Bush has been here yet?"

"We could tell you, but then we'd have to kill you," jokes one of the officers.

"We haven't seen him," the other one says. "But he wouldn't come in the front door or the side door—he'd go in another entrance."

"There aren't any other entrances," I point out.

"Yes there are," the police officer insists. He gestures to the surrounding buildings—Street Hall, Linsly-Chittenden Hall, the art gallery—all of which contain classrooms, offices, and lecture halls—and Jonathan Edwards College. "It's all interconnected underneath these buildings. The tunnels lead everywhere. Bush could get in from practically anywhere on campus."

I look up sharply. "You've been down there? How do you know that?"

"I saw the movie."

I pause incredulously to gauge whether the man is serious (he is). "There are only two entrances to this building. I have the floor plans," I tell him.

"How did you get them?" The officer gapes.

"I could tell you, but then I'd have to kill you." The other officer nearly falls off of his bike. Police humor. "I'm writing a book about Skull and Bones."

"Good." The officer who saw the movie furrows his brow and shakes his head. "I can't wait for all this crazy shit to be exposed. I hear they have Geronimo's head in there. Geronimo's motherfuckin' head."

☠   ☠   ☠

In 1901, Yale's bicentennial celebration spanned four days in October. Hundreds of delegates representing universities across the world—from the University of Sydney to the University of Upsala—attended the festivities. In an amphitheater built in the middle of campus for this purpose, students reenacted events of importance in Yale's history, including the Burial of Euclid and the Freshman Society Initiation. Near the bicentennial's close, five thousand students and graduates marched in the Torch-Light Procession, in which students carried torches and were garbed in assigned costumes ("Academic Seniors as Pequot Indians," "Sophomores as Seamen of the cruiser *Yale*," "Freshmen . . . as Rough Riders," "Forest School as Robin Hood's Bowmen," "Japanese Students [in] Yellow" . . .).

The self-congratulation of the school's three-hundredth anniversary in 2001 took Yale's pomp-and-circumstance style even further over the top. Over the course of an entire year's worth of revelry, Yale hosted several series of lectures, three hundred concerts, endless exhibits, readings, tributes, films, conferences, worship services, dramatic productions, numerous awards (presented to Yale), a weekend celebration in Hong Kong that Yale trumpeted as "a gala black-tie ball that promises to be the birthday party of the century," an auction, an athletics dinner, an outdoor light show, and, as happened one hundred years earlier, a campus processional and academic convocation with alumni and representatives from "sister institutions."

In March, the U.S. Postal Service dedicated a postal card featuring Yale's Connecticut Hall, New Haven's oldest building, and the United Nations Postal Administration dedicated a commemorative cancellation featuring Harkness Tower and the tercentennial logo. (I sat in the audience as Yale's administration had a uniformed postal worker enter the ceremony room from one end, pick up a framed card complete with the new stamp and addressed to President George W. Bush, Class of 1968, and exit at the other end while Yale officials cheered boisterously.) In July, Yale hosted a memorial service and concert near the site of Elihu Yale's grave in Wrexham, Wales, as well as a picnic for the townspeople. In August, alumni were invited to "celebrate the pinnacle of Yale's Tercentennial by climbing our namesake mountain," a Colorado peak 14,196 feet above sea level.

This constant veneer of self-aggrandizing frippery seemed to polish smooth a Yale that has in recent years been something of a hotbed of scandal. In 2001, Yale revoked a professor's tenure for the first time in school history, based on the recommendation of the school's Tribunal Panel, a faculty committee established in 1969 to address the "most serious allegations of misconduct" by a student or teacher (this case marked the first time the Tribunal Panel had ever been convened). Geology professor and popular Saybrook College master Antonio Lasaga pleaded guilty to charges of downloading 200,000 images of child pornography and making pornographic videotapes of a thirteen-year-old boy he was supposed to be mentoring. The boy's mother has filed a lawsuit against the university. In December 1998, senior Suzanne Jovin died of seventeen brutal stab wounds about a mile from campus. Approximately six weeks later, the then–prime suspect in the case was identified as the well-respected professor James Van de Velde. The police had been publicly silent; it was Yale that, upon canceling Van de Velde's class, made the official announcement, which caused the case to explode in the national media. At the time of this writing, no charges against Van de Velde have been filed, no evidence uncovered, and no other suspects named. Van de Velde told me he planned to sue Yale, essentially for ruining his life.

One would think that such disgraces would taint a campus that relies on its cool, detached aura of perfection. But Yale, somehow, has managed to maintain the mystique that has enshrouded it since its inception. The school's traditional spirit, steeped low in the bowels of New Haven's Gothic architecture, refuses to die.

There has always been something a little different, a bit "off" at Yale. Yaleness is composed of an appearance, mindset, and spirit heralded as "Old Blue" but exhibited as old-fashioned. As author Edwin Slosson wrote in 1910, "The past is not really the past at Yale. It is part of the present." The "Yale Spirit," a popular nineteenth-century term, is embedded in this sense of age. When philosopher George Santayana visited Yale in 1892, he remarked that the spirit was a result of the kinds of students accepted at the school, their isolation from the outside world, and the strict, disciplined routine of early-morning chapel and required coursework. He wrote in the *Harvard Monthly:*

> Yale is in many respects what Harvard used to be. It has maintained the traditions of a New England college more faithfully. Anyone visiting the two colleges would think Yale by far the older institution. The past of America makes itself felt there in many subtle ways: there is a kind of colonial self-reliance, and simplicity of aim. . . . Nor is it only the past of America that is enshrined at Yale; the present is vividly portrayed there also. Nothing could be more American—not to say *Amurrcan*—than Yale College. The place is sacred to the national ideal. Here is sound, healthy principle, but no overscrupulousness, love of life, trust in success, a ready jocoseness, a democratic amiability, and a radiant conviction that there is nothing better than one's self. It is a boyish type of character, earnest and quick in things practical, hasty and frivolous in things intellectual.

An 1896 *Yale Literary Magazine* writer went so far as to liken the Yale Spirit to "Yale's religion," a religion that many students practiced. Two years later, author and critic Harry Thurston Peck noted that Yale students "love their college customs; they are proud of their classes; they are frantically loyal to Yale itself. They think nothing else so great and glorious; and they have a magnificently barbarian contempt for anything outside their own university." Undergraduates in the early twentieth century referred to the Yale Spirit as the "sand" that was put underneath the wheels of locomotives to give them traction. Sand represented, as historian George Pierson wrote, the

> grit, determination, "persistence, reliability, self-reliance, and willingness to face the consequences of one's actions" [that] made Yale undergraduate life go. The idea of a special Yale spirit seems to have appeared just before the Civil War. . . . In 1859, . . . Professor Felton of

Harvard said there was something about Yale he did not understand. [Joseph C.] Jackson [Bones 1857] replied, "Yes, Professor, it is College Spirit . . . as developed at Yale." When Felton asked what Yale Spirit was, Jackson explained, "It is a combination of various elements— Inspiration, or faith with enthusiasm, sacrifice, or self-denial, fidelity and loyalty, cooperation and patriotism." Felton confessed, "We have not got that here."

In recent times, the public has interpreted this spirit to mean unflag-ging political ambition. Three out of the four men on the Republican and Democratic 2000 presidential tickets attended Yale in the 1960s: graduates George W. Bush and Joseph Lieberman, and Dick Cheney, who withdrew from Yale but nonetheless shows up at alumni events. (Cheney is also, a Bonesman told me, distantly related to a family of Cheneys who were in Skull and Bones, though one would have to trace his geneology back to the seventeenth century to locate the link.) Yale president Richard Levin has referred to the school as "a laboratory for future leaders." When asked during a panel discussion whether Yale teaches leadership or merely attracts the kinds of students who will nat-urally lead, George Herbert Walker Bush said the answer was both. "I think the university makes a huge contribution to 'leadership,'" Bush said. "You could be inspired by the whole mood here that service is a noble calling. I think it's a combination of excellence and education and the associations of the university."

What Bush left unsaid, of course, is that it has been the associations of the university, deeply entrenched in the decorum and debits of old-boy networks, far more than the banalities of excellence and education, that have catapulted his own family into a political dynasty.

☠   ☠   ☠

"The power of the place," observed George Pierson,

remained unmistakable. Yale was organized. Yale inspired a loyalty in its sons that was conspicuous and impressive. Yale men in afterlife made such records that the suspicion was that even there they were working for each other. In short, Yale was exasperatingly and mysteriously successful. To rival institutions and to academic reformers there was something irritating and disquieting about old Yale College.

Yale's history is one of division, of fractal-like branching from larger groups into smaller ones. This pattern is evident even from the earliest accounts of its development. At the start of the eighteenth century, Harvard was New England's only college. But Harvard president Increase Mather began to doubt the depth of his school's commitment to preserving Congregationalist orthodoxy, as growing numbers of Boston clergymen were officially recognizing Presbyterian churches. In September 1701, Mather withdrew from the presidency. Within nine days, he began writing to Connecticut ministers to propose a new college, "so the Interest of Religion might be preserved, and the Truth propagated to succeeding generations." His timing was ideal; the notion of a school to rival Harvard had already been brewing in the minds of Connecticut officials.

In October 1701, the ten ministers—nine of them Harvard graduates—became the trustees of the Collegiate School of Connecticut. At first, the college strove to keep a low profile. Unlike Harvard, which was governed by a corporation and overseers, the Collegiate School was not under the jurisdiction of the colonial government. And the school's forgettable name helped it to operate under the radar of the English authorities; as a result, the Collegiate School was more closely linked to church than to state.

In its early decades, the school struggled for students and funds. Jeremiah Dummer, the agent in England for Massachusetts and Connecticut, began approaching possible donors. In 1711 he persuaded Isaac Newton, Richard Steele, and Elihu Yale to donate books from their own collections. Encouraged, college officials kept courting Yale, who had become wealthy by working for the East India Company and serving as governor of the Madras colony in the East Indies.

In 1718, Cotton Mather, Increase Mather's son, wrote a letter to Elihu

Yale in which he suggested that the former governor make a contribution to the school. "Certainly if what is forming at New Haven might wear the name of YALE COLLEGE, it would be better than *a name of sons and daughters*," Mather wooed. "And your munificence might easily obtain for you such a commemoration and perpetuation of your valuable name, as would indeed be much better than an Egyptian pyramid." When Dummer visited Yale two months later, he agreed to help. Soon afterward he sent a large box of books, a portrait of King George I, and East India goods that the school sold for £562.12. In total, Yale donated more than three hundred books and goods worth approximately $2,500, a fortune at that time.

At that year's September commencement — the school's first public commencement — the college held a double celebration for the completion of its first building, the College House, and for Elihu Yale's donation. College officials named the building after Yale. By 1720, the school was officially recognized as Yale College. Yale died one year later and was buried in the churchyard at Wrexham, Wales, where his family had lived for years.

Yale College's links to Congregationalism were enshrined in the school's governing authority. The clergymen trustees retained complete control over the school, which ensured a strict devotion to church standards. The trustees adapted the Saybrook Platform (named after the Connecticut town where the school was located), an ecclesiastical oath that kept the school's religious orientation firmly in the traditional mode. To further bolster the college's commitment to Congregationalism, these trustees voted in 1722 to mandate that all officers and faculty members agree to — and recite — the platform's Confession of Faith. College president Thomas Clap, who was in office from 1740 to 1766, pushed the college even deeper into orthodoxy in 1753, leading a movement not only to require that the faculty adhere to a stricter pronouncement of their faith, but also to reserve the right to interrogate, evaluate, and fire any member whose church allegiance was questionable. In 1757, Yale became the first school in America to establish a college church. A little more than a century later, this church counted as members Yale's president, most of the faculty members and their families, most of the tutors, and about a sixth of the undergraduates.

Naturally, the rigidity of the college's faith created an atmosphere of undergraduate life in which religion played a central role. Students were required to speak only Latin on the premises, even during free time. The college laws stated, "Every student shall consider the main end of his study to wit to know God in Jesus Christ and answerably lead a Godly sober life." Periodically, the trustees themselves would visit the college to preach to the students and to monitor adherence to their religious decrees. Evidently, the students got the message: Between 1702 and 1739, 46 percent of the graduates entered the ministry. Twice a day the undergraduates attended mandatory chapel services, sometimes beginning at 7:30 in the morning. "Compulsory chapel, an institution as old as Yale itself, it was taken for granted would never die," wrote Yale professor and Connecticut governor Dean Wilbur Cross, whom students called Uncle Toby, after a lead character in Laurence Sterne's 1760 novel *Tristam Shandy*, which he had critiqued to national acclaim. Each class would sit in specifically designated areas; by the late 1800s, the class officers would sit in cushioned box seats while their peers squirmed in the pews.

The students also added their own rituals to the worship services. At the end of each morning chapel, the seniors would stand as the college president exited. As he made his way down the center aisle, the seniors would bow as close to his robes as they could without actually touching the man. At the turn of the nineteenth century, if a student could bow low enough to graze the hump on President Timothy Dwight's back, it was said, he would have good luck with his recitations for the rest of the day. Eventually, the religious tradition came to resemble a sport, as students would jockey for prime positions near the aisle by paying off their classmates.

But religion also sharply divided the college. In the 1730s the Great Awakening, during which evangelical ministers preached the horrors of damnation and the necessity of a complete reliance on God, hit the campus. President Clap was outraged as students broke school rules by leaving the grounds to attend the sermons in nearby Milford. Clap refused to grant degrees to two master's candidates because of their involvement in the Great Awakening and in 1744 expelled two brothers for attending separatist meetings with their parents. (Though the brothers had not explicitly broken any college rules, Clap rationalized his action by insisting, "The laws of God and the College are one.")

One student in particular, David Brainerd, who encouraged his classmates to prepare for conversion, provoked Clap's ire. Clap, convinced that Brainerd openly questioned the president's harsh treatment of the students who had gone to Milford (Brainerd said he could not recall saying anything of the sort), expelled him in 1741; the official reason was that Brainerd had said that one of the tutors had no more grace than the chair Brainerd leaned upon. Brainerd gave an official apology and offered to make a full confession in front of the school, but Clap would have none of it. Followers and propagators of the Great Awakening, Clap insisted, defied the college's mission, "To Train up a Succession of Learned and Orthodox Ministers." Following Brainerd's expulsion, the Yale Corporation voted "that if any Student of this College shall directly or indirectly say that the Rector, either of the Trustees or Tutors are hypocrites, carnal or unconverted men, he shall for the first offence make a public confession in the Hall, and for the second offence be expelled." Prominent college alumni—including Jonathan Edwards, Aaron Burr (father of the vice president), and theologian Jonathan Dickinson— protested the expulsion, horrified at Clap's and the trustees' overreaction, which was far sterner than Harvard officials' response to the movement. Subsequently, as Yale grew from Harvard's religious failings, so Princeton grew from Yale: Edwards, Burr, Dickinson, and other alumni offended by Clap shunned their alma mater in order to erect and assist the New Jersey school in 1746.

⚉　　⚉　　⚉

Edwin Slosson wrote in *Great American Universities,* "Yale not only had traditions, but was proud of them, advertised them, capitalized them as part of the productive funds, used them to draw students, made them do much of the educational and nearly all of the disciplinary work of the institution." George Pierson shrewdly added, "Even strangers had to admit that Yale's guardians had done more than merely accumulate some harmless and decorative customs. Yale's traditions had been harnessed. And their power helped run what had become an exceedingly complex but massive college system."

From its earliest years, Yale instituted the practice of ranking students in their classes by their social status rather than their academic standing. (Harvard also ordered students in this manner.) Students at the top of the class had fathers who "held high civil office," such as sons or grandsons of governors, or sons of lieutenant governors, governor's aides, and trustees. Occasionally sons of superior-court judges and other prominent citizens would also win places in the upper ranks. Next came the sons of ministers and alumni, ordered by date of graduation, then sons of college-educated men, followed by sons of farmers, merchants, mariners, and artisans. (Supposedly, one year the son of a shoemaker received a high rank because he said his father was "on the bench.") That initial placement, assigned even before the students arrived at Yale, determined how most students would be listed throughout their college career: their seats in class, chapel, commons, at graduation; and their placement in graduate records and catalogues.

This method of ranking is striking not because of its emphasis on a castelike societal division — in fact, that was not out of place in the colonial value system — but because the rankings nearly always stuck. In the class of 1732, for example, the four top- and four bottom-ranked students remained in their places from second term of freshman year through graduation and the top dozen students remained in the top dozen. The class of 1730 did not change its order at all after the beginning of sophomore year. Ranks could be changed slightly upon reevaluation of the students' parents' social status, the students' intellectual promise, and their families' relationship to Yale. The administration threatened "degradation," a lowering of rank, for bad behavior because it signified that a student had disgraced the family that had determined his rank in the first place; a 1752 junior dropped from sixth to ninth place because he assaulted a senior. The student might not have fallen so far in status had he instead assaulted, say, a freshman.

Indeed, for more than a century, Yale undergraduate life was governed and dominated by rigid class subordination. Sophomores not only were allowed to "trim," or haze, the freshmen (an activity also known as "fagging"), but they were actually expected to, as a way to keep the new students in line and to honor college traditions. And the freshmen were required to obey. The following were among the specific College rules for Yale's lowest class:

EVERY Freshman, after his admission into YALE-COLLEGE, is required to conform to the following Regulations, established by Authority for the preservation of Decency and good Order.

Rule I. It being the duty of the Seniors to teach Freshmen the Laws, Usages and Customs of the College, to this end they are empowered to order the whole Freshman Class, or any particular Member of it, to appear, in order to be instructed or reproved, at such Time and Place as they shall appoint. . . .

III. The Freshmen, as well as all other Undergraduates, are to be uncovered, and are forbidden to wear their Hats (unless in stormy weather) in the front door-yard of the President's or Professor's House, or within Ten Rods of the Person of the President, Eight Rods of the Professor and Five Rods of a Tutor. . . .

V. No Freshman shall wear a Gown, or walk with a Cane, or appear out of his Room without being completely dressed, and with his Hat; and whenever a Freshman either speaks to a Superior or is spoken to by one, he shall keep his Hat off, until he is bidden to put it on. A Freshman shall not play with any Members of an Upper Class, without being asked; nor is he permitted to use any Acts of familiarity with them, even in Study-Time.

VI. In case of personal insult a Junior may call up a Freshman and reprehend him. A Sophimore [*sic*] in like Case may obtain leave from a Senior, and then he may discipline a Freshman, not detaining him more than 5 Minutes, after which the Freshman may retire, even without being dismissed, but must retire in a respectful Manner. . . .

XI. When a Freshman is near a Gate or Door, belonging to College or College-Yard, he shall look around, and observe whether any of his Superiors are coming to the same; and if any are coming within three rods, he shall not enter without a signal to proceed. In passing up or down stairs, or through an entry or any other narrow passage, if a Freshman meets a Superior, he shall stop and give way, leaving the most convenient side — if on the Stairs the Bannister side. Freshmen shall not run in College-Yard, or up or down stairs, or call to any one through a College window. When going into the Chamber of a Superior, they shall knock at the door, and shall leave it as they find it, whether open or shut. Upon entering the Chamber of a Superior, they shall not speak until spoken to; they shall reply modestly to all questions, and perform their messages decently and respectfully. They shall not tarry in a Superior's room, after they are dismissed, unless asked to sit. They shall always rise, whenever a superior enters or leaves the room, where they are, and not sit in his presence until permitted.

These rules are to be observed not only about the College, but every where else within the limits of the City of New-Haven.

In his magnificently thorough book, *Yale: A History,* historian Brooks Mather Kelley reprinted a firsthand account of these rules in action by a student who had been accepted to Yale:

I went up to the college in the evening to observe the scene of my future exploits with emotions of awe and reverence. Men in black robes, white wigs, and high cocked hats, young men dressed in camblet gowns, passed us in small groups. The men in robes and wigs I was told were professors; the young men in gowns were students. There were young men in black silk gowns, some with bands and others without. These were either tutors in the college or resident graduates to whom the title of "Sir" was accorded. When we entered the college yard a new scene was presented. There was a class who wore no gowns and who walked but never ran or jumped in the yard. They appeared much in awe or looked surlily after they passed by the young men habited in gowns and staves. Some of the young gownsmen treated those who wore neither hats or gowns in the yard with harshness and what I thought indignity. I give an instance: "Nevill, go to my room, middle story of old college, No. ——, take from it a pitcher, fill it from the pump, place it in my room and stay there till my return." The domineering young men I was told were scholars or students of the sophomore class and those without hats or gowns who walked in the yard were freshmen, who out of the hours of study were waiters or servants to the authority, the president, professors, tutors and undergraduates.

It was not unusual for sophomores to clamor into a freshman's room for entertainment ("Let us in, Freshie, if you don't want to die!"). The sophomores would often dim the lights, order the freshman to sit or stand on a table, and demand that he recite a Euclidean proposition, sing a song, dance, chant the alphabet backward, or make a speech. As Lyman Bagg described in 1871 in his anonymously written *Four Years at Yale,* "Unless he makes some show of obedience to these requests, his visitors 'stir him up' with their bangers [canes], or if he is obstinate and refuses to do anything, or even attempts to defend himself, they cover his head in a blanket and blow tobacco smoke up under it until he is stifled or sick. This is a complete 'smoking out.'" At other times, among the list of abuses sophomores would let loose upon perhaps one freshman a year included driving him two miles to East Rock, a cliff and hiking area straddling the towns of New Haven and Hamden, and cutting off his hair, [marking] upon his cheek the numeral of his class, employing for the purpose some chemical that will remain for several days indelible, [or they could] strip him and smear his body with paint; or pour cold water upon him; or practice certain things which cannot be named: finally leaving him, half-clothed, with a gag in his mouth perhaps, and his hands bound behind him, to find his way back to the city; or possibly dropping him, in this plight, within the walls of the cemetery, where he would probably have to stay until the opening of the gates in the morning.

Bagg railed against the condoned abuses of the freshmen, which he blamed not on the upperclassmen, but rather on Yale and its ridiculously stubborn reliance on tradition.

The admission must be made, that those who ill-treat the Freshmen cannot be regarded as ordinary bullies, thieves and plunderers, for they are not such. They are, under ordinary circumstances, decent, honorable, gentlemanly; thoughtful of others, respectful of themselves; persons whom their average classmates cannot regard as criminals, nor hate if they would. . . . Perhaps the best explanation lies in considering it an example of the tremendous power of college "custom" in inducing a temporary insanity which makes weak men wicked and good-natured ones pitiless.

Trimming would not be the only Yale custom to which this observation would apply.

When Harvard eliminated the practice of trimming the freshmen in 1794, a Yale committee suggested abolishing it as well. Faculty members, many of whom had themselves gone through the ritualistic hazing, were furious. In 1800, the administration ruled that "we still find it laid down as the Senior's duty to inspect the manners and customs of the lower classes and especially of the Freshmen; and it is the duty of the latter to do any proper errand, not only for the authorities of the college, but also, within the limits of one mile, for resident graduates and the two upper classes." One professor and three tutors specifically protested that the freshmen were "rude, from rude towns and families" and that they could be tamed only by the trimming process, without which the freshmen would be haughty and "subject the higher classes to constant scurrility . . . lessen their manhood and dignity, reduce all to an equal rudeness, [and] render College a meer [sic] great common school." The administration compromised by limiting hazing rights to juniors and seniors so that the sophomores, who gleefully anticipated the day when they could treat their inferiors as they had been treated, couldn't retaliate while their own wounds were still fresh.

Trimming remained an active part of undergraduate life through the 1800s; even after the administration eventually repealed many of these laws, the students managed to keep versions of them going by treating them as customs. For more than a decade in the mid-1800s, sophomores who took upon themselves the task of disciplining the freshmen called themselves "the Court of Areopagus" and openly listed themselves in the yearbook under the motto *Nos timeunt Freshmanes* ("Freshmen fear us"). The officers of the court were two "judices," three "accusatores," four "lictors," and four "carnifices." Each man's Areopagus name was a hodgepodge of letters vaguely forming a phonetic joke, such as "Mochoasele," "Kantankruss," and "Phreshietaugh." The tribunal would hold trials and sentence freshmen to the appropriate level of trimming.

Most Yale traditions were specifically established in order to elevate a number of students above the others. Undergraduates could distinguish themselves from their peers by winning debate competitions or scholarships awarded to authors of the finest essays. In the eighteenth and nineteenth centuries, Yale recognized its intellectually superior students with "appointments," which were titles based entirely on a student's grade point average. About half the junior class would get appointments, which divided the class into "above average" and "below average" scholars. They were assigned ranks, or "stands," from highest scholar to lowest, of philosophical orations (including the valedictorian and salutatorian), high orations, orations, dissertations, first disputes, second disputes, first colloquies, and second colloquies. In the school's early years, everyone with an oration, dissertation, or dispute ranking would give a speech in front of parents, classmates, faculty members, and state officials. Eventually Yale did away with the public orations because as more and more students qualified for honors, fewer and fewer spectators cared to listen to the increasing number of speeches.

In the late 1700s, Yale began hosting the Junior Exhibition, an April event for juniors who received high grades. During the Exhibition, which lasted an entire day, these scholars gave speeches in front of the administration, faculty, and students. The Exhibition was accompanied by the Junior Promenade. In 1847 some enterprising juniors, bent on spoofing the Exhibition, hosted a few days after the Exhibition a Wooden Spoon Presentation and Promenade, in which a wooden spoon was bestowed on one of the juniors with the lowest appointments, usually someone from the bottom of the list of second colloquies. Eventually, the juniors scrapped the satirical recognition entirely and awarded the Wooden Spoon to their most popular classmate instead. By the 1860s, the event was so organized that the junior class elected a committee called the Society of Cochleaureati (from the Latin *cochlear,* for spoon, and *laureatus,* crowned with laurel), the class's nine "best fellows," who would then choose one of the Cochleaureati to receive the coveted Wooden Spoon. Generally, the Spoon Man would not be a student who held an office, but rather someone who was simply well liked. The Cochs—for whom puns, yes, ran rampant—each received a two-inch gold spoon badge, as well as a three-foot-long black walnut spoon on which their names and class were engraved. The initiation of the Cochs included a banquet, after which the new Cochs would tear around the college, waking up their peers and chasing them with their new spoons. The Spoon Man would receive an elaborately carved rosewood or black walnut spoon with an engraved silver plaque in a velvet-lined case. The Spoon Exhibition, which became the biggest, best-attended event of the year, with regular crowds of more than three thousand spectators—eclipsing the Exhibition it was intended to spoof—lasted annually until 1871.

The event wasn't as unusual as it sounded: older ceremonies included giving a pair of red-topped boots to the most popular junior, a jackknife to the ugliest (and then a leather medal if he refused the jackknife), a cane to the best-looking, and, in earlier days, a wooden spoon to the junior who ate the most. (Today's closest equivalent would probably be the Doodleburger Challenge, hosted by a campus restaurant known fondly as the Doodle and consisting of a competition in which students battle for the honor of being named Doodleburger Champion—and having their name engraved on a plaque—by wolfing down as many greasy Doodleburgers as they can in as little time as possible. And, typical Yale, certain traditions survive regardless of context. The day before graduation, for example, Yale students continue each to be presented with a pipe, a handkerchief, and a bag of tobacco. So it was, so it continues to be.)

One of the most important traditions at Yale during the 1800s was the Fence. Located on what is now Old Campus, the freshman courtyard at the center of Yale, the Fence served as meeting spot and lounge, podium and auditorium. Mostly, students would sit and sing there—singing was such a cherished custom at Yale, with its Fence and society songs, that it would publish the country's first college songbook in 1853, with subsequently updated editions. Every class had a particular place along the Fence except for the freshmen, who were not allowed to sit there unless they won their annual class baseball game with Harvard. In 1899, author Lewis Welch wrote that the Fence was Yale

in miniature, and sometimes in life size. . . . As to some pedestrians' great embarrassment walking down the sidewalk in front of a row of two or three hundred young men squatted on those rails . . . from the middle of April to the end of the summer term, . . . it was the one place to be sure of finding anyone. . . . You could go to the Fence and be moderately sure to find within a reasonable length of time the most peripatetic individual. . . . Whomever you were looking for, the surest way was to sit on the Fence and watch and wait.

The students' tendency to bellow songs and provoke each other to mischief there eventually became cause for complaint. In the mid-1800s, the faculty twice warned students not to sit on the Fence, but to no avail. The administration then tried to lure the students from their beloved Fence by installing seats nearby, but the students wouldn't budge. Eventually, to make way for another building, the administration moved the Fence to another corner of the quad, where it gradually lost its cachet among the students.

It is not too difficult to understand how some of the institution's older, sillier traditions eventually grew into Yale's vaguely cultlike society system. A case in point is the Burial of Euclid, which, despite numerous faculty prohibitions, continued annually from Yale's early years through 1863. When the sophomores had completed the study of Euclid, usually in late October, they would burn or bury their books in an elaborately constructed midnight ceremony accompanied by poems, tragedies, and processions. First the students, garbed in devilish masks and costumes, would silently march to a building called the Temple, all the while pointing toward their destination. As they filed up the building's winding staircase, they recited the assigned Homeric password to the "committee," which presided over the ritual with shining swords. In the Temple's ceremony room, an effigy of an old man representing Euclid lay on the stage. The sophomores surrounded the effigy while chanting tongue-in-cheek songs such as:

> *In the arms of death old Euclid sleepeth,*
> > *Sleepeth calmly now;*
> *And corruption's ghastly dampness creepeth*
> > *O'er his pallid brow.*
> *His* triangles, *which so often floored us,*

> *Soon shall find their grave;*
> *He'll try angling with the lines that bored us,*
>   *In the Stygian wave.*
> *His accounts all squared, he hath departed*
>   *From his earthly sphere;*
> *On a narrow bier his body's carted,*
>   *Not a la(r)ger bier.*
> *We've described the space of his existence,*
>   *In these given lines,*
> *And we'll burn old Euclid in the distance,*
>   *'Neath the waving pines.*

The students would then deliver a poem, a speech, and a funeral oration between pieces of music from the student band of choice. Then, as described by a writer in 1843 in the solemn language that properly fits the occasion:

> The huge poker is heated in the old stove and driven through the smoking volume [pile of books], and the division, marshalled in line, for once at least "see through" the whole affair. They then "understand" it, as it is passed above their heads; and they finally march over it in solemn procession, and are enabled, as they step firmly on its covers, to assert with truth that they have "gone over" it — poor jokes, indeed, but sufficient to afford abundant laughter. And then follow speeches, comical and pathetic, and shouting and merriment. The night assigned having arrived, how carefully they assemble, all silent, at the place appointed! Laid on its bier, covered with sable pall, and borne in solemn state, the corpse (*i.e.,* the book) is carried with slow procession, with the moaning music of fiddles, and thumping and mumbling of a cracked drum, to the opened grave or the funeral pyre. A gleaming line of blazing torches and twinkling lanterns, moves along the quiet streets and through the open fields, and the snow creaks hoarsely under the tread of a hundred men. They reach the scene, and a circle formed

around the consecrated spot; if the ceremony is a burial, the defunct is laid all carefully in his grave, and then his friends celebrate in prose or verse his memory, his virtues, and his untimely end; and three *oboli* are tossed into his tomb to satisfy the surly boatman of the Styx. Lingeringly is the last look taken of the familiar countenance, as the procession passes slowly around the tomb; and a moaning is made — a sound of groans going up to the seventh heaven — and the earth is thrown in, and the headstone with the epitaph placed duly to hallow the grave of the dead. Or if, according to the custom of his native land, the pyre, duly prepared with combustibles, is make [*sic*] the center of the ring; a ponderous jar of turpentine or whisky is the fragrant incense, and as the lighted fire mounts up in the still night, and the alarm sounds dim in the distance, the eulogium is spoken, and the memory of the illustrious dead honored; the urn receives the sacred ashes, which, borne in solemn procession, are placed on some conspicuous situation, or solemnly deposited in some fitting sarcophagus. So the sport ends; a song, a loud hurrah, and the last jovial roysterer seek short and profound slumber.

☠   ☠   ☠

In 1886, because the standard curriculum was replaced with elective courses, rendering each student's schedule different from his peers', the administration decided to stop naming valedictorians and salutatorians. It is not surprising, then, that in the next twenty years, Yale witnessed a flurry of organizational proliferation to prod some students to the forefront of the campus in other ways. Yalies, it seemed, could turn practically anything into a time-honored custom. In 1893, for one, a freshman was roused from sleep by the racket of two drunks arguing beneath his window, so he dropped a bottle of ink between them. Thus began the annual tradition of Bottle Night, during which students would make use of the bottles of spring water that constituted much of the dormitory water supply by hurling them out the window. During Omega Lambda Chi, a spring parade that began after the faculty prohibited freshman societies in 1880, sophomores, juniors, and seniors marched by the college build-ings, cheering each one in turn. After the parade came the Pass of Thermopylae, during which the freshmen ran a gauntlet of upperclass-men between two tightly spaced buildings with the sole object of not getting pummeled. In 1903, the Pundits, a group of well-organized pranksters, surfaced (they are still in existence); 1909 witnessed the founding of the now legendary a cappella group the Whiffenpoofs, which took its name from a character in the Victor Herbert operetta *Little Nemo,* a recent arrival on Broadway. Herbert's narrator bored a hole in an icy lake and placed cheese around the hole. The Whiffenpoof creature shot up the hole for the cheese, squawked, and got caught. Apparently, the Whiffenpoofs felt the name was appropriate because, they said, "If you infuriated us with food and drink, we came up and squawked."

And more: On a snowy winter night in 1934, the plaster fell from the newly installed ceilings of the Timothy Dwight residential college. Once the ceilings were fixed, the T.D. master (the college's faculty administra-tor) threw a banquet and rewrote songs to fit the occasion to "Ceilibrate the End of the Plastercine Age." Thus began the annually commemo-rated Plaster Night. In the mid-twentieth century, students started cele-brating Bladderball Day, which they would usually begin by consuming mass quantities of alcohol at breakfast. At about eleven in the morning, campus police would close the gates to Old Campus, the freshman courtyard, where students from every residential college staggered, awaiting the drop of a five-foot ball from the top of Phelps Gate. The object of Bladderball was for a college to navigate the ball, amid the chaos, over the gate that signified its goal. Once the ball was tipped over a gate, the throng would rush out after it in gleeful, delirious pan-demonium.

For at least its first two centuries, Yale had no student government. So these sons of privilege felt they needed some other way to recognize a minority before multitudes. They came by their earliest solution in strange manner. Beginning in the late 1700s, town–gown relations had soured into open hostilities, particularly with the sailors who spent off-duty hours in the port of New Haven. In 1806, the fighting escalated into a major riot, during which the townspeople called one of the students "the College Bully." In true Yale style, the delighted students turned insult into an elected office, and from then on annually voted on a College Bully, as well as a bully for each class. The Bully led not only fights, but also every class procession and meeting in a role akin to that of class president. At first, the Bully was the beefiest man in the senior class. Eventually, each class would elect a major bully (a popular class-mate) and a minor bully (the smallest classmate, who would serve as vice president in the absence of the major bully). Each bully was ceremoni-ously presented with an elaborately gilded "banger," or cane. The senior major bully, who was the official College Bully, was outfitted with a large weapon known as the Bully Club.

Naturally, the transfer of the Bully Club from the College Bully to the junior bully at the end of each year became an elaborate ritual, replete with speeches, music, and parades. But by the late 1830s, some students began to feel that calling the leader of the class a bully was unrefined, as opposed to electing a class president, leader, or moderator. A reform party quickly grew, and elected its own leader to rival the College Bully. On the morning of commencement in 1840, the two elected class leaders decided to sort out their powers the old-fashioned, Bully way. Neither the faculty, the police officers, nor the chief magistrate of the state could break up the fight. Soon afterward, the faculty abolished both groups and decreed that, from then on, there would be no class leaders at Yale at all. The last College Bully, a Skull and Bones man from the class of 1841, deposited the Bully Club in Bones headquarters, where it was last seen.

Probably the most prominent way that Yale students divided them-selves was by forming societies. The first major societies, the literary so-cieties, were harmless, open, and nonexclusive. They merely served as a way to make the students feel as if they belonged to something more in-timate than the Yale community. First sprouted the short-lived Crotonia, about which virtually nothing has been documented, except that it existed before 1750. In 1753 the Honorable Fellowship Club, rechristened the Linonia Society, was established as a result of President Clap's efforts to promote literature and oratory in the college. It was a large, open literary group that would eventually count among its number Yale's hero, Nathan Hale. In 1768, seven upperclassmen Linonians seceded in order to found its rival, Brothers in Unity, which became the first Yale group to admit freshmen, who were beneath the totem pole in those days. (By coincidence — or perhaps not — the class of 1768 was the first class whose names were listed alphabetically instead of ranked by social status.)

Once Brothers in Unity had been established, the two literary societies halved the campus as they battled for membership, leaving no undergraduate without an affiliation. In 1801, Linonia and Brothers agreed to divide the freshmen so they could save the time and energy of campaigning for membership by doling out students alphabetically, one by one, alternately to each society. In 1819, Linonians became embroiled in a fierce political fight that resulted in the election of a Northern student as the society's president. In protest, the Southern members of both Linonia and Brothers withdrew from their societies to form a third literary society, Calliope, which never grew to the size of its predecessors but nonetheless endured for several years. Instead of Calliope having to pledge the freshmen, it was generally known that all Southerners would automatically flock to that society, which in 1853 became the first major literary society to fold.

The societies met in separate alcoves at opposite ends of a building that resembled a Gothic chapel; they charged dues of about eight dollars per year. At the weekly meetings, students would debate, give speeches, write poems, and perform plays. Oration and composition topics included the likes of "What is the square root of 16/99ths?," "What is the reason that, though all rivers run into the sea, yet the sea doth not increase?," and "Ought old maids be taxed?" These gatherings allowed students to discuss the kinds of subjects that their conservative curriculum left no room for, such as current events. The authors of *The American College and American Culture* (1970) would note that these kinds of societies' "debates, libraries and publications were often more effective modes of study than the formal academic exercises; and their ability to exclude some students gave gratifying recognition of the distinction of those admitted." Occasionally the societies would hold an exhibition, during which each would aim to outperform the others in a series of events, including an originally written dramatic poem, a tragedy, and a comedy. Eventually the administration abolished these oratory Olympics because the students were devoting more time to them than to their actual classes.

These literary societies were the first undergraduate intellectual societies in the country. F. A. P. Barnard, the president of Columbia from 1864 to 1889, would write: "No part of my training at Yale College seems to me to have been more beneficial than that which I derived from the practice of writing and speaking in the literary society to which I belonged." Although the societies' purpose was mainly to develop intellectual character, one of their greatest initial benefits was their libraries. At a time when the Yale library was rarely open, lacked liberal borrowing privileges, and was limited mostly to conservative academic books, the literary societies offered a wide selection of light reading.

As the literary societies solidified, students continued to funnel into progressively more exclusive groups. In 1780, the Connecticut Alpha branch of Phi Beta Kappa was founded at Yale as a secret society, with a regular program originally known only to members. In 1797, some students formed the short-lived Moral Society, a secret society that emphasized the importance of religion. In 1812, students established a music society later known as the Beethoven Society. The 1820s and early 1830s saw the Philencration Society, which preached moderation of and eventually abstinence from alcohol. Society fever hit even the faculty: in 1819 Theodore Dwight Woolsey established the Hexahedron Club, which hosted meetings during which members read poetry. In 1821, students appalled at a classmate's wardrobe—"an entire suit of light changeable silk"—formed the Lycurgan Society to oppose wasteful indulgence in life, clothes, and demeanor. Also in 1821, the distinguished professor James L. Kingsley founded Chi Delta Theta to encourage interest in literature; only the best writers of the senior class were elected. Chi Delta Theta met every other Tuesday night to read and discuss essays, usually at Kingsley's house. Nineteen members of the class of 1831 established the Philagorian Society, or Phi Alpha. Phi Alpha, which lasted two years, met weekly in a room on Orange Street to improve members' extemporaneous speaking skills. Phi Alpha cloaked itself in secrecy; all members had to recite the oath: "You and each of you promise on your faith and honour, in presence of these witnesses, that you will never directly or indirectly, betray, discover nor reveal any of the laws, ceremonies or transactions of this Society."

By the 1830s, the literary societies had begun their slow descent into extinction. Linonia and Brothers both folded in 1872, when their libraries were transferred to the university library, which to this day maintains the "L&B" collection in a comfortable reading room popular with students. While their loss of popularity was partly due to the proliferation of so many new opportunities for students to feel as if they "belonged" to something, it is undeniable that their death was directly attributable to the way they were overshadowed by a more insidious, exclusive Yale entity: the class secret society.

Skull and Bones, the first of these societies, was established in 1832. For seniors only, the group consisted of fifteen surreptitiously elected members who met regularly—and quickly piqued campus curiosity. By 1840, every class had at least one society; by the late 1800s, the campus was dominated by the three prestigious secret senior societies, Skull and Bones, Scroll and Key, and Wolf's Head. These societies served to emphasize class divisions as a centerpiece of the Yale experience at a time when the trimming system had begun to wane. But the societies also narrowed the divisions further by actively excluding students, something that the larger literary societies had not done. Suddenly, for a Yale undergraduate, it was not enough to win a debating contest, triumph on the athletic field, or graduate at the top of his class. The societies quickly came to represent the pinnacle of success at Yale, and the undergraduates wanted in.

It didn't take long for the faculty members to decide that they wanted in as well. Six years after the establishment of Skull and Bones, a group of six prominent New Haven residents, including professors Josiah Willard Gibbs and Theodore Dwight Woolsey, founded the Club, a society for the Yale faculty elite and, initially, also for the upper echelon of the New Haven intelligentsia. "The Old Man's Club," as some outsiders referred to it, offered about twenty-five lifetime memberships to the university's social and intellectual elite (the members' families usually called the organization "The Old Gentlemen's Club"). Eventually the range of members would include William Howard Taft, future Connecticut chief justice Simeon E. Baldwin, scholar Thomas Bergin, neurosurgeon Harvey Cushing, and Skull and Bones founder William H. Russell.

The meetings, held every couple of weeks, consisted of supper — usually scalloped oysters, cold tongue, biscuits, raised cake, tea, and coffee — and intellectually stimulating discussions on such topics as "Slavery: How Should It Be Treated By Literary Men" in 1856 and "Pre-Frontal Lobotomy" in 1947. The presiding member, who usually hosted the discussion at his home, would call on the men to opine on the given topic in order of their seating.

The Club wielded considerable power on campus, mostly because, at least through 1963, two-thirds of its members were or had been members of the university administration. In fact, on several occasions the members of this exclusive organization specifically discussed a university issue, came to a decision without the rest of the faculty and administration, and steered the issue's outcome. "The Club has never aimed at action or influence outside itself, but has sought simply to provide social pleasure and intellectual intercourse," the Club's historian tried to spin in a book about the organization. "But in the very nature of the case its members informally make decisions unrelated to it but certainly not unrelated to the University, as they chat informally before and after dinner." Then again, there were also serious discussions about less controversial topics, like "the development of a horse's hoof from a three-toed to a one-toed formation."*

☠   ☠   ☠

While Yale would undergo many changes as it progressed into the twentieth century, its core and its atmosphere would hardly move with the times. In 1951, *Time* magazine noted on the occasion of Yale's 250th anniversary that

> consciously or unconsciously, Yale has traditionally waited for others to lead, observed their course, then picked the middle road to follow. Thus if its progress has not been speedy, it has been selective and generally sound. If it has opened few new frontiers, it has at least held fast to old and solid principles. In the best and truest sense of the word, Yale has stood from its earliest beginnings for conservatism triumphant.

Earlier, in 1885, the *Nation* observed this trend of conservatism when it remarked that Yale clung

> pretty stoutly to the original theory of its establishment. It is still an institution practically governed by a few clergymen of a single denomination in a single State. It is still insisted by the believers in the old theory that the first requisite for a President is that he shall be a clergyman of the "orthodox" church. The conservative party may carry their point in the election of a new President, but they will only postpone the

---

*The Club still exists today. So does the Saturday Morning Club, an organization formed about 125 years ago for the daughters of Yale faculty members. Now an all-female, limited-membership group of about twenty active professors and faculty spouses, the Saturday Morning Club meets about eight times a year to deliver speeches and presentations.

inevitable. A great modern college cannot be permanently conducted upon the same lines as a colonial divinity school.

Perhaps not, but Yale would stubbornly try to stay the same as it ever was—and churn out the same kinds of students. In 1913, the *Yale Daily News* chairman decried "the Yale type," who wore the right clothes, conducted himself properly, was "offensive in being utterly inoffensive," and didn't think for himself. "The dismal sands of the Desert of Sahara could not be more neglected by Yale undergraduates than the art of thinking," the chairman wrote. "And it has nearly the mental power of the original Yale Bull Dog." In 1923, Upton Sinclair wrote in *The Goose Step* that there was a clear directive of "This is the way we do it at Yale" and contempt for those who tried another way. He charged that the senior societies in particular left room for "no smallest trace of eccentricity in ideas." Even Bonesman William F. Buckley would reproach in his 1951 *God and Man at Yale,* "sonorous pretensions notwithstanding, Yale (and my guess is most other colleges and universities) *does subscribe to an orthodoxy:* there are limits within which its faculty members must keep their opinions if they wish to be 'tolerated.'"

Yale never denied nor apologized for its homogeneity. At the 1935 commencement, President James Rowland Angell warned students that the unwillingness to change which they had cultivated as undergraduates would only intensify when they graduated. "Now as alumni, your conservatism will in most cases be instantly raised to the n'th power and anything which was not done in your time at Yale will seem to you irrational and demonstrably evil," he said. One year later he would make the blunter statement, "You have been alumni ten minutes, and already there has been crystallizing in your souls, perhaps unconsciously, that typical attitude of critical resentment of all change at Yale which is one of the most engaging and exasperating traits of the graduate."

In 1952, George Pierson described Yale's attitude as a conflicting mandate of conformity and competition. He wrote:

Yale conformed. There was no doubt about it. A true Yale man was not at Yale just for what he could get out of it. He was not even being educated to rely on himself or to pit his judgment against popular opinion. At some of the institutions of the newer West everything old was automatically suspect. At Cambridge, as a Harvard editor confessed, the Harvard man was apt to be such a law unto himself that team play and concerted effort were often impossible. But at Yale individualism was not encouraged. Campus sentiment was against it, and traditions stood in the way. A man's classmates valued his cooperation far more than his criticism. Originality of ideas was suspect and, outside of a tolerated range, eccentricity of dress or conduct was frowned on. To succeed at Yale one must avoid queerness, make friends, do something. And whatever the activity or however calculated the underlying motive, the assumption was always the same. To "go out" and do something was to work for the welfare of the College.

About a quarter-century later, Brooks Mather Kelley would make a similar observation: "Yale was, it is clear, *too* traditional, *too* conforming, *too* much of a creature of the age. The elaborate structure grew decadent and began to disintegrate. . . . The extracurriculum became more important than anything else."

In 1926, the Yale Corporation agreed to end the longstanding tradition of compulsory attendance at chapel services. But the biggest change was to come a few years later. Edward Harkness, an active Wolf's Head society member from the class of 1897, voiced his disappointment that he knew of many "average" men like himself who had not been tapped for the intimate bonding experience of secret-society life and therefore missed out on something he considered crucial to the Yale experience. In 1930, he pledged a donation of more than $15 million to Yale in order to develop a residential college system patterned after those at Oxford and Cambridge. Harkness hoped in this way to crumble some of the barriers between classes, and, more strikingly, between the insiders and outsiders of Yale's exclusive clubs.

The first seven residential colleges opened in September 1933. (Freshmen remained unaffiliated until they were assigned a college in time for sophomore year. This practice differed dramatically from the "house" system at Harvard, in which students chose where they would live.) Faculty members assigned to the colleges mingled with students in the dining halls. College-specific organizations bloomed. If a student couldn't get a position on the *Daily News,* a varsity team, or in a play, he could still work for his college's paper, play intramural athletics, or be a college thespian. More important, each college now had its own honors, its own means of recognizing student standouts, who could now compete in these smaller communities rather than flounder in the larger university pool.

And, of course, new traditions particular to the residential colleges solidified. Each college had its own ties, blazers, plates, holiday parties, and picnics. At commencement the colleges marched together behind their master, dean, and fellows, who wore the college colors on their hoods. Each college had a symbol. Calhoun College carried the senator's cane, Berkeley College bore two silver maces, Pierson College spun a staff topped with a sun, and Davenport College walked with a wooden mace atop a carving of a felon's head. By mid-century, each college had its own banner, carried aloft on the march to graduation. (Yale's official seal includes the Hebrew words *Urim v'Thummim,* commonly translated as Light and Truth. College secretary Theodore Sizer, who created the banners, one year designed a special banner for the commencement's master of ceremonies to march behind. On it, Sizer put the Hebrew for "God damn it" above the phrase *"Deus id dampsit,"* a pun on *"Deus id dempsit,"* meaning "God took it away." When Sizer presented the banner to the master of ceremonies, spectators erroneously translated the Latin to mean "My God, it may rain.")

Throughout the twentieth century, Yale placed an increasingly greater emphasis on the residential college system. In the fall of 1962, freshmen were incorporated into the colleges. Though almost all freshmen would spend their first year living on Old Campus, this meant that before students even got to Yale, they already "belonged" to something smaller and more intimate than the university. A student's most important means of identification became his college, which is why, even today, the first question undergraduate strangers ask each other is, "What college are you in?" When Yale went coeducational in 1969, the women were more likely to associate with the men in their residential college than with the other females on campus. College loyalty came to supersede class loyalty, as students recognized each other less frequently by class than as a Stilesian, Branfordian, or Piersonite.

☠   ☠   ☠

"The struggle for existence outside in a business world is not one whit more intense than the struggle to win out in the *News* or *Lit* competition. We are like a beef trust, with every by-product organized, down to the last possibility," says a character in Owen Johnson's 1912 novel *Stover at Yale*.

> You come to Yale—what is said to you? "Be natural, be spontaneous, revel in a certain freedom, enjoy a leisure you'll never get again, browse around, give your imagination a chance, see every one, rub wits with every one, get to know yourself." Is that what's said? No. What are you told, instead? "Here are twenty great machines that need new bolts and wheels. Get out and work. Work harder than the next man, who is going to try to outwork you. And, in order to succeed, work at only one thing. You don't count—everything for the college."

Johnson's descriptions, however fictionalized, do ring true. Even *Time* would rhapsodize, "Like the British constitution, the Yale code is unwritten; it is simply in the air. . . . Yale undergraduates still 'play the game'—on the field and off—in an atmosphere of calm but unrelenting competition: From the moment a freshman begins to 'heel' for the *News,* the *Banner* or the *Lit.,* his life becomes a purposeful drive upward—but a drive he must pretend to ignore." With its strict traditionalism and conservative conformity, Yale became—and certainly has remained—an institution that presents itself far less as an academic school than as a social game. As George Pierson unflinchingly observed in his history of Yale,

> A considerable element had come to College to learn not from books but from each other—not how to be scholars but how to succeed. Success was really their goal, not Veritas. What they were surely preparing for in their competitions was the struggle of making a living. . . . The undergraduates knew that, provided they first learned the rules of the game, they were destined for great prizes, sure to make fortunes, and bound for the managing posts in society.

To succeed at Yale meant to engage in the fierce competitiveness and boundless, calculated ambition that the university fostered. Pierson astutely added that Yale's "unprinted curriculum" could fill a second catalogue:

> To the innocent or the unawakened the first plunge into the maelstrom could be a bewildering experience. But to the sociable it was sheer pleasure, and to the more mature and ambitious it had all the excitement of a game: a game for influence and power, a contest whose rewards stretched far beyond graduation. He who became a big man in his Class and was tapped by Bones or Keys seemed already made. His would be the pick of the job opportunities. For him the big law firms would be waiting and the doors of the Wall Street houses swing open.

The police officer I spoke to in front of the Skull and Bones tomb was indeed correct in his assertion that an intricate maze of tunnels runs beneath Yale. But it isn't literally underneath the campus. Rather, it exists in the undertones of the Yale experience. This is what makes Yale different from any other university in the world: Running beneath and parallel to Yale college life is a matrix supporting the institution's power structure. And, it is taught, if one solves the New Haven labyrinth, he will be given the keys to a next set of tunnels, passageways that connect the corridors of power in the world beyond. It is a labyrinth that undergraduates always keep in the back of their minds as they doggedly navigate their way through traditions unyielding as walls, past gauntlets thick as those of the Pass of Thermopylae, to where the most prestigious of the paths converge — as the officer suggested, at the door to a secret society.

Chapter Two

THE SOCIETY SYSTEM

I should be glad if the whole system of petty *perpetuata* societies in this college should perish," wrote Yale professor Thomas Thacher in a letter in the 1870s.

But I feel bound to add that it is not their *secrecy* which makes them an evil. Almost all the evil which they cause here, except the waste of time and money, would cease, if every one of them should become really secret, if their places and times of meeting, the names of their members and even the names of the societies and their very existence were absolutely unknown except to the members. It is what is known about these societies, not their secrets nor their secret doings, which works evil among us.

That such a strange defense-within-an-accusation would come from a well-respected Yale professor seems odd. What makes the contents of this letter fall into place, however, is that Thacher, like his son and grandson, was a member of Skull and Bones. Clearly a Bonesman would state publicly that secret societies should stay secret. The more secret they become, the more powerful the public imagines them to be. This debate about secrecy is important because it courses through the core of what Skull and Bones has always been about. The society is mired in the paradox of its own self-image: Members claim to be secret, insist they want privacy, and then flaunt their membership in this elite group. This contradiction is directly in line with the way Bones breeds its initiates. It is also very Yale.

Yale's secret societies, which have always mirrored the zeitgeist of the university, rein in the unconventional with a decided proclivity for blind traditionalism. The system is, as future Yale president Arthur Hadley (Bones 1876) said in 1895, "a characteristic product of Yale life, with its intensity of effort, its high valuation of college judgments and college successes, and its constant tension, which will allow no one to rest within himself, but makes him a part of the community in which he dwells." Generally, society members—less than one-tenth of the senior class—meet for "sessions" every Thursday and Sunday night of their senior year. Though they are dogged by charges of elitism—up until the mid-twentieth century, it was considered a given that the ideal society candidate was "Greenwich born, Andover nourished, Fence polished and Bones tapped"—secret-society members like to say that the fifteen seniors in each organization represent a cross-section reflective of campus demographics. But Yale's Old Blue mystique and secret societies are synonymous; they smell like the long wooden tables that stretch across campus, from the old dining halls to the classrooms in Harkness Tower to the *Yale Daily News* boardroom to the favorite campus pizza joint, on which Yalies have etched their initials with keys for more than a century. They operate confined by custom like over-constricted neckties, as if the ivy vines snaking around the stone towers, stained to convey more age than they possess, cage the walls in rather than deck them out. They bear the same attitude as the staff at Mory's, a central campus membership-only restaurant where the waiters serve Welsh rarebit or filet mignon with the haughtiness of British butlers and raise a permanently arched eyebrow ever so slightly should a patron request extra chutney. Secret societies are that arched eyebrow personified. They embody the spirit of "For God, For Country and for Yale," with God and Yale transposed.

"It would, of course, be foolish to judge an individual solely by his society connections," Lyman Bagg wrote in 1871, but it would be far less foolish than to judge him solely by the number of prizes, or scholarships, or honors he could lay claim to, as is not infrequently the practice. To set up any one arbitrary standard whereby to judge character is manifestly unfair, yet, if it is to be done, there is no single test which embraces so many, in making an estimate of a Yale man's importance, as his share in the society system.

This statement is no longer true for some Yale students, partly because the society system is only a quarter of what it once was. There are enough ways now to stand out that a student can distinguish himself as a big man on campus without a society membership. But what is remarkable about the Yale society system is that even today, 170 years after it began, society membership still holds for many students the same pull it always did. The present-day secret societies still thrive as bastions for overachievers; at a college without formal GPAs, class rank, or merit scholarships, where Greek life is off-campus and peripheral, secret societies serve for many students as the ultimate means of recognition.

As soon as freshmen arrive at the New Haven campus for the start of "Camp Yale," those few days after registration ends and before classes begin, they hear stories about the university's infamous secret-society system. Often wide-eyed, sometimes afraid, and always curious, they can't help but wonder—when they see tight-lipped, black-hooded students silently single-filing into a windowless building, when they hear about the seniors who never show up in the dining hall on Thursdays and Sundays, when they encounter the strange insignias stamped menacingly on campus—what goes on in these organizations. Some students become obsessive about compiling all the information they can about a particular society that intrigues them. In 1998, one prominent senior was so mortified that she had not been tapped for a secret society, she spent every Thursday night hidden in a remote top-floor room of Sterling Memorial Library so that her friends would think she was attending society meetings. Even her roommate, too, was fooled until she caught the senior soon before graduation.

One reason these organizations so quickly became an integral part of Yale culture is that they were never typical student clubs. *Scribner's* magazine noted in 1897, "Except for the curriculum itself, no force in the college is to be compared with the senior societies. The bond among their members lasts through life, and so close is it that even the college world knows nothing of their proceedings, and can only conjecture their purposes." Members of the Yale faculty and administration—many of them society members themselves—were often as enthralled with the system's mystique as the students. Administrators not only frequently took part in society ceremonies and programs, but also, with the senior societies in particular, used society networks to influence university issues. Inside their walls, the societies did not draw lines between generations: faculty members, administrators, undergraduates, and graduate students were equal brothers. The students in societies therefore had direct connections with administrators, who in turn considered their brothers' opinions to be representative of the entire undergraduate body or, at least, any undergraduates worth listening to. Consider the description by Yale president Timothy Dwight, Skull and Bones 1849, of the society that he mentions a few times in his autobiography but always refuses to name:

> With reference to the friendly relations between the younger members of the Faculty and the students, I think that in these years the smaller and secret societies began to exert an influence of a special character. These societies, during the larger portion of my tutorial career, drew into their fraternal fellowship, more fully and frequently than they had done before, their members who were already graduates, and, among them, those who had been appointed to offices of instruction in the College. An opportunity was thus opened for a very free and unrestrained intercourse, from time to time, between the teachers and their pupils. The two parties were easily rendered able to understand each other's thoughts and feelings, and to gain, each from the other, opinions or suggestions which might have the best and happiest influence. For

myself, I am sure that such opportunities, in my younger days, were of very great service and benefit. They gave me the knowledge of the student mind, as well as a familiar and friendly acquaintance with the ideas and sentiments of individual students.

It was my privilege, for which I have been ever grateful, to know by this means, and even to know with much of intimacy and affectionate feeling, many members of the successive classes which came under my instruction while I was in the tutorial office. It is a pleasure to me, as I review the past history, to feel that they and I worked together not only, as I believe, for our mutual upbuilding in knowledge and character, but also for the introduction of better life in the student community and more truly kindly relations between the younger and the older portions of the College world; in a word, that we took part as friends — our part, whatever it may have been as to its measure — in making the University a brotherhood of educated men, bound together in a common earnestness of purpose and having, each and all, the generous feeling which pertains to liberal scholarship.

During the late 1800s, President Dwight, Secretary Franklin Dexter (Bones 1861), Dean Henry Parks Wright (Bones 1868), and several of the most powerful professors regularly attended society meetings to maintain ties with the student leadership.

The administration realized that despite the societies' exclusivity and occasional notoriety, they did serve a crucial purpose at Yale: They provided keen motivation. "The inauguration of the society system which now exists at Yale was one of the most important steps in the evolution of the old simple college into a life of humming organized activity," *Scribner's* stated.

This is the highest honor which a Yale man can receive from his fellows, and because it comes from them he sets it above scholastic distinction. . . . The writer, the debater, the scholar, the athlete, each is goaded to the full measure of his abilities. Life is tenuous and eminently practical because success is tangible. The organization of effort, carried to its highest development at New Haven in athletics, debate, or the different phases of social life, which is the "Yale spirit" upon its tangible and mechanical side, is due in large measure to the society influences which concentrate into channels of efficiency all the diffuse and vagrant energies of the college.

While the societies certainly strongly divided the undergraduates into insiders and outsiders, it also united them—as it pitted them against each other—in that they largely worked toward the same goal: getting in. This factory-like drive formed the "machinery" that Owen Johnson famously referred to in *Stover at Yale*. And this was also why, despite fierce opposition, Yale would not shut all of its societies down—it could not avoid the inescapable fact that while these strange clubs tore the campus apart, they also glued it back together again.

Still, a significant portion of the Yale community found the societies problematic and threatening. "Under the outward appearances, below all the so-called joys of these few years lurks a poisonous undercurrent, that spreads itself into all the roots and fibres of our college life, and anon rises menacingly and lowering into view. On the sustinence [*sic*] that such a life-blood can give, grow and foster all the branches of our work," wrote Edwin S. Oviatt in an 1896 issue of the *Yale Literary Magazine*.

> There is no man, whether he be high or low, whether he be strong, or weakly in the current, who does not feel it. . . . If he lacks the ambition to attain position by questionable means, if he has not in him the worshipful spirit of reverence to a would-be Hero, his life here is dwarfed, narrowed, browbeaten into a sullen silence, and he leaves at the end with tears in his eyes, perhaps, for the tender associations of the few friends as noble and as independent as himself, and with inward cries of rage at the system of things that has brought it thus.

The college society system, to many people on campus, was not the system but The System, a macabre, Machiavellian matrix designed to weed out the weaklings and brainwash future leaders of the world—this on a campus created expressly to develop ministers, not minions. An anonymous writer in the *Nation* charged that "the evil worms itself into our religious life, it introduces friction into our religious development."

Others felt differently. In his spirited 1939 *Lit.* article titled "For the Defense," future Kennedy adviser McGeorge Bundy opined:

> Although the traditional way has sometimes in the past seemed to constrain men from devoting their time to more important things, it is highly questionable whether in general the microcosm has not tended in general to elevate rather than to depress the quality of the work done in college; certainly it has always operated to discourage mere idleness and wild oats. It may be bad that we should have a system that attracts a blind desire and rewards on arbitrary and only half-true bases. It would be worse if the ordinary aspiring Freshman were drawn by nothing more compelling than the double-feature at Loew's Poli or the dubious glories of the Knickerbocker.

Soon after he published this impassioned defense, Bundy was rewarded with a tap from Skull and Bones.

Once the first secret society was established in 1832, students didn't take long to develop alternatives to and imitations of Skull and Bones; the period up until the Civil War saw the most such activity. The first junior society was founded in 1836, sophomore societies started in 1838, freshman societies in 1840, and the second prestigious senior society, Scroll and Key, in 1842. These groups constituted what many Yale historians have referred to as a social pyramid because the process successively narrowed down the elite of a class, from the all-inclusive freshman societies to the two senior societies, which took fifteen members apiece, until only the best, brightest, most popular, and, in some cases, luckiest were deemed spectacular enough to merit recognition.

As a result, the college experience was hardly the norm—Yale wasn't a college; it was a pageant and a proving ground. As the campus publication *Harkness Hoot* charged in the 1930s, "For most undergraduates, the activities of their first three years are consciously or unconsciously focused on election to a senior society. . . . A set of social values, ulterior, material, degrading in their premeditation, is imposed upon almost every aspect of campus conduct." The societies did more than merely enhance Yale campus life. They drove it.

☠   ☠   ☠

In the nineteenth century, a Yale student's introduction to the secret society system came long before he even arrived on campus. Kappa Sigma Epsilon (founded in 1840) and Delta Kappa (1845), the oldest and most prominent of the freshman societies, regularly sent representatives to the preparatory schools to pledge some of the students who would be attending Yale the next fall. At first, "Sigma Eps" and "Delta Kap" inducted about twenty members apiece. But the competition for the best men became so fierce that they soon changed their practice in order to initiate, instead, as many members as they could, regardless of worth. The rivalry then became a contest to see who would "win the campaign." Sigma Eps and Delta Kap would usually trade off years, with the nonsecret Gamma Nu (1855) and the short-lived Sigma Delta (1849) societies drawing a few dozen freshmen as well.

The rush to pledge members was feverish; every freshman was expected to choose a society. Barely into their freshman year, graduates of the preparatory schools would return to their alma maters to recruit as many "sub-Fresh" as possible. It was common, in this way, for a society to "control" a prep school. Andover students, for example, often went in packs to Delta Kap—and thus frequently dictated its president, whom they had likely elected even before setting foot at Yale. When freshmen arrived at the train stations, not just in New Haven, but also in New York, New London, and Springfield, society representatives would accost them with frenzied pitches, sometimes even jumping on the platforms of moving trains to be the first to reach their recruits. In the mid-1800s, zealous recruiters would scour the depot for incoming freshmen twenty-three times a day in addition to visiting the docks morning and night.

The freshman societies, like the sophomore and junior societies, each took their acronymic names from the letters beginning a phrase in Greek that was considered the group's motto. (Or sometimes the founders would come up with a trio of Greek letters that sounded nice and create a motto to fit the name.) Each society, like the older societies at Yale, also had a pin, or "badge." Freshmen would wear the pin always, from their initiation until the initiation of the next year's group. Often they would attach to the pin a chain with a small gold letter representing the society. They also had gold or colored notepaper and envelopes stamped with the society's insignia, as well as a steel plate or lithographic framed poster of the design hanging in their rooms. In the societies' early years, they would publicize announcements by posting on campus trees cards bearing the societies' logos and meeting times. Later, the societies regularly met on Saturday nights from about eight o'clock to eleven in rented rooms—which had to have a stage, necessary for dramatic exercises—in buildings around town. There the members would debate, give speeches, read essays and passages, and put together the society's "papers," which consisted of members' written work, culled by a designated society editor. On some occasions or at the end of literary activities, the society would hold a "peanut bum," during which a member dumped a couple bushels of peanuts on the floor and laughed with his classmates as guests scrambled to pick up as many as possible. This activity inevitably was followed by cigar smoking and postulating. Society membership cost a freshman about $35 to $40.

The freshman society initiation was probably at a fitting level of puerility, given that freshmen in the 1800s were often age sixteen or younger. On the day of initiation, each freshman received a black-bordered envelope and note card marked with the society's logo. The card read something like, "You will be waited upon at your room this evening, and be presented for initiation into the dark and awful mysteries of the [name] fraternity. Per order." Enclosed would be another, elaborately designed card with a corner missing. The freshman was told to wait until the sophomore with the matching edge appeared at his door.

In the early evening, freshmen would hear the racket outside their windows as sophomores marched around campus, blowing tin horns and banging their canes on the ground to frighten the initiates. Later that night, the sophomores took the freshmen, one by one, to a rented public building from which emanated wild, chaotic sounds. Each freshman, blindfolded, was thrust inside the building; the blindfold was whisked off to reveal only pitch blackness — and the other freshmen waiting to be initiated.

A hidden door creaked open and someone would bellow the initiate's name. He was blindfolded again, by sophomores dressed as a devil and a skeleton, who then pushed him up a few flights of stairs. Then he was shoved off the landing, from which he fell blindly downward until he was caught in a blanket by the society members. They tossed the freshman around in the blanket for a bit. Then, as Lyman Bagg recounted in *Four Years at Yale* (1871),

> He is officiously told to rest himself in a chair, the seat of which lets him into a pail of water, beneath, though a large sponge probably saves him from an actual wetting; his head and hands are thrust through a pillory, and he is reviled in that awkward position; he is rolled in an exaggerated squirrel wheel; a noose is thrown around his neck, and he is dragged beneath the guillotine, when the bandage is pulled from his eyes, and he glares upon the glittering knife of block-tin, which falls within a foot of his throat, and cannot possibly go further. Being thus executed, he is thrust into a coffin, which is hammered upon with such energy that he is at length recalled to life, pulled out again, and made to wear his coat with the inside outwards.

This kind of chaotic cacophony would come to characterize the initiations of nearly all of the societies at Yale.

In the freshman societies' early years, the initiations were often public events, with tickets issued depicting freshmen being violently tortured in various manners. These proceedings were often more elaborate than later initiations. Sometimes the freshman was placed in a coffin that was raised to the top of the initiation hall. The bottom would drop out, plummeting him into a blanket.

In 1880, the faculty closed down the freshman secret societies because they had grown out of control and caused strife between the freshmen and the sophomores. The suspension was supposed to be temporary, but the societies never reopened.

Like the freshman societies, sophomore societies, too, sent representatives to the preparatory schools to pledge members, even though the students would not actually be initiated for more than a year. To elect members, the societies used a ballot box with one compartment containing white cubes and one with black balls. The voter selected a cube or ball and placed it into the opposite compartment. If a candidate received even one negative vote, he was "blackballed" and unlikely to be elected. Preparatory school ties carried great weight.

The first sophomore society, Kappa Sigma Theta, formed in 1838, and would later be joined by Alpha Sigma Phi (1846), Phi Theta Psi (1864), and Delta Beta Xi (1864), the latter of which was created by the junior society DKE. Other, later entrants included Hé Boulé (1875), Alpha Kappa (1878), Eta Phi (1879), Beta Chi (1883), and Kappa Psi (1895). Membership cost roughly $45 to $55. Sophomore society meetings were initially held Saturday nights from about ten o'clock until midnight and later shifted to Fridays. For several years, at least one of the societies reportedly branded its members with a hot iron. On the way home from the meetings, the groups would march back to the dormitories, sometimes stopping to sing society songs. Theta Psi and Beta Xi both happened to pass the Fence at about the same time during this march. When they crossed paths, they would sometimes get into a singing duel—on good days alternating society songs, and at less sophisticated moments trying to drown each other out by belting the songs as loudly as possible. It was probably this latter maneuver that drove the administration to ban all society singing outside of the halls in 1870 because other students were trying to sleep.

By the late 1800s, the senior societies were electing a total of 45 members, the junior societies about 120, and the sophomore societies about 50. A strong sentiment emerged on campus that the increasingly rambunctious sophomore societies were far too exclusive, and the spurned sophomores far too young to experience such rejection. The faculty tried to ban the sophomore societies on three separate occasions, but the students found ways to resurrect them until December 1900, when Yale president Arthur Hadley shocked the sophomore societies by announcing to their representatives that they had been abolished, effective immediately. For a while, at least, the societies lived on through rumor—a quarter-century later, some students still believed that every year one senior society man was also initiated as an honorary member of each of the supposedly dead sophomore societies in order to keep the tradition of the sophomore organizations intact. But Hadley's edict stood, and the sophomore societies never returned.

It is unclear when Yale began calling its junior organizations "fraternities"; some early histories of the university refer to them as junior societies and some as junior fraternities. In any case, they served as the third tier of the funneling of students toward the senior societies—and some were able to survive to the twenty-first century by acting as fraternities instead of societies while their freshman and sophomore counterparts were eliminated. Although numbers dictated that not nearly every junior society member would be tapped for a senior society, generally the junior societies wouldn't tap a man unless they thought he was a possible candidate for the greater honor. Junior society membership was often crucial if a student desired election to the Cochleaureati or an editorship of a campus publication, because the society members banded together like political parties to nominate, or "run," as they called it, their own.

Psi Upsilon (1838), Delta Kappa Epsilon (1844), Alpha Delta Phi

(1836), and Zeta Psi (1889) had campaign committees that would distribute the best sophomores so that the groups were fairly even. Each group took twenty-five men for the incoming junior class and about ten more over the course of the junior year. They held meetings on Tuesdays from about nine o'clock to midnight. Initially the junior societies met in rented rooms near the College Yard, but eventually they built tombs like their senior counterparts. In 1870, Psi U built a house that reportedly cost $15,000.

Elections to junior societies were announced ceremoniously on the Tuesday before the senior societies' Tap Day in a procedure known as Calcium Light Night. The societies would march—"Deke" in red gowns and hats, Psi U in white, "A.D." in green (Zeta Psi announced its elections at a banquet instead)—in double file behind a large calcium light. Each society member carried fireworks or burning red or green lights as the lines wove around campus and into dormitories to notify candidates of their election, frequently intersecting to the visual delight of the hundreds of onlookers.

Initiation rituals varied according to society, but the following early-twentieth-century account of one society's ceremony was typical. Huddled in the cellar of the society house, the initiates were dragged upstairs, one by one, by two "guards" (usually large athletes), and tossed to the floor in front of burning coals. When the initiate looked around, he saw hooded figures clad in black robes, groaning like demons. Suddenly, a loud, low voice seemingly from everywhere would fire a passage in Latin before bellowing, "Candidate! Translate!" As the surprised initiate attempted to translate, the hooded figures would shriek loudly enough to drown him out. The voice again: "Candidate, you have failed." The guards lifted the initiate, dragged him down the three flights of circular stairs (hitting every fifth step), and threw him out the door in a heap on the street. The battered student would eventually walk away dejected. At the first street corner, a junior would meet him and persuade him to come back to the cellar. The guards again seized him and thrust him up the stairs to throw him disdainfully on the floor, this time directly in front of the voice representing the "judge." As the coals glowed red, the voice would speak again: "Candidate, you have failed the test of learning. Now we must try your courage. Pick the sacred fruit out of the fire." Incredulously, the initiate would look up to see that the thunderous voice belonged to none other than the college dean, Frederick Jones, Skull and Bones 1884. Presumably, initiation ended soon afterward; anything that followed would have seemed anticlimactic.

☠   ☠   ☠

The attempt to make an outsider realize the overwhelming fascination, which a senior society exerts upon the mind of the average Yale undergraduate, would probably be useless. An election thereto is valued more highly than any other college prize or honor; and in fact these honors derive a good part of their attractiveness from their supposed efficacy in helping to procure the coveted election. There is nothing in the wide world that seems to him half so desirable. It is the one thing needful for his perfect happiness. And if he fails in gaining it, the chances are that he becomes a temporary misanthropist.

When Lyman Bagg wrote those words anonymously in 1870, the influence of the two senior societies, Skull and Bones and Scroll and Key, at Yale alone was tremendous. Between 1872 and 1936, of the thirty-four consecutively elected alumni fellows, seventeen were Skull and Bones men and seven were Scroll and Key men. Between 1862 and 1910, forty-three of the forty-eight university treasurers were Bonesmen. Every university secretary from 1869 to 1921 was a Bonesman. So were 80 percent of the university's professors between 1865 and 1916. Between 1886 and 1985, the university president was an alumnus of Bones, Scroll and Key, or Wolf's Head for sixty-eight of the ninety-nine years.

Scroll and Key had joined Skull and Bones in 1842 and quickly solidified its presence on campus as a powerful secret society. In its first year it kept a live eagle in its quarters for use during ceremonies. By the late 1800s, Keys not only rivaled Bones, but in some circles surpassed it.

The campus publication the *Yale Illustrated Horoscope* proclaimed in 1887:

> The ill-mannered customs and haughty mien of the Skull and Bones society are, of course, obnoxious to all outsiders and to these airs and notions can be laid the loss of that prestige . . . which now rests as a golden crown on the head of Scroll and Key. The objections . . . against the system . . . apply almost exclusively to the Skull and Bones organization. No other society has the brazen gall to attempt to crush the will of the majority. No other set of men are so brainlessly puerile and lack the title of gentlemen at times, as the dwellers of 322 High Street. . . . Not another living clan will refuse to salute you on the way to and from the society hall.

Members of Scroll and Key have included Cole Porter, Dean Acheson, Calvin Trillin, Garry Trudeau, Harvey Cushing, Benjamin Spock, Paul Mellon, A. Bartlett Giamatti, several Rockefellers, and many of Jackie Kennedy's Auchincloss step-relatives.

Over the next forty years after Scroll and Key's founding, several groups attempted to form alternative senior secret societies, but none of them was taken seriously. Star and Dart, a short-lived society established in 1843, had a pin depicting the eagle of Scroll and Key picking apart a skull and crossbones. In one corner a dart hovered, about to pierce the eagle; in another was a star that was supposed to represent "the prosperity and final success of the society over its rivals." The experience of Spade and Grave was a typical one for these imitators. Formed in 1866, Spade and Grave grew out of hostility toward Bones and plotted to overthrow it. An argument with three Bonesman editors of the *Lit.* inspired two "neutral" editors to launch the aspiring rival society. Its insignia was based on the *Hamlet* scene in which the gravedigger tosses up Yorick's skull with his spade. But the society immediately met with derision on campus as the students, probably spurred by the Bonesmen themselves, dismissed it by calling it "Bed and Broom," and, later, "Diggers." When

Diggers couldn't persuade any members of the class of 1870 to accept election, it disappeared.

The hostility toward the secret societies that sparked the formation of Diggers also led to the establishment of a more threatening group. In 1866, a group of seniors, armed with the knowledge that since they had not been tapped for a secret society, they had no one left to try to impress, created a satirical society at first called Bowl and Stones and later changed to Bull and Stones. The object of the organization was to attack its skewed namesake, Skull and Bones, by roaming about the campus during and after senior society meetings. The Stones men blocked the senior societies' doorways, sang mocking songs ("Haughty Bones is fallen, and we gwine down to occupy the Skull"), and wrought general havoc. The Stones men also offered fake taps to the more naive undergraduates, often successfully persuading them that they had been elected to the real thing. In 1867, the Stones men shattered ink bottles on the front of the Skull and Bones tomb and ripped the chain from its fence. Class of 1870 members wore in public a gold pin portraying a bull standing on stones, as if it were an authentic secret-society badge. In 1870, the Stones men overtook the confectioner who was delivering food to the Bones tomb for initiation night and confiscated the ice cream and other items that caught their fancy. (Eventually, Bones stationed a police officer in front of the tomb to discourage such behavior.) By that time, the group had become so well known that any student not elected to Bones or Keys was said to "belong to Stones." Anti-society sentiment continued, with society members occasionally becoming the targets of violent attacks, particularly when they returned home from meetings. In 1878, a group of students painted grafitti on the facades of the Bones and Keys tombs. The vandals were tried in City Court, facing some of New Haven's top lawyers, but were let off on a technicality. That year, students launched a daily anti-society newspaper. In the early 1880s, students vandalized the tombs yet again.

In 1884, before the annual class meeting to elect a class secretary and committees for the Promenade (a ball), Class Supper, Class Day, and Ivy (each graduating class ceremoniously planted ivy at the foot of the southern tower of the library), a group of seniors spread the word that at this session they would introduce a resolution to abolish the two senior secret societies. After a debate (none of which was published by the mainstream college press, which stuck to its longstanding policy of co-operating with the societies by not reporting their news), the seniors voted, many of them sure from their polls that they had enough support to rid the college of secret societies finally and abruptly. They did not. The societies won out, shocking both the neutrals and the society members, by a vote of 67 to 50. It turned out that the anti-society campaigners had counted on the votes of 15 students who, unbeknownst to the public, had quietly formed a third secret society the previous year. The society was Wolf's Head.

Wolf's Head first privately called itself "Grey Friars" and publicly referred to itself as "The Third Senior Society," out of respect for its predecessors, but because its pin portrayed a wolf's head, other students called the society by that name and it stuck. Unlike the other upstart societies, Wolf's Head was quickly accepted on campus. The *New Haven Register* wrote in 1886, "Wolf's Head is not as far out of the world, in respect to public knowledge of its doings, as are the other two. There is a sufficient veil of secrecy drawn around its mechanism, however, to class it with the secret societies, and this gives it a stability and respectability in Yale College circles that it might not otherwise obtain." Wolf's Head moved into its tomb, funded by alumnus Edward Harkness, in 1924. Wolf's Head members would eventually include future senator Thurston Morton, and ambassador Douglas MacArthur, Jr. Its tomb of Gothic stone contains a full bar, billiard room, mullioned windows, and an Egyptian motif centered on Isis and other Egyptian deities.

☠   ☠   ☠

"The secrecy of at least three-fourths of the so-called secret societies here has, in a great measure, passed away," professor and Bonesman Thomas Thacher wrote in his letter in the 1870s. "This is owing, in part, to the fact that, as the students pass on from the secret societies of their Freshman year to the new ones of their Sophomore year, and so on through the successive years of their college life, they enter into new combinations and hold more loosely to the obligations of their earlier years." The senior societies never allowed this to happen because their tight rein on their members began with only a year of college left. In addition, by carefully electing only the "proper" men, with the proper qualifications and the proper kinds of friends, the societies retained a certain respect. They were exclusive and elitist, but many agreed that they were so for good reason.

Not everyone, however. In 1844, the faculty voted to advise students not to join the societies, and in 1849, it voted to deny financial aid to students who became society men without requesting permission from the faculty (which did not necessarily grant it). In 1857, the faculty decided that non–society members would receive preference when the college doled out financial support. In 1862, Yale took this policy further, declaring that members of secret societies that did not require dues would receive half the usual financial aid, while secret-society members who paid dues would receive nothing. Not only did these stipulations fail to deter the students but those students eventually replaced the administrators who had voted against them. By 1884, half the faculty and the Corporation were members of a Yale secret society. In control, they were careful to quash efforts at restricting the societies.

Meanwhile, a similar system had evolved at the Sheffield Scientific School. Begun by Professor Benjamin Silliman (Bones 1837), "Sheff" operated both separate from and as a part of campus. One could be an undergraduate at Yale and study either science at Sheff or the core curriculum at the Academic Department, which housed the rest of the students. Sheff and the Academic Department would gradually commingle until they finally merged into one undergraduate body in 1945 (Sheff continued graduate-level instruction until 1956). Although Sheff was not integrated with the rest of the college, its students quickly became familiar with their counterparts' society system and soon set up their own.

The most prestigious secret societies at Sheff, which endure today, were Berzelius (1848) and the Literary and Scientific Society (1860); the latter, which grew out of resentment toward Berzelius, was renamed Book and Snake after three years, and counts among its membership Henry Ford II and Bob Woodward (who some people suspect found Watergate's "Deep Throat" through secret-society connections). Berzelius and Book and Snake began as four-year societies that kept their activities as secretive and private as Skull and Bones did. Initially these societies met for literary and academic discussions and debates—Berzelius members exchanged scientific papers—but in the 1870s they rented houses as well, and became the first college societies in the country to have their own dormitories. The names of the dormitories, Colony for Berzelius and Cloister for Book and Snake, became nicknames for the societies, which donated the buildings to Yale in the 1930s, when they moved into tombs and became true Yale societies.

But until then, Yale devoted its attention almost exclusively to Bones and to Keys. The rules for these societies were stringent—and there were plenty of them, both for getting in and then for comporting oneself as a member. The societies wouldn't necessarily reject a candidate because he was impoverished, but they might be more inclined to elect a man whose wealth could contribute to the society's upkeep. During the late 1800s, the rich, social-climbing underclassmen hoping for society election paid handsomely for entrance into a private dormitory called the Hutchinson, where through their "Hutch" connections they were more likely to make their way up the society ladder. These were the men who could afford good tailors and fine food, ordered cigars by the hundreds, gambled fives and tens on minutiae, and ruined expensive suits during their old-boy romps without a thought.

To even be considered for society election, an underclassman had to monitor his character as well as his achievements. Though success was far more important than scruples, immorality was frowned on, and displays such as necking with a girlfriend in public would "queer" a student, or take him out of the running. For this reason, juniors were more likely than other classes to abstain from drinking in public, lest they taint their all-important image. As the *Yale Daily News* explained in 1878:

> Now is the time of year when the Junior creeps into his hold and re-mains there, keeping as much out of sight as possible, and spending his time in waiting and praying, if perchance fortune may so smile upon him as to grant him the boon of a Senior election. Now is the time when the jolly Junior swears off until the summer vacation. Not because of the Senior societies, oh no! not he, but because you know, the liquor don't agree with me. Now he forgoes the Saturday evening walk, and the Church street opera house, and shut up in the solitude of his study, em-ploys his time in writing essays, and making himself solid. Now he is circumspect as to his bows, and bows low and obsequious or lofty and condescending, according to the great or little influence possessed by the party. Now is the time when the trembling Junior walks around the block to avoid meeting Mr. So and So, of Scroll and Key, or Mr. ___, of Skull and Bones, fearful lest he may not bow according to the aforesaid gentleman's pleasure, and by so doing, diminish his so considered sure chances, for was not the step-brother of his brother's most intimate friend, a member of Skull and Bones, or rather would have been if he had not declined an election. Certainly, and this is what gives to many a Junior a confidence in his chances, which bears him up until the bit-ter end, rendered all the more so by his former aspirations and hopes. Never mind, Junior, come forth from your hold, long suffering patience, buy the *News,* and drown your mournful thoughts in a good laugh at the follies of those false gods whom ye adore.

Literary critic and Princeton man Edmund Wilson argued in a 1923 *Forum* article that students were molded by this strange, sinister censor-ship. And other Yale students were well aware that they paradoxically sacrificed their individuality in order to become eligible for individual recognition; in 1896, junior Nathan Smyth railed against this aspect of the society system, a vehicle through which "evil creeps in under cover of good." He wrote:

The society member is becoming too much a hero among us. The desire to become society men ourselves is so great that we are sacrificing to it higher ends and principles. Freedom of speech and act is threatened by a subtle system of wire-pulling and toadying. The aspirant for social honors is so continually haunted by the fear of being "queered," that he can neither act nor speak without first considering whether he is endangering his chances for election.

Nevertheless, when Smyth was tapped for Skull and Bones later that month, he accepted.

For at least the first century and a quarter of the societies' existence, members were not allowed to speak of their own or a rival society or discuss anything remotely related to society business in the presence of outsiders. Bones and Keys men also usually did not speak when entering, exiting, or merely passing by their tombs—a rule that is still in effect today. When a neutral mentioned any senior society in the presence of a society member, or even hummed a bar of a society song, the member would look offended and, in the case of Skull and Bones, often leave the room. Sometime during the late nineteenth century, a theater troupe came to New Haven to perform *The Pirates of Penzance.* As a few Wolf's Head men attending an afternoon performance found out, the pirate king donned a Napoleon hat bearing a skull and crossbones. Later that day, the Wolf's Head men paid a visit to the actor at his hotel, where they told him that he would "make a local hit" if he displayed the numbers 322 below the skull and crossbones. That evening, when the character came out on stage wearing the altered hat, several students immediately stood up and left the building—while the rest of the Yale members of the audience apparently were tickled silly.

Seniors were never supposed to remove their engraved society pin. During the day a society man would display his pin on his necktie; at night he slept with it firmly attached to his nightclothes. Faculty members usually refrained from wearing their pin openly during official business, but young tutors, not far removed from their society heyday, were

sometimes too proud to hide theirs. Seniors who were gymnasts or row-
ers made sure to fasten their pin during practices and competitions on
whatever skimpy clothing they wore. Senior swimmers, to adhere to the
societies' policy, would compete with the pin in their hands or mouths.
(Perhaps it was one of these swimmers who in the 1880s reportedly had
to have an operation in nearby Bridgeport after swallowing his Skull and
Bones pin.)

The pins presented a bit of a paradox: A society man would proudly
flaunt his membership by wearing his glimmering pin practically at eye
level, but if anyone were to make even a passing comment about a society, the man would act outrageously insulted. As a Wolf's Head member
outlined in 1934:

> If we grant that an election to a senior society had become, like an elec-
> tion to Phi Beta Kappa in the days of its glory, "one of the greatest hon-
> ors in college"; if we grant that the failure to receive an election was one
> of the greatest disappointments; if we grant that any mention, direct or
> indirect, of the society system, or any of its trappings, was taboo in the
> presence of a society man; if we grant all this—and we must on the ev-
> idence, then it must have been annoying in the extreme, when condi-
> tions were most favorable, and almost unbearable when they were not,
> to sit across from a man at table; to meet him on the Campus; to talk
> with him in front of a fire in a College study or travel with him during
> vacation time, and to be aware every moment of his society badge star-
> ing at you from the necktie of his throat.

Wolf's Head members decided to do what they considered bucking the
trend by wearing their pins not on their neckties but on the supposedly
less egregious locale of their vests instead. (Apparently, nineteenth-
century Yale students gazed only at eye level and did not, in fact, look
down their noses. . . .) Eventually, Skull and Bones followed Wolf's
Head's example and within the society referred to that change as one of
the most momentous in the society's recent history.

Tap Day, an event that began in the 1870s and endured as an excruciatingly public ceremony for nearly a century, was the culmination of the selection process. Before Tap, juniors could only guess, hope, and place bets on who would go where and why. (The finer New Haven tailors, who fitted society members and society aspirants with their suits, also kept a pool going.) On a Thursday afternoon near the end of May, the juniors would group together, regardless of the weather, on what is now Old Campus, huddled with friends for support and consolation. Other students, faculty members, administrators, alumni, and even New Haven townies would line the perimeter, watching the event from windows, steps, rooftops, and streets. When the campus clock struck five, each of the senior societies would dispatch one member, often black-suited, who silently, soberly emerged from his tomb and made his way alone to campus without acknowledging anyone. As he wove his way into the crowd of white-faced juniors, he would often appear to approach one person and then move on to someone in the opposite direction. He would maneuver to the thickest part of the crowd, where the best candidates grouped, slap his man hard on the shoulder, and thunder, "Go to your room." The junior would turn around to see which society had tapped him by the pin the senior wore. Without a sound, the junior would head toward his room with the senior on his tail. Once there and alone, the senior would offer election to his society. Afterward, the senior would wind his way back to his tomb, where he would remain until the end of the evening. This process would repeat approximately every five minutes until each society had filled its roster of fifteen. When societies tapped men whom the crowd felt were deserving, the undergraduates would erupt with cheers and applause. Taps of men whose merit was questionable were met with cold silence.

Usually, Scroll and Key was known to tap the well-rounded achievers who were congenial, Wolf's Head chose the gregarious prep-school men, and Skull and Bones selected the successful. Athleticism, notably, was perennially prized—in 1905, of the forty-five juniors tapped for senior societies, thirty-two were athletes. Skull and Bones was the only society not to condone the practice of "packing," or tapping a small group of friends who insisted that either a society accept all of them or none of them.

Tap Day always scarred. The painfully public procedure left many men broken, because there were always more qualified students than there were society slots. Occasionally the tenseness of the afternoon caused a candidate to faint, reported Ernest Earnest in his 1953 book *Academic Procession*. In 1899, Lewis Welch explained:

> That afternoon has left in the hearts of a score and more of men as sharp and painful and deep wounds as perhaps they will ever suffer in all the battles of life. They have lost, generally for reasons which they cannot tell, that which they most desired of all the honors their fellows could give them. Their friends, and the college at large, have seen them conspicuously fail. The decision is irrevocable. A peculiar mystery is closed to them, a peculiar experience denied them, and a certain choice and helpful association prohibited. There is no undoing it all. The word has been given, and judgment has been passed.

But the feeling on campus was that a Yale man should be able to take this humiliation with class.

The prospect of facing a final judgment in such a public arena, how-ever, actually deterred some students from coming to Yale, and caused many fathers who doubted their sons' grit to refuse to send them to a school that could potentially cause such devastation. Even Yale gradu-ates would brag that they had successfully dissuaded prospective stu-dents from coming to Yale, and that they themselves would not give Yale a penny, precisely because of the existence of the society system.

In 1933, the chairman of the *Daily News* galvanized the juniors in an anti-society movement: that year the best candidates for society election did not appear in the quad for Tap Day. Instead, the societies had to hunt the juniors down by locating their rooms in order to offer election. But while some underclassmen exhorted, "Tap Day is dead!" the next year the event was back, held in Branford College court (where it was held for nearly two more decades), with Berzelius and Book and Snake added as first-time participants. The Sheff societies acclimated quickly by following the older societies' lead. Berzelius (BZ to its members), for example, marched in reverse order of height in black suits and ties from the library to its tomb for meetings.

The fifties and the sixties constituted an era that, at Yale and throughout the country, was fraught with changes that helped to set up new boundaries for the societies. The residential college system gathered steam; by 1963, each college had its own dean. In 1967, distributional requirements were dropped and the numerical grading system was replaced temporarily by the classifications of Honors, High Pass, Pass, and Fail. By the mid-sixties, Yale's admissions policies had been altered tremendously so as to recruit minorities and to place less emphasis on preparatory schooling and legacy ties. In 1969, Yale began to admit women. "Seldom was there such rapid change at Yale," Yale professor and historian Gaddis Smith said to me. "The climate of the sixties was one that looked down on distinction, elites, and special privilege. The societies experienced a withdrawal from self-congratulatory publicity, because there was embarrassment over that. There was some discussion that the societies were in their last years because they were so out of touch with the new cultural–social climate. The mood of protest against established authorities was connected with first the civil rights movement and then the Vietnam War. With the war going on, people wondered why they should give a damn about whether they got into a society."

The public Tap Day was finally done away with in 1953, when public outcry outweighed conventional sentiment. The change in the society system garnered national media attention as a momentous event. It also altered the way the senior societies attracted members. Some societies would begin to woo candidates early in the second semester, in a kind of masked pledging process. In 1966, the dean's office, which had drawn fire for releasing information from juniors' academic and extracurricular records to society members for review, persuaded the societies to agree not to contact juniors until one week before Tap Day. Today that practice has fallen by the wayside. Societies now get to know potential members in a strange, superficial courtship, in which both the courter and the courted must pretend that their meetings are purely social. In most cases, a society member, perhaps through a mutual acquaintance, will set up an informal social occasion with a candidate. Feigning fast friendship, the society member will then invite the candidate to many group activities (where the group will consist of society brothers, though their membership remains unacknowledged) so that he can introduce the candidate to as many members as possible. That way, the society member can drum up support and familiarity in time for the actual voting process.

Other societies formed to keep up with Yale's growing enrollment. The Elihu Club, which was founded in 1903 as a nonsecret society, tried to gain more respect in the mid-1900s by emulating its predecessors. In 1962, future *Washington Post* managing editor Robert Kaiser and future vice presidential candidate Joseph Lieberman were Elihu officers, but it was Lieberman, not Kaiser, who edited the society's regular bulletin. By the end of the century, however, Elihu had become more of a joke — the only society that accepted formal applications for membership. A group called Manuscript began as an underground society in the 1950s, and later moved up to a tomb (its members include current Yale dean Richard Brodhead and *Skulls* screenwriter John Pogue). St. Elmo, formerly a Sheff society, became a senior society in 1962. St. Anthony Hall, a three-year society (and the haunt of future deputy secretary of state Strobe Talbott and Washington, D.C., mayor Anthony Williams), also moved from Sheff to Yale. Aurelian, which began as an honor society in 1910, and Torch, an honor society founded in 1916, changed over to senior societies sometime during the late twentieth century.

By 1968, George W. Bush's senior year at Yale, there were eight "above-ground" societies, or societies with tombs, and about ten underground societies, which rented rooms in buildings around town. Desmos, Gamma Tau (informally known as Gin and Tonic), Ring and Candle, Mace and Chain, and Sword and Gate were among this latter bunch. The underground societies, knowing that they would have to work harder than their better-known counterparts to persuade juniors to join their ranks, would approach candidates well in advance of the week preceding Tap Day, before which the societies technically were not supposed to court juniors. The underground societies were generally much more lax than their entombed counterparts. Activities included listening to recorded music and telling dirty jokes for an entire evening. In the 1990s, these elite organizations often spent their nights bowling. But some of the programs were at least in the same vein as those of the more ambitious above-ground societies. One underground society game called "Guns," popular at least in the 1960s, revolved around a toy weapon located in the center of the room. The society held elections to choose the member who would get to "shoot and kill" any other member, thus eliminating him from the next election. In between ballots, during the "campaign period," players would try to form parties and gain votes. The frenzied politicking and inevitable backstabbing were supposed to teach the students interpersonal strategies, group dynamics, and cutthroat survival tactics.

Two of the underground societies in 1968 were coed with Vassar women and all of the societies except for Bones, Keys, and Wolf's Head admitted women soon after Yale became coeducational in 1969. But with the women came a more relaxed attitude that led to open society events in the tombs. Book and Snake, for example, still holds an annual Naked Party for invited outsiders. Elihu's "House Rules" declared that "Graduate members shall use discretion in bringing in guests and all guests must be accompanied by members." Even Wolf's Head occasionally admitted guests.

While the three oldest societies were castigated for refusing to open their doors to women until the 1990s, they also retained a higher level of respect and prestige—especially from old Yale alumni—than the other

societies did. They also had more money. (All of the societies are controlled by alumni trust associations that handle the endowment, pay the
bills, and act as a governing body.) In 1970, the *Daily News* reported "the
assets and endowments of five of the societies, which filed as non-profit
educational organizations, with the Hartford IRS. Scroll and Key's combined total was more than $2.7 million, Wolf's Head more than $2.3 million, Book and Snake more than $800,000, Manuscript more than
$300,000, and Elihu had assets of $700,000."

Relations between the societies were, and are, generally amicable.
While they compete against each other for certain students, there is an
unspoken sentiment of brotherhood, especially among Bones, Keys, and
Wolf's Head. Representatives from each of the major societies form an
inter-society council that meets occasionally to govern society life and re-
solve disputes. Moreover, because the societies understand each other's
purpose and secrecy, they respect one another. In 1942, to commemorate
Scroll and Key's centennial, Wolf's Head sent one hundred thornless
American Beauty roses accompanied by a poem composed for the occasion by Wolf's Head member and author Stephen Vincent Benét.

On occasion, though, the societies' territorialism could get fierce. For
example, when electing a new Yale president, society men in the administration usually stuck to their own party lines. When Yale secretary
Anson Phelps Stokes, a Bonesman, was up for the presidency in the mid-
1900s, he drew votes from the Bonesmen, but the Keysmen actively organized against the candidate, who eventually lost the election.

☠   ☠   ☠

In 1982, Henry Chauncey, a 1957 Wolf's Head member who served as
university secretary until 1981, said that the society system of his time
was "not unlike today—there was a good deal of worry if you could succeed in the world. It was perceived that getting in was the road to
success." The attitude of Yale neutrals toward these stalwart institutions
was and is still a mixture of respect, revulsion, and haughty ambivalence.
But most of all there remains the intense curiosity about what goes on in

those strange, seemingly lightless buildings that shut fifteen seniors and powerful alumni in and the rest of the world out. In 1934, the campus anti-society publication *Harkness Hoot* satirized this curiosity in a poem titled "A Freshman's Prayer on Thursday Night":

Perhaps some day if I am good,
I may be of that brotherhood . . .
There is something grand about a club,
So few can join it, there's the rub . . .
O Lord I pray them let me
Be a God in such society.
For, tho I know not what they do,
I greatly want to do it too!

Nineteen thirty-four was the last year the *Hoot* ever published an issue.

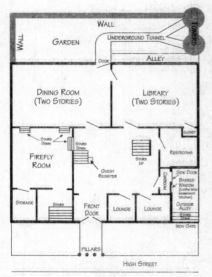

FIRST FLOOR

SECOND FLOOR

Floor plans to the Skull and Bones
tomb. Map by George Ward

Chapter Three

INSIDE HEADQUARTERS

The Old Brown Jug

Across the way from our Commons' Hall,
In sunshine and in storm,
A dark and mystery-haunted pile
Uprears its gloomy form.

A poison-vine o'erspreads its walls,
To rank luxuriance grown,—
Perhaps from feeding on a soil
Enriched by Skull and Bone.

Its portal dark and sombre is,
And on its plated door
Two massive locks of quaint device
Keep guard its secrets o'er.

No windows grace the darksome pile,
And all is black within,
Black as the deepest, darkest crime,
Black as the blackest sin.

A strange, oppressive sense of ill
About it seems to cling,

And all who pass its frowning door
Are filled with shuddering.

But when the night has grown apace
And stillness rules the earth,
Those massive doors and silent stones
To fearful sounds give birth.

"A sound of revelry by night,"
A sound that seems to tell
That demons wild instead of men
Within its portals dwell.

And often at the dark midnight,
When earth is draped in gloom,
The beings weird are seen emerge
From out their living tomb.

They step so proud, they look so loud,
Their bearing is so high,
That common folk are fain to shrink,
Whenever they pass nigh.

Like spirits from another world,
Down, deeper down than ours,
They seem to come all furnished
With dark and deadly powers.

And on their breasts they wear a sign
That tells their race and name;
It is the ghastly badge of death,
And from his kingdom came.

The son of Satan, son of Sin,

The enemy of man,
Still claims these worthies as his own
And counts them in his clan.

The sign they bear, in former days
The pirates of the seas,
The foes of God and scourge of man,
Unfolded to the breeze.

Where'er they steered their bloody backs
Their pennon stained the air;
They flung aloft the Skull and Bones
And bade the world beware.

Are these the pirates of our day?
Have they with petty crime
Together joined in evil league
In this, our later time?

Strive they to emulate the deeds
Whose fierce and fiendish thought
Upon the outlaws of the main
The curse of man has brought?

Whate'er they be, from whence they come,
Where'er they seek to go,
Their badge defies an honest world
And brands it as their foe.

O! may our Yale so fondly loved,
The Skull and Bones beware;
Avoid it like a faithless friend,
A serpent in his lair.

—anonymous, *The Iconoclast*, October 13, 1873

Phi Beta Kappa, which founded a Yale chapter in 1780, stood for *Philosophia Biou Kybernetes*, or "Love of wisdom, the guide of life." Its purpose was the "promotion of literature and friendly intercourse among scholars." PBK sponsored speeches and debates throughout the year in order to discuss topics such as philosophy, religion, and ethics. At Yale, PBK took a form similar to the literary societies Linonia and Brothers in Unity, except its membership was limited and its activities were shrouded in secrecy. Most members were elected and initiated during their junior year. Although members were supposed to be, and usually were, chosen from a list of top scholars submitted by the faculty, occasionally students were able to sneak a few scholastically inept friends in or to keep deserving foes out.

Yale chapter meetings, at first held twice a month, then reduced to once a month, were said to be conducted in a building that belonged to the Freemasons. The evening sessions, which began promptly at 6:30, usually consisted of a speech and a debate. Members were fined sixpence for arriving late, ten dollars for absence, and twenty dollars for "flunking an appointment." In December, the members annually celebrated the PBK chapter's anniversary by serving dinner, listening to an oration delivered by a graduate, and electing the next year's officers. Despite the fairly bland nature of the society's activities, its secrecy apparently sparked intrigue. Nonmembers, provoked by the organization's aura of mystery, broke into the PBK building twice in the late eighteenth century, supposedly "under the united influence of envy, resentment and curiosity," a chronicler reported at that time. In 1786, three seniors broke down the door of the office of the PBK secretary and stole his trunk, which contained society papers. Members tracked down the thieves, retrieved the papers, and forced the men to appear before the society membership to deliver a "voluntary" written confession in which they vowed never to reveal the secrets they had learned. Eighteen months later, the trunk was stolen again by unknown individuals.

In 1830, students and faculty sparred over what came to be known as the Great Conic Sections Rebellion. While the cause seems simple, the battle was fierce. The faculty insisted that because Yale tradition dictated that students had to conduct their recitations of conic sections (geometrical curves such as ellipses, circles, parabolas, or hyperbolas) with only the aid of a diagram, they would have to continue to do so. The class of 1832, however, argued that some classes had had the privilege of being able to use the book during the recitation, so they should be given the same opportunity. When it came time for recitations, the students refused to follow the faculty's orders. Enraged, the administration, citing "a combination to resist the government," suspended classes and demanded that students sign a written agreement to obey college laws. When forty-three of the ninety-six members of the class of 1832 refused to sign, they were expelled — and their names were distributed to other colleges on a blacklist so that they would never be admitted by another school.

During this time, the students' inability to overthrow the stringent rules of an institution set in its ways was accompanied by the country's more broadly influential period of Anti-Masonic reform. In 1832, the Anti-Masons were so intent on decreasing the influence of secret societies on America's ruling elite that they sponsored a candidate for president, former U.S. attorney general William Wirt of Maryland. The Anti-Masonic fever that blanketed the nation threatened to wipe out any organizations so much as hinting at mystery. At Yale and other elite institutions, the craze hit home by forcing Phi Beta Kappa to strip away its secrecy.

The organization's handshakes and signs were published and it was forced to stop performing secret ceremonies. As the mystery was ripped from Phi Beta Kappa, so was the prestige. The society steadily declined in popularity for several decades until it disappeared entirely from Yale's campus in the 1870s amid charges that it was electing socialites over scholars. Phi Beta Kappa was not resurrected at Yale until early in the next century.

The proliferation of many new literary societies in the 1820s, combined with the demystification of Phi Beta Kappa, Yale's most secret society at the time, probably set the stage for a new, more secret, more prestigious, more impenetrable organization. Another Phi Beta Kappa incident also bears relevance. During the 1832–33 academic year, the secretary of Yale's PBK chapter was valedictorian William H. Russell, class of 1833, who later became a member of the Connecticut state legislature and a general in the Connecticut National Guard. That year, a prominent undergraduate scholar, Eleazar Kingsbury Foster, class of 1834, was conspicuously left out of Phi Beta Kappa elections. Reportedly, Russell was furious and openly condemned the society for its conduct. In December 1832, Russell took Foster under his wing and joined with thirteen other students, including the future judge Alphonso Taft, to form the bigger, badder, better society they eventually called Skull and Bones. Many of the Bonesmen themselves, at least in the twentieth century, have been told a story along similar lines: In 1832, their version goes, a group of students were extremely dissatisfied with the quality of the faculty at Yale. As a result, they met separately as a group of elite scholars. They had to meet secretly, because if the faculty found out what they were doing and why they were doing it, they would have been thrown out of school.

The society's name and symbols were not entirely original. In the early 1800s, several American educational institutions followed German models of both schools and societies; the Germanic societies' emphasis on songs, for example, is clearly manifest at a place like Yale. When William Russell took some time off from Yale to study in Germany, he could very well have been introduced to a German student club with the death's-head logo, and then returned to Yale and set up a branch of that club. The evidence is compelling: Nineteenth-century raids uncovered documents suggesting that Skull and Bones is but a chapter of a mother organization. A thirtieth-anniversary celebration invitation describes "a Jubilee Commemoration of the History of Our Establishment in New Haven." An accompanying historical address bears a title page pronouncing "The Eulogian Club: An Historical Discourse Pronounced before our Venerable Order on the Thirtieth Anniversary of the

Foundation of our American Chapter in New Haven July 30th 1863 Thursday evening. By Timothy Dwight of 1849 New Haven 1863." A 1933 society document refers to "the birth of our Yale chapter."

The Bones building itself supports this theory. A room known as the German room is rife with German artifacts (many predating the Franco-Prussian War), and German phrases are engraved in the dark wooden walls, accompanying an iron cross. One print in the tomb portrays an open burial vault with four human skulls lying on a stone slab around a jester's cap, an open book, several mathematical instruments, a beggar's scrip, and a crown. The picture is accompanied by the phrases *"Wer war der Thor, wer Weiser, wer Bettler oder Kaiser?"* ("Who was the fool, who the wise man, beggar, or king?") and *"Ob Arm, ob Reich, im Tode gleich"* ("Whether poor or rich, all are equal in death"). Next to the print hangs a card reading, "From the German chapter. Presented by Patriarch D.C. Gilman of D. 50." Five parlor-type photographic pictures of scenes from "German Student Life" are also in the tomb. Furthermore, Bonesmen confirmed for me that one of their traditional songs is sung to the tune of "Deutschland über Alles," the German national anthem. (One Bonesman carefully pointed out that this anthem was penned not by Hitler but by Haydn.) Skull and Bones "has Germanic origins, but there is no longer a connection to any German organization now," another Bonesman elucidated. "When they started, the founders were not college kids as we know them. They were a very adult set of the ruling elite who were into codified ways of pursuing what they understood to be dignified activities. If there was relative racism or sexism in the German national anthem, it came from the culture at that time."

Given how societies have generally worked at Yale—students upset with one incumbent organization would pull away to form another—it is likely that all three theories are correct: Russell was probably provoked by the injustices of the Phi Beta Kappa process and by the inadequacy of the faculty, and inspired by his experience in Germany. In any case, the Germanic influence has faded. None of the Bonesmen with whom I spoke were quite sure how or why Skull and Bones was founded. When

I ran the different lines of thinking by them, most said the Phi Beta Kappa thread sounded more familiar. This ignorance isn't particularly shocking, even at an institution so determined to preserve its past. In most Yale societies, there is no requirement that members pore over the often dense tomes of their society histories.

But if Skull and Bones' Germanic origins have faded, Bones itself has stayed strong—and unyielding. As the first page of a Skull and Bones booklet titled "Continuation of the History of Our Order for the Century Celebration," dated June 17, 1933, reads, "I hereby confess: That there is no History of the Bones. How could there be? It is the very essence of our traditions that there is no change. The heavy thinkers of the barbarian twentieth century may be much perplexed by the problem of time and space, but the Goddess knows that there is only one time, Skull and Bones time, and only one place, Her Temple, and that nothing else exists."

☠   ☠   ☠

At first, the organization, called the Eulogian Club, operated unbeknownst to the rest of Yale and tapped the majority of its members from the junior society Alpha Delta Phi. After about a year, the club called a special meeting and officially adopted the insignia of the skull and crossbones, at which time the members fastened a drawing of the logo to the outside of the door to the chapel in which they met, thus sparking the mystery for outsiders. On Christmas Eve 1833, the club held such a raucous meeting that the faculty convened a special session on Christmas Day to discuss the group. The faculty sent to nine members of the society—including a future congressman, Yale treasurer, and associate justice of the Supreme Court of Louisiana—a warning and a letter to their parents. Sometime early on, the society took as its symbol the number 322. The Greek orator Demosthenes died in 322 B.C., when, according to Bones lore, Eulogia, the goddess of eloquence, ascended into heaven and did not return until 1832, when she happened to take up residence with Skull and Bones. Bones lore refers to the "First Miracle of the origin of <u>Our Goddess</u>" and her arrival at Skull and Bones as "the equally miraculous transmigration of Her Spirit to Yale College two thousand one hundred and fifty-four years after her birth." Since then, Bonesmen have traditionally signed their intra-society letters "Yours in 322." The number gained such a mystical significance at the university that in 1967, the year George W. Bush became a member, a well-off graduate student with no connections to Skull and Bones reportedly donated $322,000 to the society. "A lot of guys use the number as a code to remember things by. John [Kerry] even uses it," said David Thorne (Bones 1966), who is the Massachusetts senator's ex-brother-in-law, onetime campaign manager, and close friend. Thorne chose 322 as the number for his office telephone extension.

In 1856, Daniel Coit Gilman (Bones 1852), the founding president of Johns Hopkins University, officially incorporated the society as the Russell Trust Association. On March 13 of that year, Skull and Bones stopped meeting in apartments scattered around campus (including, for a few years, rooms on the corner of Chapel and College Streets, behind the room used by the Linonia Society) and moved into its present tomb on High Street. The size of the building was precisely doubled in 1903, and was last renovated during the summer of 1998. The initial structure cost between $7,000 and $8,000 to build, including the furniture, with the walls and foundation comprising about $5,200 of that amount. Renovations have cost close to $50,000.

On the outside, the Bones tomb, which members also call the Temple, the T, or the Boodle, is a cold, foreboding Greco-Egyptian structure of brown sandstone with sparse narrow windows of dark glass. Stairs guarded by a black latched gate on the right side of the building lead down to a small barred window that looks into a corner of the kitchen, where servants prepare the society's meals. The kitchen looks something like a butler's pantry in an old estate house, or the kitchen in a preparatory school dormitory, with stainless steel tureens and worn walls. The emergency door, an iron monstrosity, is also located down in this corner. The yawning iron doors standing approximately twelve feet

high at the front of the tomb are zipped in padlocks and usually surrounded by barren, skeletal trees, as is much of New Haven.

In its three stories and an attic, the Bones tomb houses a great morass
of, simply, stuff, as if the building were not so much a foreboding crypt
as a multistory storage space. Scattered throughout the tomb are a pot-
pourri of stuffed moose heads, candles, mannequin knights in armor,
antlers, boating flags, manuscripts, medieval artwork, old photographs, a
samovar, a Buddha on an elephant, a trunk full of woolen blankets, and
statuettes of Demosthenes. Many of the items are gifts from Skull and
Bones alumni. Architect John Walter Cross (Bones 1900) decorated the
hallway, which is dotted with war portraits provided by other graduates;
Russell Cheney (Bones 1904) donated a painting of skeletons dancing
in a garden and another painting of Bonesmen sitting in the sun;
a "Patriarch Miller" gave the tomb the Aldine edition of the works
of Demosthenes; Ganson Depew (Bones 1919) offered a first edition of
Laurence Sterne's *Tristram Shandy*. Though daunting on the outside,
the inside of the tomb of Skull and Bones resembles more the Victorian
house of a pack rat.

In one corner of the building, a glass case exhibits several gilded
baseballs printed with dates and scores of Yale games. In another hang a
few pieces by distinguished painters such as J. Alden Wier. In more recent years, the interior of the tomb has lost a bit of its elegance because
its rooms have become too crowded with relics. "Bones is like a college
dorm room," a Bones graduate of the 1980s told me. "On the desk there
were one hundred thousand pens, half with caps off, old drafts of term
papers. There were socks underneath the couch, old half-deflated soccer
balls lying around."

Behind the large green curtain that blocks light from the inside of
the door, the decor of the rooms is hardly consistent, save the high ceilings, wood paneling, and a tendency to reflect Gothic overtones and
Teutonic influence. In some cases it may be difficult to distinguish between coincidence and camp; take as exhibit the two staircases that consist of thirteen steps apiece. Near the front door is a bulletin board onto

which members tack notes, announcements, and letters. While one room is adorned with Chinese panels and dotted with bones from the hand of a monk and one is sheathed in a Brussels carpet, another's colored-tile floor reflects gaudy walls done up in red and black with white woodwork. Nineteenth-century tapestries abound. During an earlier period, any permanent decorations differing from the conventional Gothic norm were largely forbidden — one undated Skull and Bones House Committee report discloses, "Due solely to the strenuous efforts of the secretary of RTA [Russell Trust Association] the painter of the job was dissuaded from scattering a few cumulus clouds among the resplendent stars on the dome of the IT [Inner Temple]." Periodically, the society's House Committee chooses portions of the tomb to renovate: walls, ceilings, woodwork, and floors will be painted, waxed, and refinished, carpets will be replaced, roofs redone, and basement rooms whitewashed.

War runs as a prominent motif within the building. During and after the Civil War, founder General Russell sent muskets that Bonesmen managed to incorporate into the society's initiation rites for several years. The tomb houses a large collection of Civil War and World War I and II memorabilia, including German helmets and a machine gun from a plane in which a Bonesman was shot down and taken as a German prisoner. Another member wore a single pair of boots throughout his active duty with the Allied forces and shipped the pair back to the tomb immediately upon the armistice.

But the tomb seems like more of a shrine to those who do not survive: death imagery is everywhere. One Latin phrase engraved in the tomb is *"Tempus fugit"* ("Time flies"). Dozens of skeletons and skulls, both human and animal — elk, buffalo — grip the walls. A mummy lies prone on a mantel in the upstairs hall. The death's-head logo stamps everything from crockery to painted borders on the wall to glittering Exit signs printed with letters composed of tiny skulls. In the kitchen, each piece of silverware bears the mark S.B.T. (for Skull and Bones Tomb or Skull and Bones Treat). Cups and mugs of all sizes are skull-shaped. In the dining room, dim and intimate, light shines through the gaping eye-holes of fixtures in the shape of skulls.

When a Bonesman once mentioned the tomb's "steadily daunting collection of the Dance of Death," he may have been referring to, among other things, a colored wood engraving titled *Death and Napoleon* that depicts the caricatured conqueror confronting a grinning skeleton astride carrion (in the nineteenth century, this picture inexplicably hung in the kitchen). The walls celebrate death as if it were a victory, or at least some measure of glory, with artistic adornments such as a variety of framed pictures of skulls as well as *The Signing of the Death Sentence of Lady Jane Grey* and *The Earl of Strafford Going to Execution.* One of the gravestones in the tomb, marked "Sperry," sits near a decrepit skull that may or may not have been Sperry. William Blake's prints, though apparently not his poetry, abound. In the main foyer lies a tablet inscribed *"Memento mori"* ("Remember that you must die") dedicated "to the departed Bones."

Despite the surplus of silent companions, some interlopers agree that the ambience within the tomb is less *Sixth Sense* than *Bride of Chucky.* Marina Moscovici, a Connecticut art conservator who in 1999 completed a six-year effort to restore fifteen paintings in the building, described the atmosphere to me as "spooky, but funny spooky. Everything has that Skull and Bones theme to it. It's sort of like the Addams Family; it is campy in an old British men's smoking club way. The place is very musty and old. It's not glamorous by any means. It's just like a funky old house with dark, narrow passageways and little tiny stairwells everywhere." The bones in Bones, a Bonesman added, "were probably taken from bio classes," and the death motif, he said, was comparable to "a college dorm room where a guy will have Marilyn Manson and Motley Crüe posters. At that time [in the nineteenth century] they used Gothic and Teutonic images instead."

A Bonesman from the 1970s explained to me the society's philosophy behind the dark ornamentation. In a place bent toward self-aggrandizement, the motif of mortality is apparently intended to bring the brothers down to size. "Skull and Bones is not about the scary stuff. It's a context for what becomes an experience at a young age of the finitude of this existence. Every time we looked around we were reminded that a king's skull looks just like a pawn's skull. You leave this world the same way as everyone else," he said. Constant reminders of their own mortality may also serve to prod society members to realize that they do not have that much time during which to accomplish the achievements that would make them worthy of Skull and Bones.

In fact, when the art does not focus on death or war, it tends to center with bravado on the Bonesmen themselves. Moscovici said the mostly nineteenth-century, mildly impressionistic portraits, at least ten of which blanket the walls of the dining room at five feet by three feet apiece, are works commissioned by the society that depict only the most illustrious Bonesmen, such as President and Chief Justice William Howard Taft and Chief Justice Morrison R. Waite. One of these portraits depicts in the background a skull with a bird perched on it. The latest portrait added to the collection — and one of the most prominently placed in the building — is of George Herbert Walker Bush, whose photographs (of him alone and with dignitaries) have adorned several rooms for years. "These paintings are sentimental, historical," one Bonesman has said. "We are the stewards of history, and these portraits were given to us in honor." Nonetheless, the society had to call in Moscovici because of spots and tears in the paintings apparently caused by Bonesmen throwing food, footballs, and Frisbees. "It's as if once a painting got a small tear in it, they figured, 'Well, there goes that one,' and felt free to ruin the rest of it," Moscovici told me. Other artwork includes a picture of George Washington delivering his inaugural address, a picture titled *Youth in the Voyage of Life,* and engravings of the pseudo-Latin gibberish phrases *"Nihilne te concureus Bonorum omnium morir?"* ("Don't you realize that all good men die?"), *"Irr ossitus amor"* (roughly, "Love turns into bone"), and *"Ossa Patriarchuns tradeba ut deos ornerannes"* ("The Patriarchs handed down the bones to us to honor the gods").

Most of the paintings hang in the dining room, by far the most impressive chamber in a building that is hardly luxurious. From atop the doors to the ceilings, windows standing thirty feet high overlook a court-yard. On one end of the room, also called the Boodle, looms a grand, expansive fireplace—large enough to stand in—that roars beneath a mirror in a scene that one observer said is "like a Gothic scary movie." Above the fireplace, a mantel with skulls and bones carved into the stone bears small silver and bronze skulls engraved "322," gifts from Bonesmen past (one reads "322 from the S.E.C. of 1858"). Across the room is an-other, slightly smaller fireplace. The "shades" to the windows are actu-ally scrolls that display the lyrics to the Skull and Bones songs; they unfurl from the wall like old-style slide projector screens.

Other quarters include a library containing sofas, textbooks, and every book or pamphlet written by Bones alumni, called "patriarchs" or "pats." At one point, the library also contained the Constitution of Phi Beta Kappa. An elegantly framed dark velvet cushion bears the pins, like decapitated foes, of every other society that has existed at Yale, including the mocked Spade and Grave and the foiled pests of Bull and Stones. The library, which is carpeted in crimson, has in the past contained to-bacco, pipes, and decks of cards. Pipe bowls in the shape of skulls and stamped "M. Gambier, Paris" were marked in red ink with the names of Skull and Bones members.

A reading room has old, 1940s club-style leather chairs, and another fireplace. One brownish-red carpeted office (there is another, smaller one, too) is complete with computers and a printer, reading lamps, a bed, and walls decorated with letters from William Howard Taft and George Bush, two of the society's presidential patriarchs. A small closet holds Bones membership catalogues and a set of bound books, one for each year of the society. In another room lie the costumes used by the nineteenth-century literary societies Linonia and Brothers in Unity and an oil painting of Calliope, the Muse of epic poetry, that used to hang in Calliope Hall, as well as the pledge that initiates of the Calliope literary society had to take to receive membership. Throughout the building, the furniture and adornments are old and worn. "There isn't gobs of money spent anywhere," said a person who has been in the tomb. "It's just being maintained with whatever they can just get by with."

Several of the rooms are numbered. In 323, a mantelpiece supports a silver pitcher and two goblets marked 323. The main hall, 324, has a ceiling of dark wood and is lined with dozens of approximately 12 x 20-inch photographs of the fifteen members of each year's club grouped around a table bearing a human skull and crossbones. A safe, approximately 20 x 26 inches and 15 inches deep, is set into the wall. In 1902, Skull and Bones formally dedicated the newly constructed rooms of 324½, 325, 326, 327, 328, 329, and the "Kit." (A society document jokes, "So that by the naming of the coat-closet, bsc as the *Whole,* we then had the *Whole Kit and Boodle.*")

Members call the most private room, where the most sacred activities have always taken place, the Inner Temple, IT, or room 322. Guarded by a large, locked iron door that has thwarted trespassers during break-ins, the Inner Temple stands approximately fourteen feet square, with four-foot-high black walnut wainscoting and walls spread with valuable oil paintings, interrupted only by a fireplace. Immediately in front of the door lies an inlaid floor mosaic of the number 322, which mirrors the 322 engraved beneath Greek letters spelling out Demosthenes' name on the opposite wall. A skull and crossbones hangs on brackets on the inside of the entrance above the door, which is flanked by two "bell clappers." Beneath a blue-painted dome (sans cumulus clouds) with a skylight in the center of the ceiling, a card table displays a skull on a cushion and a five-minute sandglass. In the southeast corner of the room stands a tocsin that is sounded during ceremonies and before certain activities; it is likely the bell Yale used in its earliest days. A life-size rendition of the objects of the Bones pin—which was mocked by outsiders for many years as "the crab"—is inlaid in a black marble hearth. Below the mantel, the Latin phrase *"Bari Quippe Boni"* (one translation could be "Bars indeed are good"), in old-English-style typography, is also inlaid in marble. At one end of the room, on a small platform underneath the Yale College flag, stands a chair in front of a large grandfather clock with a skull and

crossbones on the face. This clock has appeared in many of the Skull and
Bones annual group photographs; elsewhere in the tomb is a smaller
clock with the same figure on its face. Above the platform a cane and a
spade are attached to the wall. On a marble mantelpiece in the Inner
Temple rest several more small treasures, such as the spectacles of Yale
president Ezra Stiles, a pipe with a skull and crossbones, a silver goblet,
a bronze statuette of Demosthenes, and a ballot box.

In this room looms a huge case containing a skeleton, which with a
chivalric irreverence Bonesmen refer to as "the Madame," out of their
conviction that it was once Madame de Pompadour, the fashionable so-
cialite mistress of King Louis XV and one of the most influential women
of the eighteenth century. Each side of the case divides into compartments that keep some of the society's valuables and manuscripts. At the
base of the skeleton a child-size coffin once lay, the skeletal former occu-
pant of which dangles above the mantelpiece. One of several crew-
related relics in the building, "Pioneer Yale No. 1," which hangs above
the Madame, was the first flag flown from a Yale boat in the New Haven
harbor. On each side of the case hangs a picture beneath a sword fixed
to the wall. Also in this room are a wardrobe that holds some initiation
materials in a drawer, and a case that displays an old black robe. Perhaps
the most important item in this room is a gilt frame with a gold door that
hangs over the mantel and below the child's skeleton. When a spring at
the back of the piece is pressed, the door opens to reveal a tinted wood
engraving of Eulogia.

The large skeleton key to the Inner Temple is kept in a safe—"cave,"
in Bones-speak—in a locked room called the Outer Temple, the key to
which is in a room down the hall, known as the "nest" or "dark room."
The door to the Outer Temple, or OT, is also covered by a steel plate.
Inside, a chandelierlike light with a dangling pull chain illuminates a
mess of group photographs of varying sizes crammed together. From the
floor of the northwest corner of the Outer Temple, a wooden step leads
up to a large, black walk-in vault with a combination dial lock and a yel-
lowed engraved picture of a skull and crossbones. Given the ways other

societies hide their valuables, it is likely that Skull and Bones' most important documents, most valuable possessions, and the best information it has culled on the other societies are all located in here. Next to the vault is a storeroom of sorts, piled high with junk, including a skull and, according to at least one account, a fake gorilla head.

The obsession with locks, or "puzzles" in Bones lingo, is most noticeable on the front door to the tomb itself (though some Bonesmen are more likely to use the keypad on the side door rather than the combination lock on the front door). Woe to the visitor who guesses wrong; in a manner comparable to the circumstances in "The Lady or the Tiger," the outsider who yanks the wrong padlock will actually ring the doorbell. When someone is in the tomb, the door handle is flipped a particular way and locked from both sides. Another Bonesman can gain entrance if he presses a "secret buzzer," I was told, and, when prompted, utters the passwords, "Uncle Toby sent me."

Despite the security, some raids have succeeded. In a short booklet titled "The Fall of Skull and Bones/ compiled from the minutes of the 76th regular meeting of the Order of the File and Claw," published on September 29, 1876, the authors describe a break-in of gargantuan proportions. (The Latin on the cover, *"De ossibus—quid dicam? Ilium fuit!"* translates to "About Bones what should I say? Troy once existed!") Beneath the subhead "Babylon is fallen," the writer describes in painstaking detail how, over the course of several hours, the intruders managed to cut the inch-thick iron bars covering the outside of the back-cellar windows of the tomb (hence File, one would imagine), to remove the long nails fastening a strong iron netting spanning the wood frame of the window (hence Claw), and to break down several other security obstacles in the way. The members of the Order of File and Claw published a map of the interior of the tomb with analytical descriptions of some of the more interesting items they encountered, such as a framed set of "Directions to Freshmen," signed by Thomas Clap and dated Yale College, 1752, and manuscripts by well-known ancient Greek, Latin, and German writers. When the group cracked open the building's safe, they found only a bunch of keys and a small gilded flask half full of brandy.

There was, the group seemed surprised to discover, "a total absence of all the 'machinery' which we had been led to expect." They found no documents bearing what they deemed to be Skull and Bones secrets — and no written constitution, except for "a few directions similar to the suggestions appended to the Delta Kappa by-laws." The Order of the File and Claw debated whether or not to open up the doors of the tomb for the good of the greater public. "We think no one will deny that we had it in our power at one stroke not only to take away forever all the prestige which her supposed secrecy [sic] has given this society, but to make her the laughing-stock of all college, and render her future existence extremely doubtful." But the group kept the tomb closed because members did not want to offend the good friends they had in the society. Instead, they were satisfied with the souvenirs they smuggled out of the building. Soon after the burglary, the society thoroughly sealed up the window through which File and Claw gained access — and it has presumably remained sealed ever since.

☠   ☠   ☠

In the movie *The Skulls,* soon after main character Caleb Mandrake is initiated into his New Haven college's secret society, which is clearly modeled after Skull and Bones, he is taken to the society's retreat. As described in the movie's original screenplay, the society transports Mandrake on a restored 1920s Herreshoff cruising yacht to a lush island described as "a green jewel." Among verdant lawns and tennis courts, forest growth and "a magnificently restored 1800s lodge," Mandrake speaks with some of the society's most powerful alumni, who include a senator and a member of the Harvard Law admissions committee, the university provost, and Mandrake's own father, a judge about to enter Supreme Court confirmation hearings.

Long ago, Skull and Bones' real-life retreat may have seemed relatively this indulgent an Emerald City to its newly inducted members.

The tomb, before the building was expanded and the ivy cut away, from the 1879 Skull and Bones photograph album. Manuscripts and Archives, Yale University Library

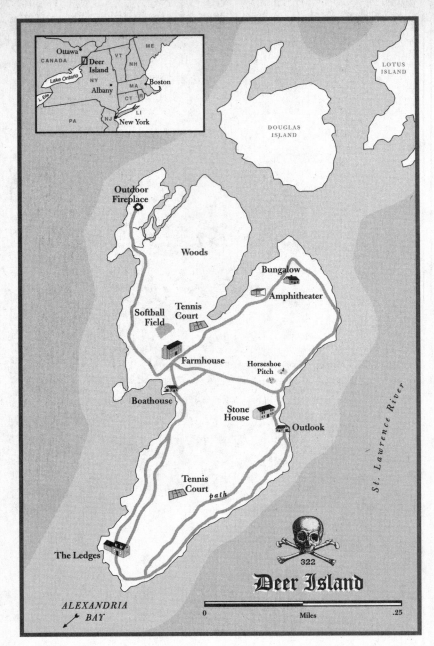

Map of Deer Island, a forty-acre island in the St. Lawrence River owned by Skull and Bones and used as a society retreat.

Map by George Ward

Deer Island—a gift to the society, a member told me, from a Patriarch Miller—is a forty-acre span of private woodlands with a two-mile shoreline, 340 miles from New York City, on the St. Lawrence River two miles north of Alexandria Bay, New York. To get there, Bonesmen can call Rogers Marina for a chartered boat to pick them up. One 1937 Skull and Bones letter details, "Next week twelve of the latest vintage p-ts (D-135) will clamber out of the ample-beamed 'Madam' at Deer Island, claim rooms in the higher reaches of the Stone House, strip themselves of barbarian vestments, and settle down to the business of undisturbed relaxation in the crowning week of the college year."* In its heyday, Deer Island was a frequent club reunion and family vacation spot. Heralded in an early-twentieth-century brochure as "The Best of All Ways to Lengthen Our Days," Deer Island offered turn-of-the-twentieth-century lodgings for "a Club to get together and rekindle old friendships." Softball fields and tennis courts were at one point surrounded by rhubarb plants and gooseberry bushes, and cat boats waited on the lake for lazy afternoons of swimming, fishing, and aquaplaning. Guests could also, if they chose, do nothing more than relax on the sand. In the early to mid-1900s, servants presented guests with three daily meals of delicacies such as clam chowder and strawberry shortcake. (Guests were instructed not to tip Deer Island servants, who already "receive good wages," according to a Bones document.)

Visitors can hike from their guesthouses through wooded paths, wildlife, and patches of wildflowers to an outdoor fireplace or to a horseshoe pitch located in a pine grove. Instead of mile markers, the fifteen miles of hiking trails are spiked with carved stone Skull and Bones markers engraved with the number 322. A large, grassy, Greek-inspired

---

*Society documents, even those that are not supposed to leave the tomb, are coded. Many Bones words and names are abbreviated, such as C.T. for Corporal Trim or SAs for sacred anthems, or have some letters replaced by dashes, such as C—b (Club) or P-t (Pat, for Patriarch). Most documents are signed for authenticity with the farewell "Yours in 322," though William Howard Taft often signed his intra-society letters "Yours in Bones."

outdoor amphitheater hosts gatherings and dramatics. The brochure, which points out that the island is complete with hot water and electricity, advertises the sanctity of the place. It cajoles:

NO telephones   NO dirty dishes   NO interruptions
Just PEACE and QUIET

Several buildings on the island are available for Bonesmen's use. The Outlook, located on the eastern part of the island, is the main clubhouse, with a dining room, a "lounging room," a semicircular library, fifteen bedrooms (seven with balconies) that overlook the water from a tall granite ledge on the riverbank, and a main hall that is "filled with a collection of curious and beautiful mementos and relics gathered from many lands." A hundred yards away, the Stone House contains a large hall decorated with a collection of ancient armor that was once housed at the Albany Historical Society, two galleries, and eleven bedrooms. On the southern tip of the island, the Ledges, a group of semidetached houses on the shore, has a large open veranda that serves as a dining room, and nine bedrooms expressly for the use of Bones spouses and families. Both the Ledges and the Outlook include boathouses. The Bungalow at one end of the island was at times specifically designated "for the entertainment of ladies."

Today Skull and Bones still tries to impress each new batch of initiates by sending the group on a field trip to the island, usually around the time of Yale's "Dead Week," which is the stretch after exams and before graduation. Patriarchs still plan reunions and getaways there, especially between the beginning of May and Labor Day. They sometimes bring their families to the island for the summer-camp-like environment; to encourage visits, Bones hires a few members, like camp counselors, to supervise activities each summer. A woman who went with her boyfriend to the island in the late 1980s during a reunion week told me that the island unquestionably had a summer-camp feel. "Mostly WASP-y, mainstream lawyers and insurance guys were there with their families. It was pretty relaxed; people were wearing shorts and sneakers. The Bonesmen put on a show. I remember we made arts-and-craftsy Skull and Bones things—I guess it was an activity for the kids. We made a big Skull and Bones, but I forget if we traced it or made a gravestone rubbing," she said. "It was sort of dorky. I had thought the island was going to be gazillionaire luxurious, and it wasn't very glamorous at all. There was a cocktail hour, but the dressiest people got was Talbots-type preppy clothes."

Deer Island is run by the Deer Island Club, a membership-only group of Bonesmen who contribute a certain amount for maintenance. The Deer Island Club is controlled by the Deer Island Club Corporation (established in February 1907), the purposes of which, according to the corporation's articles of association, are

> to promote the social intercourse of its members, and to provide for them facilities for recreation and social enjoyment; and to this end, to purchase, hold and convey any property, real or personal, which may be necessary or convenient therefor; to maintain a Club House for the use and benefit of its members; and to adopt by-laws and generally to exercise all the usual powers of corporations not prohibited by said statutes.

Any member of the Russell Trust Association, the corporation's bylaws read, is eligible for membership in the Deer Island Club Corporation.

Skull and Bones has always subsidized the upkeep of the island with alumni donations. In 1937, for example, individual Bones guests paid all-inclusive rates of $5 a day or $25 a week; Bones "clubs"—the groups of fifteen—paid $300 a week. To stay in the Ledges, which was equipped with its own separate facilities, including food and housekeeping service, families paid $250 a month. For some frequent or long-term visitors, the society would keep "Deer Island Club accounts" to maintain records of milk, meat, groceries, and railroad fare. Occasionally, the society explicitly solicited contributions from patriarchs to help cover the costs of maintaining the island. In one such plea, dated August 1921, five

Bonesmen pointed out to their fellow society men that sixty members had already joined the Deer Island Club—and that they hoped to persuade all the other alumni to join "in the delightful fellowship of Deer Island, and to make a pilgrimage to the 'Abode of Bliss' an annual affair." They signed their note, "Each for All and All for Each. Cordially yours in 322."

Like the tomb itself, the retreat has been eroded by time and dwindling finances. These days, the kitchen staff is the Bonesmen themselves, and guests often have to help cook. The society hires graduates just out of college who might not know what else to do, so they can stay at the island, help maintain the buildings, and figure themselves out. The central dining room resembles a mess hall, with rows of picnic tables. Guests sleep in cots in cabins—granted, some of them are double-bedded cots—if they can slumber through the blare of the tour boat that sometimes circles the island with a guide shouting through a megaphone, "And there is the secret island that belongs to Skull and Bones!"

"Now it is just a bunch of burned-out stone buildings," one alumnus sighed to me. "It's basically ruins." Another Bonesman said that to call the island "rustic" would be to make it sound too chic, though the sandy shores still make an impression on the wide-eyed new members who are whisked there soon after they are initiated into the society. "It's a dump," he said, "but it's beautiful."

In truth, Skull and Bones does possess a green jewel, but it cannot be found on Deer Island. Instead, in the society's New Haven complex is a tiny area that has been carefully shielded from the media and from the prying eyes of conspiracy theorists. The society has one underground tunnel, lined with candles and leading to towers in which long spiral staircases wind beside more candles and old splatters of blood-red paint to windows at the top, where a Bonesman can, as one told me, "overlook the realm." In between these towers lies a quiet, enclosed courtyard, "like that of a monastery," within which stone walls embrace a secret garden of greenery that is a private pride of Skull and Bones. The lush, medieval-style garden, which includes a patio, a brick mosaic, cool, carved stone sculptures, and a bench, was built in 1918 at the instruction of Patriarch Theodore Woolsey (1872), who initially cared for it. It is a space of solitude, a place for Bonesmen to retreat both from the society and within it, to take respite from the hours of stringent traditions and to commune with the past. This private spot, as disparate as it is from the rest of the complex, could be a metaphor for Bones, where, withdrawn and protected from the invasive cacophony of a city known among college students for its anger and dilapidation, there is a hush like a wind from the past that erases everything but the fifteen students inside.

The Outlook, a building on the eastern shore of Deer Island, serves as the island's main clubhouse and includes a dining room, lounge, library, and fifteen bedrooms.
Deer Island Club, 1908

Secretary of State Henry Stimson,
Skull and Bones 1888.
*Quarter-Century Record, Class of 1888 Yale
College,* Manuscripts and Archives,
Yale University Library

W. Averell Harriman,
Skull and Bones 1913.
History of the Class of 1913 Yale College,
Manuscripts and Archives,
Yale University Library

Senator John Forbes Kerry,
Skull and Bones 1966.
Yale Class Book 1966,
Yale University Library

Senator Prescott Bush,
Skull and Bones 1917.
History of the Class of MCMXVII,
Manuscripts and Archives,
Yale University Library

President George Herbert
Walker Bush,
Skull and Bones 1948.
Yale Class Book 1948,
Yale University Library

President George W. Bush,
Skull and Bones 1968.
Yale Class Book 1968,
Yale University Library

Doonesbury cartoon, May 25, 2001.
Doonesbury © 2001 by G. B. Trudeau. Reprinted with permission
of Universal Press Syndicate. All rights reserved.

Chapter Four

THE INITIATION

Near the inside of the entrance to the tomb hangs a sign, perhaps stolen from some obscure hideaway in Middle America (or maybe snatched from Mory's), announcing, "THIS IS A PRIVATE CLUB: BE PREPARED TO SHOW MEMBERSHIP CARD." One can just hear the Bonesmen cackling at their find. If only getting in were quite that simple.

In April 2001, journalist Ron Rosenbaum, who has spent more than a quarter of a century chasing Skull and Bones, published in the *New York Observer* an account of what he believed to be the Skull and Bones initiation ceremony. He reported that "a member of the Yale community" had approached his research assistant to inquire whether the two of them would be interested in a videotaping expedition. The Yalie presented an audiotape of what was described as the April 2000 ceremony. On Saturday, April 14, 2001, Rosenbaum's confederates used "high-tech night-vision video equipment able to peer through the gloom into the inner courtyard" of the tomb. They witnessed, according to Rosenbaum's article, someone representing George W. Bush who repeatedly yelled versions of, "I'm gonna ream you like I reamed Al Gore"; individuals saying, "Take that plunger out of my ass, Uncle Toby," in what Rosenbaum called a reference to Abner Louima, the Haitian immigrant tortured by New York police; and people crying, "Lick my bumhole, neophyte." At the end of the "ceremony," the group videotaped this scene:

They were forced face-to-face with a shocking tableau: a guy holding what seemed like a butcher knife, wearing a kind of animal-skin "barbarian" look, stood over what *seemed* to be a woman covered in fake blood and not much else. The neophyte then approached a skull a few feet away from the knife-wielder-and-victim tableau. The neophyte knelt and kissed the skull, at which point the guy with the knife knelt and cut the throat of the prone figure. (Well, pretended to cut the throat.)

Rosenbaum made all sorts of inferences based on what his team taped that night. He claimed that the initiation "has bonded diplomats, media moguls, bankers and spies into a lifelong, multi-generational fellowship far more influential than any fraternity, " that "the founders of Time Inc. and the C.I.A., as well as several Secretaries of State and National Security Advisors—the men who made the decision to drop the Hiroshima bomb, invade the Bay of Pigs and plunge us into Vietnam, the Tafts, the Bundys, the Buckleys, the Harrimans, the Lovetts—all took part in this initiation ritual." Following the release of the article, Rosenbaum rode an international media wave. ABC News ran clips from the videotape, as Peter Jennings intoned:

Finally this evening, getting under the skin of the Ivy League. Those eight, old, definitely distinguished colleges that are known for their ivy-covered buildings and their sometimes superior attitudes to other colleges and universities, which often gets under the skin of people who went elsewhere. Yale University is three hundred years old this year and were you to visit its campus you would see that it still has exotic club houses which look like tombs, where Yale's legendary secret societies meet. Their prestige and importance have largely evaporated, but the rituals are still a secret. And so when we heard that some enterprising characters had managed to spy on the famous Skull and Bones Society, well, we couldn't resist.

Reporters chattered about the uncloaking of the ritual: "This is a great day in the annals of American journalism," *Slate*'s Timothy Noah, perhaps sarcastically, crowed. Newspapers as far away as Sweden called me for comment, because I had written an article on Skull and Bones for the *Atlantic Monthly* the previous year. "I," Rosenbaum proclaimed in his article, "am the Ahab of Skull and Bones, pursuing the white whale (or white male) leviathan to the utmost depths." And unlike Melville's doomed captain, Rosenbaum implied, he had beaten the whale.

As a veteran of Yale secret-society initiations myself, I believed that the ceremony described in Rosenbaum's article sounded much too vulgar for Skull and Bones. The initiation of new knights—Bonesmen are called "knights" from the time they are initiated to the time they initiate the next group—is a ceremony that surely has its sophomoric moments, but my understanding is that it is intended to introduce new members to the society's culture, rituals, songs, history, and lore in a way that will impress and awe them, not disgust and repel them. Skull and Bones does use some silly methods to evoke temporary fear in the initiates, but to my knowledge its most important ceremony is not full of the "ooga-booga" embarrassment that Rosenbaum detailed. Instead, the rites are, as a Bonesman from the late 1970s explained to me, "a passing on of something of importance." Perhaps Rosenbaum observed a society skit, perhaps Skull and Bones had known he would be watching; but from my secret society experience and from my interviews with Bonesmen, the videotaped ceremony certainly seemed far from authentic. In fact, one Bonesman I spoke with laughed heartily: "We wanted to fuck with that prick."

☠   ☠   ☠

During Skull and Bones' early years, the procedure for tapping new members was private. On the appointed evening at midnight, all fifteen Bonesmen would skulk together about campus. They would enter a candidate's room, display a human skull and bone, and ask only, "Do you accept?" No matter the answer, the group would silently file back out again. But as the years went on, word spread more quickly about the Skull and Bones procession. Neutral students would heckle the society men, following them and jeering them as they crossed campus. Occasionally the outsiders would even bar the doors to the entryways. As a result, the society gave up on the midnight hour and instead called on juniors at earlier, unspecified times. One senior, sometimes accompanied by a graduate member, would enter a candidate's room, make sure that the two men were alone, and then say, "I offer you an election to the so-called Skull and Bones. Do you accept?" If the junior accepted, the Bonesman shook his hand and returned to the tomb to relay the answer. If the junior rejected the offer, the senior would report back to the society, which would, depending on the junior, sometimes send a more powerful graduate member to try to persuade him.

Beginning in the 1870s, however, Tap Day became a public event, both celebrated and dreaded. In his 1912 novel *Stover at Yale,* Owen Johnson dramatized the nervous frenzy of the moment:

Tap Day arrived at last, cloudy and misty. He had slept badly in fits and starts, nor had the others fared better, with the exception of Regan . . . — but then Regan was one whom others sought. The morning was interminable, a horror. They did not even joke about the approaching ordeal. No one was so sure of election but that the possible rejection of some chum cast its gloom over the day.

. . . "Four-fifteen; let's hike over in about twenty minutes."

"All right."

"Say, I don't mind saying that I feel as though I were going to be taken out, stuck full of holes, sawed up, drawn and quartered and boiled alive. I feel like jumping on an express and running away."

. . . The four went together, over toward the junior fence, already swarming.

. . . "Ten minutes of five," said Hungerford, looking at the clock that each had seen.

. . . The four stood close together, arms gripped, resisting the press that crushed them together, speaking no more, hearing about them the curious babble of the underclassmen.

"That's Regan."

"Story'll go first."

"Stand here."

"This is the spot."

"Lord, they look solemn enough."

"Almost time."

"Get your watch out."

"Fifteen seconds more."

"Five, four, three, two—"

"Boom!"

Above their heads the chapel bell broke over them with its five decisive strokes, swallowed up in the roar of the college.

"Yea!"

"Here he comes!"

"First man for Bones!"

"Reynolds!"

From where he stood Stover could see nothing. Only the traveling roar of the crowd told of the coming seniors. Then there was a stir in the crowd near him, and Reynolds, in black derby, came directly for them; pushed them aside, and suddenly slapped some one behind.

A roar went up again.

"Who was it?" said Story quickly.

"Hunter, Jim Hunter."

The next moment Hunter, white as a sheet, bumped at his side and passed, followed by Reynolds; down the convulsive lane the crowd opened to him.

Roar followed roar, and reports came thick.

"Stone's gone Keys."

"Three Wolf's Head men in the crowd."

... About them the curious spectators pressed, staring up into their faces for any sign of emotion, struggling to reach them, with the dramatic instinct of the crowd. Four more elections were given out by Bones—only three places remained.

"That settles me," said Stover between his teeth. "If they wanted me I'd gone among the first. Joe's going to get last place—bully for him. He's the best fellow in the class."

He folded his arms and smiled with the consciousness of a decision accepted. He saw Hungerford's face, and the agony of suspense to his sensitive nerves.

. . . Suddenly Hungerford caught his hand underneath the crowd, pressing it unseen.

"Last man for Bones now, Dink," he said, looking in his eyes. "I hope to God it's you."

"Why, you old chump," said Stover laughing, so all heard him. "Bless your heart, I don't mind. Here's to you."

Above the broken, fitful cheers, suddenly came a last swelling roar.

"Bones."

"Last man."

The crowd, as though divining the election, divided a path towards where the two friends waited, Hungerford staring blankly, Stover, arms still folded, waiting steadily with a smile of acceptance on his lips.

It was Le Baron. He came like a black tornado, rushing over the ground straight toward the tree. Once some one stumbled into his path, and he caught him and flung him aside. Straight to the two he came, never deviating, straight past Dink Stover, and suddenly switching around almost knocked him to the ground with the crash of his blow.

"Go to your room."

. . . He began to move mechanically towards his room, seeing nothing, hearing nothing. He started towards the library, and someone swung him around. He heard them cheering, then he saw hundreds of faces, wild-eyed, rushing past him; he stumbled and suddenly his eyes were blurred with tears, and he knew how much he cared, after the long months of rebellion, to be no longer an outsider, but back among his own with the stamp of approval on his record.

Before "tap," most societies sent out feelers to determine how many alternates to line up should any first-choice prospects reject them. Skull and Bones, believing itself above the fray as an institution that no one would reject, long refrained from any pre-tap procedures. But it eventually had to shift its approach. On Tap Day in 1928, Skull and Bones reportedly received eight rejections. In one case, a junior thought the Bones senior who tapped him was somebody else, but the other refusals could be attributed to the society's lack of preparation: because Bones hadn't bothered to find out which men were considering other societies, it lost out on the candidates who had decided to "pack"—go en masse with their friends—to other organizations. In 1929, the society took care to find out the rival groups' intentions and, when the clock struck five, Skull and Bones immediately tapped five juniors instead of one or two. Members wore their Bones pins on their neckties so that they could not be mistaken for others. Still, there were always some who resisted. In 1940, future Yale president Kingman Brewster, Jr., who, as the chairman of the *Yale Daily News* in the class of 1941, was a shoo-in for Bones, gave the society another shock. "Instead of making himself available for tap . . . he was ensconced in a cubicle of his dormitory bathroom when the tower clock struck," wrote future Clinton White House special counsel Lanny Davis in the 1968 Yale yearbook. "A senior Bonesman yanked the door and shouted the awesome words. 'Reject,' said Brewster calmly, which may explain why students today refer to their president very simply as a 'stud.'"

Skull and Bones has a history of trying to dupe the other societies so that it could tap the best men first. In 1871, when commencement and end-of-term events were pushed earlier in the spring, Scroll and Key suggested that the two societies move their initiations earlier as well so that there would be enough time for the outgoing clubs to teach the incoming clubs the ways of society life before the students dispersed for the summer. When Skull and Bones never answered Keys' letter, the latter society assumed that initiation would proceed at the usual time. Instead, Skull and Bones tapped students three weeks ahead of schedule. Local newspapers took notice of the change and wondered why Bones had elected its members so hastily. Meanwhile, the Skull and Bones editor in charge of the June issue of the *Yale Literary Magazine* gloated over the society's triumph by publishing the notice, "Elections to Skull and Bones were accepted on Thursday evening, June 8th, by the following gentlemen. . . . No elections were refused." Clearly, elections wouldn't likely have been refused if Skull and Bones were the only society making offers at the time.[*]

In 1917, the three major societies decided to elect their members early because of World War I. The year before, a group of Yale students had formed a Naval Aviation Unit to prepare in case the United States entered the war, when F. Trubee Davison (Bones 1918) convinced Robert A. Lovett (also Bones 1918) to form a flying unit. Davison's father financed them so generously that local newspapers referred to the group as "the millionaires' unit." In early spring of 1917, when anticipation of formal American entry into the war had escalated, one society proposed that Tap Day be held immediately so as to accommodate undergraduates who would likely be leaving campus soon. Skull and Bones, which had not had the foresight to finish its election process early, was not ready and instead insisted that the event be delayed until April 19. That date turned out to be nearly two weeks after the declaration of war.

Meanwhile, the Yale unit had enlisted with the U.S. Navy and, under the new name Aerial Coast Patrol Unit No. 1, was sent to West Palm Beach to finish flight training. Because of the large number of eligible junior candidates in the unit, the societies sent representatives to West Palm Beach to perform a special Tap Day ceremony. The juniors gathered in the living room of the unit's headquarters, in an old building called the Salt Air Hotel. When the clock struck noon, Skull and Bones, Scroll and Key, and Wolf's Head tapped their men. The Bones and Keys

---

[*]It so happened that a Scroll and Key man was slated to edit the July issue of the *Lit.* He included in that issue the announcement, "Elections to Scroll and Key were given to the following gentlemen on Thursday evening, June 22, the usual time," in order to inform the public that Skull and Bones had jumped the gun. But Bones editors on the staff intercepted the copy before it reached the printer, changing the statement to read "men" instead of "gentlemen" and ending the sentence at "June 22."

taps went upstairs to their rooms as they would have done on campus, while the two men tapped for Wolf's Head, who refused the society's election, instead remained downstairs with the rest of the unit. Following the ceremony, the society representatives sent a telegram to New Haven that listed the West Palm Beach election results, which were confirmed by a telephone call to an office at J. P. Morgan in New York. Society members there then relayed the message to headquarters in New Haven. A 1917 Bonesman who had arrived by train from New Haven and a 1906 member who was already in West Palm Beach to supervise the unit initiated that year's group at the headquarters of the Navy's Northern Bombing Group.

Skull and Bones again interfered with the campuswide election process in 1940. That May, all senior members of Bones, Scroll and Key, Wolf's Head, Berzelius, Book and Snake, and Elihu were scheduled to meet to discuss changing the tapping procedure to a private event in juniors' rooms instead of a public event at the center of campus. But at the last minute, a group of Yale administrators who were Skull and Bones patriarchs detained and silenced the Bones seniors who had been planning to attend the meeting. Without Bones' participation, the other societies had no choice but to drop the matter.

Until the late 1900s, the *New York Times* and the *Yale Daily News* would print the names of the men who were tapped for the top societies. Other Yale publications, such as the *Banner* and the *Pot Pourri,* would also publish the lists—for a fee.

On May 16, 1919, the morning after Tap Day, the *Yale Daily News* did something unprecedented: It printed in the righthand column a large bold headline that featured the first and the last man tapped for Skull and Bones. The *News* had never previously devoted that kind of exclusive, biased attention to a single society. That year's managing editor was a Bonesman himself: future Time Inc. founder Henry Luce, whose name was also listed as one that had been selected the night before. Luce issued an apology (and shift of blame) in the next issue: "The Managing Editor hereby apologizes for his oversight in not correcting the headlines submitted by a reporter, on the Senior Societies' elections, so as to make them conform to the traditional NEWS policy of mentioning no names in the headlines of all articles dealing with society elections." But the apology couldn't erase the message he had already sent: There was only one secret society that really mattered.

From 1934 to 1952, Tap Day took place in the courtyard of Branford College, Yale's most historic-looking residential college, which houses the bell tower. There, each society used a Branford room as a headquarters and observation post. At first, tapped juniors were told to go to their rooms, as tradition dictated. But after a few years the policy was changed because Branford was so far from some students' dormitories. Instead, the society senior said, "Follow me," and led the junior to the society's designated room in Branford to proffer election. The *Yale Daily News'* 1951 nonfiction account of these proceedings is notably similar to Owen Johnson's fictional 1912 version:

The hands reached five, the arms posed themselves over three shoulders, the fingers itched on the camera trigger, a hush fell like a blanket over the crowd, nothing happened, the clock bells had been silenced by an unidentified prankster. A stink bomb in the form of a dirty sock, encasing a bottle of chemical, thudded onto the grass, providing the only comic relief of the afternoon. At 5:03 somebody in the middle of the crowd clapped his hands and with the precision of an infantry rifle drill, hands crashed to shoulders, and the show was on, it lasted exactly 28 minutes.

From the first electrical crackle of slaps on shoulders, (one junior received five in one blow) to the slam of the Skull and Bones window at 5:31 the interest of the audience at the windows, walls and gates never lagged. . . . The tension of the juniors seemed to be rivaled only by that of the seniors. Tight-lipped men watched with binoculars from society windows, and prowling tappers were eyed hopefully by several hundred standees.

THE INITIATION ⊰ 111

Some might be inclined to accuse the reporters who covered Tap Day, such as the writer of the 1951 *Daily News* coverage, of outlandish melodramatics. But to a large group of individuals at Yale and in New Haven, Tap Day, however ludicrous it sounded to the rest of the world, was truly that important. For many students, it represented the absolute culmination of one's college career, and this view surprisingly lasted well into the late twentieth century. "Come 'Tap Day,' that last Thursday in April," Lanny Davis wrote,

> if you're a junior, despite the fact that you've banged your fist at the lunch table and said, "This is 1968," and have loudly denounced societies as anachronisms, when the captain of the football team is standing by your door and when the tower clock strikes eight he rushes in and claps your shoulder and shouts, "Skull and Bones, accept or reject?" you almost always scream out, "Accept!" and you never, never, pound your fist at the lunch table, not for that reason ever again.

Tap Day was Yale's pageant of pageants. It was indeed, to quote a student from 1905, "a show, an open drama of the primeval passions — fear and jealousy; a drama in which we are the puppets of the play."

In 1953, the societies once again discussed moving Tap Day from the public to the private sphere. They dismissed one suggestion that the juniors should fill out preference cards so that an inter-society council could arrange the society lists. They also rejected Dean William Clyde DeVane's plan that the elections be divided into shifts, first to tap juniors whom more than one society wanted and then to tap those who were on only one list. Instead, that May the societies simultaneously gave their taps between 8:00 and 9:12 P.M. in juniors' rooms. A central committee kept tabs on the results and constantly telephoned each society's designated university rooms to let them know who went where. When Tap Day had ended, WYBC, the campus radio station, broadcast the results. This practice lasted at least through the 1960s. Today, the major societies offer taps on a designated day advertised in advance in an ad in the *Yale*

Daily News—usually a Thursday during the second or third week in April. The process is handled privately, frequently in a junior's room or a campus building, and the results are never announced to the press. Membership remains as secret as possible for the rest of the year and beyond.

In 1986, Jacob Weisberg, who is now the editor of *Slate* magazine, took a year off from Yale following his junior year to intern at the *New Republic* in Washington, D.C. One day in the spring, Weisberg told me, he received a telephone call from the secretary to Senator John Kerry. "Senator Kerry wants to see you in his office," the secretary said.

Perplexed, Weisberg asked, "What is it about?" He wondered whether Kerry was unhappy about a story he had written, or perhaps wanted to leak him some information.

"He won't tell me what it is about," the secretary said. "Can you just come in tomorrow morning?"

Weisberg showed up at the senator's office at 8:00 A.M. the next day. Kerry made small talk for a while, as Weisberg sat on a sofa and pondered why he was there. Then Kerry (Bones 1966) told him he was extending him an offer to join Skull and Bones. Weisberg, who had not known that Kerry was a member, was stunned.

"Senator Kerry," Weisberg said, "you're a liberal—why do you support this organization that does not admit women?"

Kerry, Weisberg said, ran down a list of his efforts to assist women throughout his career. "I've marched with battered women. I've supported women's rights. No one can question my dedication to women." The argument continued for a while. Finally, when Weisberg made clear he wasn't interested, Kerry said, "Promise me you'll think about it before saying no."

Weisberg called Kerry back—his call went straight through—and told him he was rejecting the offer. Kerry, Weisberg recalled, said he was disappointed. (Soon afterward, the *Washington Post*'s Robert Kaiser took Weisberg out to lunch and persuaded him to accept membership in Elihu instead. Weisberg lasted about two weeks before quitting, after "someone suggested we all stand in a circle and hold hands," he told me.)

A 1969 Bones document titled "Interview Presentation Outline" suggests that the society expanded its tapping policy again, perhaps because of the decline of the society and the fraternity systems at that time. The outline specifies a solemn script for presenting the society to chosen juniors:

> The *manner* of this presentation is almost as important as the content. You must address the candidate seriously, deliberately, and directly. Our demeanor will be crucial to attracting these men to the society, and the first impression will be a lasting one. There must be *no interuption* [*sic*] of your presentation. After introducing yourself and thanking the candidate for coming to the interview, tell him that you would now like to inform him of the reasons that he has been called to talk with representatives of our society. Advise him that he will be able to ask questions following your presentation of these reasons.

During this presentation, which generally occurs one week before Tap Night, one of the fifteen Bones seniors informs a junior that the society will offer him an election at eight o'clock on Tap Night. Each year, one knight is selected to be the supervisor, or "Uncle Toby," of Tap, who will oversee the proceedings. Knights were instructed to promise that no members of Skull and Bones would approach a candidate to try to convince him to join, but either the society amended its policy to allow well-known alumni to act as ambassadors or the decree was simply often disregarded by eager recruiters like Kerry.

The document may be most revealing in its insistence that Bonesmen maintain a proud, detached air; the process of approaching juniors must reflect a Bonesman's reluctance to grovel. Knights, at least of the 1960s, had to remember to keep their answers to juniors' questions "cool and concise" in order to avoid appearing as if they had to convince someone to accept a tap. They had to prioritize the society's privacy above all else, and rationalize their reticence by telling the juniors, "The life which we invite you to share in our society is based on such intangible factors that we cannot meaningfully convey to you either its nature or quality." At the end of the presentation, the Bonesmen handed the juniors a list of that year's knights, as well as the names of a handful of Bones alumni in the area whom they could talk to during the decision-making process. Unless the juniors expressly told the seniors that they would not accept the offer, they were assured of a Bones tap.

As for the tap itself, ever since the procedure became private again in the mid-twentieth century, Bones has occasionally decided to be creative. While some Bones groups, or "clubs," do still choose to knock on a prospective's door, slap him on the shoulder, and bellow, "Skull and Bones, do you accept?" other groups opt for more grandiose, melodramatic gestures. In 1975, at least two juniors received strange taps. One was hustled onto a private plane that flew over Long Island Sound. Midflight, the plane went into a steep dive, at which point the crucial question was posed: "Skull and Bones, accept or reject?" The Hamden, Connecticut, police chief—or someone posing as him—called another junior to tell him that the police had a warrant for his arrest and he was to report immediately to the Hamden police station. When he arrived, a group of Bonesmen surrounded him to ask, "Skull and Bones, accept or reject?" More recent taps have involved leading candidates to dark rooms lit only by candles illuminating a skull and crossbones. Even juniors who study abroad second semester are candidates for creative taps. "Bones finds ways to tap students in foreign countries," a patriarch told me. "Bones will go to whatever lengths necessary to get to a person, with an emphasis on trying to find a way to tap that is reflective of a person. I was tapped in a theater where I was working, by the guy directing the show I was in. He called me to come to the theater, the theater was dark when I got there, and there they all were."

☠   ☠   ☠

The Skull and Bones initiation, Lanny Davis wrote, was reportedly the most harrowing of any society. Once the initiate, or "neophyte," entered the tomb, according to 1968 lore, he "faces the old delegation and the alumni alone and is physically beaten. Next he is stripped and made to engage in some form of naked wrestling followed by a coffin ritual." The most flagrant, widespread rumor about Skull and Bones is that initiates lie naked and masturbate in a coffin. The notion prompted an *Observer Life* magazine reporter to ruminate, "If . . . George Bush did lie in a coffin and masturbate while recounting his teenage sex life to his fellow Bonesmen, as the society's initiation rite demands, then it is suddenly difficult to see the former president as a figure of gravitas." It is possible that, in its early days, Skull and Bones directed odd rituals in coffins and the kind of sexual braggadocio typical of adolescent boys. Today, however, there is no coffin in the ceremony, and any sordid sexual activity is not part of the regular program, but rather the unsurprising exploits of a coed group of college kids, or even a member sneaking a significant other into the building.

The initiation itself is a cross between an amusement park haunted house and a human pinball game, with the blind dizziness of a trip through a sandstorm—"something like a Harry Potter novel," described a patriarch who is now an engineer. "It consisted of all kinds of goofy stuff. It was one of the most exciting things ever. It was this incredible fantasy created just for you." It can also scare the bejeezus out of the anxious juniors. "You're a little uneasy when you're tapped," said one Bonesman, "so when it's your turn to tap the next group, it's funny to hear people worry about it." Although the costumes, props, and lines remain consistent, the rites may vary slightly from year to year, "particularly if there are theater guys in the club," a 1980s Bonesman said.

The Bones instructions for initiation preparation read something like a wedding planner's checklist. Knights must ensure that the tomb is well stocked with black sealing wax, black ribbon, rolls of red paper, and black ink, and that the pins, "Black Book" (bound books in which each alternating Uncle Toby records notes on each session), and scrapbook for the new group are in the tomb prior to the ceremony. The Bonesmen will rehearse the most important part of the initiation rites a few times with the Uncle Toby of elections.

Sometime after Tap, most often on a Sunday night between 8:00 P.M. and 12:00 A.M., the knights deliver to each neophyte a "red packet," a kind of valentine prepared strictly in the following manner:

> Cut out an irregular piece of the traditional red paper, approximately 18" in diameter. On the red side, write in large black letters: "[name] (B.S.C.).* Be in your room between 8:00 and 12:00 on Monday night. Rex Bone." and draw a skull and cross bones. Fold the sheet into an irregularly shaped packet. Seal the packet closed with black sealing wax, stamped with the Bones Seal. Burn the exterior surface with a candle to give it a suitably macabre appearance.

That Monday night, again usually between the hours of eight and twelve, a team of four knights—"a speaker, two shakers, and a guard"— will pay a visit to the junior. First, without speaking to each other, the four seniors walk into the initiate's entryway "quietly and with dignity." The guard determines whether the bathroom nearest to the initiate's dorm room is empty. If so, the guard signals to the speaker that it is all clear to proceed. He remains at the bathroom door to ensure that it stays empty. The two shakers stand in front of the speaker as the three of them approach the junior's door. One of the guards "knocks soundly." When the door opens, the speaker, still standing behind the shakers, asks in a "firm" voice, "Neophyte [name]?" Once the junior is identified, the shakers grab him by his arms, drag him into the bathroom, and face him into a corner. The guard shuts the door and the speaker declares, "At the appointed time tomorrow evening, wearing neither metal, nor sulfur, nor glass, leave the base of Harkness Tower and walk south on High Street.

*B.S.C. stands for "Barbarian So-Called."

Look neither to the right nor to the left. Pass through the sacred pillars of Hercules and approach the Temple. Take the right Book in your left hand and knock thrice upon the sacred portals. Remember well, but keep silent, concerning what you have heard here."

The speaker then tosses a "white packet," presumably containing the formal invitation to the initiation ceremony, at the junior's feet. With that, the group retreats from the bathroom and marches away, without speaking, in double file through the dormitory courtyard, leaving the junior standing in the corner of the bathroom. (In 1975, which was apparently a rebellious year, the group decided to overwhelm a particular candidate. One Bonesman knocked on the junior's door, checked to make sure he was alone, and then left the junior standing confused in his room. The senior returned shortly with ten additional Bonesmen for the bathroom procedure.) A Bonesman explained to me that the warning against wearing metal and glass is merely to protect the junior, who is whirled throughout the tomb during initiation. He said that Bonesmen are never allowed to wear or carry sulfur—not that anyone actually would—because of a tradition that began before lighters were invented, when knights brought matches into the crypt.

After the teams of Bonesmen have visited each junior candidate, the seniors return to the tomb to prepare for the initiation ceremony under the guidance of the Uncle Toby. Among other things, they will also double-check that the costume trunk has the complete set of costumes necessary for the ceremony. Apparently, the costumes either have irreplaceable sentimental value or members have walked off with them too many times, because the instructions for rehearsal note that the seniors should be reminded at least twice to return their costumes to the appropriate bags in the trunk immediately following the ceremony.

The heart of the initiation ceremony has evolved since the mid-nineteenth century, when a junior was simply taken before the "Devil," who would strike the junior on the back with a sword and decree, "I dub thee Knight of the Skull and Cross Bones." In the society's early years, junior candidates received formal invitations to initiation in June or July.

In the early 1840s, the initiates were instructed to meet in the office of Sheff's Benjamin Silliman (Bones 1837) in the Sheffield Scientific School laboratory, which was guarded by Bonesmen. Once the group of fifteen had assembled, they were escorted to society headquarters, one by one, for the initiation ceremony. Neutral students would often line the streets in between the buildings in a sort of gauntlet and bid the initiates good-bye. As each neophyte passed by, someone would shine a lantern on him and announce his name. As the front doors cracked open for each initiate, the neutrals on the street would hear sounds they described "as of a fish horn, as of many feet hurrying up an uncarpeted stairway, as of a muffled drum and tolling bell, . . . all mingling in a sort of confused uproar, like that from a freshman initiation a good many miles away."

The twentieth- and twenty-first-century practice is an altogether headier affair. The current procedure directly involves as many of the Bonesmen as possible, including at least eleven patriarchs. About a month before initiation, the "S.E.C.," or secretary, of the club writes to a particular patriarch—the more famous the better, so as to impress the new members—to try to persuade him to take the Uncle Toby role. In 1959, the club tried to get the poet Archibald MacLeish to preside. The S.E.C. gamely used flattery to try to convince MacLeish; he wrote in particular of MacLeish's success in the post-initiation explanation to new members of the Skull and Bones experience. MacLeish, busy with work, declined, adding that he thought recent clubs were unfortunately possessed of far less brains than brawn. "The Bones, unlike the bones," MacLeish reminded his young compatriot, "are not imbedded in the flesh."

Though the initiation takes juniors throughout every room in the tomb, the ceremony in the Inner Temple is the evening's centerpiece. Just before initiation begins, when the knights and the patriarchs are assembled in the tomb, the group receives instructions on how the events of the evening will proceed. They will go through the Inner Temple ceremony over and over again until they can perform the rituals without mistakes. The Inner Temple is cleared of furniture, except for the "chair behind the portals" and the chair to the left of the fireplace. The tocsin is moved from the southeast to the northwest corner of the room, where, the instructions say, "the dumb knights suck their thumbs."

When an initiate approaches the front door of the tomb, the door creaks open and Bonesmen immediately cover his head with a bag, hood, or, in the nineteenth century, a "bladder." First the initiate is led to the Firefly Room, which is a living room. When the hood is removed, the initiate sees that he is in a pitch-black room — except for the lit cigarettes that the patriarchs wave languidly so that the room looks as though it is full of fireflies. There the patriarchs sit the initiate down and tell him what he is about to do. With the hood placed on his head once again, the initiate is then marched throughout the tomb on a pseudo-tour, during which the knights and the patriarchs shriek in high-pitched voices jokes about the initiate's girlfriend or dog, akin to benign "yo' mama" cracks. Lore about the tomb is woven into the tour: the initiate is told, for example, that he is feeling "the coffin," as the Bonesmen brush his hand up against wood; he hears rushing water, which supports the rumor of an in-house swimming pool, but the Bonesmen are actually just flushing the toilets over and over again; the initiate is told, "This is where the Bones whore lives," as the patriarchs hide their smiles.

In the Inner Temple, which is stripped of furniture save two chairs and the card table unfolded in a corner, the players — all masked — take their places. Uncle Toby wears a distinctive robe; the knight in the role of the Little Devil, clad in a devil's costume, lies in wait; the four brawniest knights serve as shakers, who in earlier times may have worn only jock straps and sneakers; a knight with a deep voice dons a Don Quixote costume; a senior dressed as the Pope sits in the chair to the left of the fireplace with one foot, covered in a white slipper monogrammed "SBT," perched on a stone skull; a knight costumed as Elihu Yale sits in the chair behind the portals and holds an open Greek book with a Bones pin affixed upside down to the leaf; and the remaining senior Bonesmen, a crew of extras in skeleton costumes and carrying noisemakers, scatter about the room in specified spots. Everyone in the room wears a mask.

The stage is set: The oath of secrecy, retrieved from its resting place in a drawer of the card table, waits on the table. The Yorick, a skull container named for the owner of the skull the gravedigger throws in *Hamlet*, is filled with "blood"—"if it's not Kool-Aid, it's Gatorade," a Bonesman admitted to me—and rests at the foot of the Madame. First, the Uncle Toby of initiation announces the approach of a neophyte to the gathering. Then, when the initiate enters the room, the Bonesmen make as much noise as possible. The patriarchs standing outside of the room shout, "Who is it?" and the two shakers assigned to the neophyte bellow his name, which the patriarchs echo. The patriarchs shove the neophyte into the room while whisking the hood from his head. The shakers drag the initiate toward the opened oath on the card table. The Bonesmen shout, "Read! Read! Read!" and the initiate is from that point on bound to secrecy.

In a whirlwind, the shakers then carry the initiate to a picture of the goddess Eulogia as the Bonesmen shriek, "Eulogia! Eulogia! Eulogia!" Thrust back to the table bearing the oath, the initiate hears the Bonesmen yell once again, "Read! Read! Read!" After another picture and another trip to the oath (again, "Read! Read! Read!"), the shakers fire the junior toward a picture of a woman that Bonesmen call "Connubial Bliss." The crowd cries, "Connubial Bliss! Connubial Bliss! Connubial Bliss!" The Bonesmen fall silent when the initiate is rushed to the Uncle Toby, who solemnly says his full name, "Uncle Toby, Philamagee, Phimalarlico, Carnicks, Carnickesi, Carnickso, McPherson O'Phanel," to which the gathering responds, "Say it! Say it! Say it!" and quiets once again. After a pause just long enough to give the initiate palpitations, the Bonesmen shout, "He can't! He can't! He can't!" and resume their initial racket. The shakers whisk the neophyte to a picture of Judas Iscariot, whose name the crowd screams three times.

The shakers push the initiate to his knees in front of the Yorick and force his head toward the pool of "blood." To the neophyte's dismay, the crowd implores him to "Drink it! Drink it! Drink it!," which he must. The shakers hurry the initiate to the Pope, but not before the Devil whips him in the face with his tail. The initiate bends to kiss the Pope's slippered toe on the skull. When the initiate is brought to Don Quixote, who stands just in front of the fireplace with a sword in his right hand, he is pushed once again to his knees, but this time for glory as the crowd falls silent once again. Quixote taps the junior on the left shoulder and says, "By order of our order, I dub thee Knight of Eulogia." The skeleton nearest the tocsin in the room strikes it three times, then two times, then twice again, and the crowd shouts, "Bones!" The shakers rush the initiate to the open book on Elihu Yale's lap while the Bonesmen scream, "Read it! Read it! Read it!," then "He can't read! He can't read! He can't read!"

Finally, the shakers thrust the neophyte out of the room and into the waiting arms of the patriarchs. In a departure from their usual stern rigidity, the initiation instructions painstakingly admonish the knights not to get too carried away lest they hurl the junior into an unsuspecting inanimate object: "Care should be taken to avoid firing the new knight into the jamb of the portals, which has been done in the past, much to the disadvantage of both jamb and new knight." The Bonesmen will repeat that precise process for all fifteen initiates, with one exception: The four shakers will carry the new Little Devil upside down through the entire ceremony, including the part during which he is supposed to drink the blood from the Yorick. "His feet," the instructions note, "should never touch the floor of the IT." Bonesmen told me that the initiation was mildly frightening, but also exhilarating. "You are dizzy and unsure, but it is never dangerous. It's like a haunted fun house throughout the whole building," one said.

Once all the new members have officially been dubbed knights, there are skits and activities set up for them throughout the tomb. The Firefly Room, for example, has its own ceremony. Documents report without elaboration that the room has its own Uncle Toby on initiation night, as well as a patriarch to serve as "measurer" at the "measuring station" (given the racier sorts of rumors about initiation, some could make much out of this, one supposes; in actuality, the initiates are told they are being measured for their coffins, but the patriarch is only noting their height to determine which neophytes are the tallest and the shortest in the club), and two to serve in the "counting house." The couches in the Firefly Room are arranged in a U-shaped formation at the east end of the room. A table and chairs are grouped in front of the hearth. A pan of water is placed just inside the door. Benches rest against the wall of the "counting house." Lists of the neophytes' names are located in the vestibule, in order of initiation, and in the "old hallway" and "measuring station," in order of the "counting house trip." The Uncle Toby in the Firefly Room, the society notes, "sounds like the only sane person in the room."

Afterward, the patriarchs gather the initiates in the dining room, where they solemnly teach the new group about the history and the lore of Skull and Bones. Then the Bonesmen throw a party that lasts long into the night. Before the evening comes to a close, the Bonesmen take care to award the new members a copy of the society's gold pin, teach them how to work the locks, introduce them to the stewards, and share with them the Bones Bible, Black Books, scrapbooks, and a tour of the premises. The instructions are explicit about the importance of the tour: "Do not assume," the document warns the seniors, "that this shall be accomplished automaticly [sic]." By evening's end, the neophytes—now knights—breathless, wizened, are fifteen new keepers of the secrets of Skull and Bones.

Chapter Five

THE SECRETS OF
SKULL AND BONES

On campus and beyond, Skull and Bones is notorious for boasting stricter rules than any of Yale's other secret societies. Perhaps the best known of these rules requires Bonesmen to clear out of a room if the words "Skull and Bones" or "322" are mentioned in their presence. The rule was particularly immortalized in Bonesman William F. Buckley's novel *Saving the Queen,* in which Blackford Oakes "would dutifully leave the room, as tradition prescribed" when the name of his society was mentioned. A woman who had been a Vassar student in the sixties told me that when she was dating a Bonesman, all it took was "one little spoof, one '322!'" and he and his friends would dart from the room. "We couldn't believe those little secret rituals were meaningful." Harvard men used to quip that all that they had to do to beat Yale in the annual football game was to shout "Skull and Bones!"—half the Yale squad would dash off the field. In 1988, reporters on the campaign trail giddily wondered whether George Bush would bolt from a press conference if they managed to smuggle the society's name into a question. Retired history professor John Blum, who has been affiliated with Yale since 1957, told me about a lecture he delivered on Theodore Roosevelt during his first year of teaching. Roosevelt had taken pride in the fact that, as a Harvard student, he had been selected to be a member of that school's Porcellian Club. "The Porcellian Club," Blum explained to his students, "is the nearest Harvard equivalent of Skull and Bones." Blum didn't linger on the point, but instead continued his lecture, which did not mention Skull and Bones again. Two days later, at the class's next meeting, Blum arrived early to find on his lectern a small white envelope, unmarked and stamped only with a wax seal bearing the Skull and Bones insignia. Inside was an unsigned card that read, "Professor Blum, May we ask you please not to mention the name of our club in your lectures." Blum read the note aloud to the class, and then never mentioned Skull and Bones in lecture again.

Not all Bonesmen, especially in recent years, take this rule seriously. Former Major League Baseball commissioner Fay Vincent, a "barbarian"—Bones lingo for a nonmember—whose father was a Bonesman, recalled one day when he, George Bush, George W. Bush, Senator David Boren, and deputy baseball commissioner Steve Greenberg were in a room together. "President Bush said, 'Hey, look at all of these Bonesmen,' and pointed to me and said, 'and your father was in Bones,'" Vincent chortled. "I said, 'Yeah, and if I say Skull and Bones, you'll all have to leave the room.' They all laughed because that's one of the myths." Sometimes, though, Bonesmen cling inexplicably to even this most obsolete of traditions. "A friend of mine shared a shower with his brother, a Bones man," wrote Paul Moore, Jr., Yale 1941, in 1982. "Whenever he wished to use it and his brother was inside, he would open the door and shout 'Bones!' His brother vacated the shower forthwith."

While the traditions are "taken with an appropriate mix of respect and irreverence, from tapping to meetings with older members," as one Bonesman told me, members realize that the rules keep the society running as a well-oiled machine. Even during the late sixties and seventies, a time of upheaval and rebellion at Yale and in Bones, the knights "welcomed the traditions," said a Bonesman who graduated in the seventies. "Relating to other people within a structure greases the wheels of interaction, especially with strangers. If you just throw a bunch of people in a room, they won't know what to do. The rules gave us a sense of belonging and participation." A patriarch in his fifties explained, "There was a great deal of procedure and certain ridiculous steps to go through the process and who sits where and what you call each other. I saw that initially as hokum, as part of the thirties, of Dink Stover at Yale. But it was a system that was extremely cleverly designed and intended to gently prod guys like me who weren't prone to being open about themselves to other guys. It was designed to encourage that kind of interchange. I didn't see that initially." Another patriarch said, "The setup and procedure was designed to encourage people to be open with each other. In a male college where competition, impressions, and achievements were important, there had to be a place where you could talk about yourself without worrying about whether you would be perceived well or not. That seems antithetical to the view that Bones was this elite retreat. But its purpose was to give a psychological release."

The rituals of 322 go so far as to dictate how members must enter and leave the tomb. For example, Bonesmen are discouraged from entering or exiting the tomb in front of witnesses. If observers are present, the society's members refrain from making eye contact with each other and with the spectators, and silently step in a quick single file, twenty paces apart in front of the building. Up until the 1960s, the seniors wore their finest suits, which made an even more punctuated statement as they marched to meetings.

Inside the tomb, each Bonesman, on his first day as a knight, receives a new name, which the society will call him for the rest of his life. For Bonesmen, the naming comes across less as a measure of raising the society above the rest of the world than as a way to pull members further within the insular walls of the tomb. Knights may pass on names to their successors if they choose; journalist and political adviser Tex McCrary told *Town & Country* he had been "Sancho Panza," a name handed down from Bankers Trust head Lewis Lapham, the father of the *Harper's* editor of the same name. Some knights are automatically assigned traditional names: "Magog," the knight who has the most experience with members of the opposite sex; "Gog," the least sexually experienced member; "Long Devil," the tallest man in the club; "Boaz," any varsity football captain; and "Little Devil," Long Devil's rival and the shortest knight in the club. The knights who are left over are free to choose their own names, and Magog and Gog are allowed to select new names if they are so inclined.

The Bonesmen who influenced George W. Bush's life would have known him by another name: Temporary, an appellation he used because he could not think of anything else and never bothered to change it. (Neither an assigned name nor a traditional Bones name, Temporary seemed fitting for someone who reputedly spent far more time partying outside of the tomb than philosophizing within it.) George Herbert Walker Bush, by contrast, was allegedly named Magog; by the time he was initiated, he had already married Barbara Pierce and fathered George W. After I reported this detail in the *Atlantic Monthly*, however, *Washington Post* gossip columnist Lloyd Grove reprinted my claim and was immediately bombarded by "irate" Bonesmen who "jammed our switchboard" to say that the elder Bush's name had not been Magog but, rather, Barebones, which, according to Bones documents, may have been *his* father's name as well — or family friend Neil Mallon's. (But if Barebones — unlike Magog, a chosen name — had been George and possibly Prescott Bush's name, one would think that George W. Bush would have been called the same.) William Howard Taft was also a Magog, as were his son the future senator Robert Taft and, in George W.'s club, Olympic swimmer Don Schollander. College football coach Amos Alonzo Stagg and literary critic F. O. Matthiessen were Little Devils.

As the society has grown older, more knights have chosen their own Bones aliases, which reflect everything from classic literature to popular culture. In the 1850s and 1860s, during what Bones calls "the romantic period of barbarian literature," the nostalgically chosen names included the likes of Sidney, Harold, Arthur, Charlemagne, Dedivere, Launfal, Endymion, and Delores. In the early twentieth century, literature lovers chose Rob Roy, Roderick, Waverly, Dombey, Tony Weller, Barkis,

Pickwick, Shylock, and Jingle.* By the 1930s, knights tended to lean toward the diabolical: Beelzebub, Caliban, Hellbender. Several prominent Bonesmen who selected their own names include:

Averell Harriman and Dean Witter, Jr.: **Thor**
Henry Luce: **Baal**
Briton Hadden: **Caliban**
Archibald MacLeish: **Gigadibs**
William and McGeorge Bundy: **Odin**
Potter Stewart: **Crappo**
William Sloane Coffin and Henry Sloane Coffin: **Coverly**
William F. Buckley: **Cheevy**
Anson Phelps Stokes: **Achilles**
Reuben Holden: **McQuilp**
Charles Seymour: **Machiavelli**
Donald Ogden Stewart: **Hellbender**

Other chosen names have varied from the humble (Dingbat, Suffering Mike, Fester) to the obscure (Nana, Gabbo, Jiggerdibs). A 1998 senior decided to call himself Keyser Soze, after Kevin Spacey's shady character in *The Usual Suspects*. In the 1980s, a knight who had recently completed chemotherapy for leukemia called himself Lazarus. When he died a few months after graduation, one of his clubmates told me, "His name had special significance for us."

Rather than elect a leader as other senior societies still do, sometimes with disastrous results, Skull and Bones members alternate assuming the role of Uncle Toby, who leads the sessions, moderates the debates, and takes notes during debates and discussions. The Uncle Toby of the evening generally has the last word on anything society-related. The

---

*Bonesmen who went on to great achievement in literary pursuits include novelist John Hersey, journalist Brendan Gill (both 1936), Pulitzer Prize–winning biographer David McCullough (1955), who got his start at Time, Inc., and publisher John Farrar (1918) of Farrar, Straus & Giroux.

seniors, along with the rest of the society, are overseen by the patriarchs on the governing board of the Russell Trust Association, which elects, among other positions, a society president and treasurer. Three knights receive permanent titles for the year: Corporal Trim, who is in charge of the menu; the S.E.C., or Secretary of the Eulogian Club, who acts as an alumni liaison and always sits to the right of Uncle Toby; and Commissary, the club treasurer and business manager, who sits by the door. The S.E.C. is the closest position the knights have to a constant, contemporary leader; at least in the nineteenth century, he had the power to approve or veto society-related business. The Little Devil sits to the left of Uncle Toby and collects all fines, which help to pay for the Skull and Bones treats (frequently referred to as S.B.T.) in the kitchen. It is worth noting that the permanent Bones names "Corporal Trim" and "Uncle Toby," as well as recurring chosen Bones names such as "Dr. Slop," "Yorick," and "Sancho Panza," can be traced to characters and references in Laurence Sterne's 1760 novel *Tristram Shandy*.

Within the tomb, the members run on "Skull and Bones Time" (also referred to as S.B.T.), five minutes faster than the rest of the world's clocks. Announcements for alumni meetings and initiation ceremonies call for commencement at VIII S.B.T., or 7:55 "barbarian" time. On the grandfather clock appearing in all of the group photographs hanging on a wall inside the tomb, the time is 8:00. During the initiation ceremony, neophytes are introduced to VIII S.B.T. as "the time we meet." (Dinner begins earlier, at 6:30.) The purpose of the separate schedule is to promote the notion that Skull and Bones, within the tomb, is unaffected by the concept of time. Ensconced in long-ago traditions, unwilling to change, the society defies the sands of the hourglass by insisting that in Bones, I was told, "time stands still." "It was to encourage you to think that being in the building was so different from the outside world that you'd let your guard down," a Bonesman told me. Skull and Bones also eschews the standard calendar year and instead uses its own series of numerical notations on society documents and letters. The "D." of a club, for some reason, is always 1,802 less than the class year—Archibald MacLeish, class of 1915, for example, signed his letter "A. MacL. D113."

Generally, the rule has always been that every senior is required to attend every meeting. Usually the fifteen students have the tomb to themselves, but patriarchs who live in the area are welcome to visit and to stay for some presentations, as are young Bones graduates in Yale's professional schools, who are thrilled to get free four-course meals in which lobster is not an infrequent menu item.* When patriarchs enter the tomb, especially during an annual function, they are requested to sign a guestbook located near the front door. Skull and Bones strongly encourages its alumni to return often to the tomb, for several reasons, one being that the tendency for famous faces to come back provides "a sense of continuity, which reinforces the bond and the mystique" of the society, a young Bonesman explained.

There are at least two annual alumni functions held within the tomb, one in the winter, and one around the time of commencement that is called "The Annual Convention of the Order." All living members receive printed invitations to each of these events. The winter and commencement functions are also the two times a year that the board of the Russell Trust Association officially meets. When the invitation to Convention is sent, during the month before commencement, it is accompanied by a list of the newly initiated that members can insert into their personal copies of the society's membership catalogue, which details where the alumni are and what they are doing. Like all official Bones correspondence—patriarchs are mailed announcements, donation requests, and information about Deer Island—the invitations are usually

---

*The term *patriarch* first surfaced in Bones in 1836, when, the Bones Records state, "Several of the Patriarchs visited the Club this evening, and they and ourselves discussed a cold collation with great vigor. We would recommend all succeeding generations to *treat* the Patriarchs when honored with their company" (emphasis in original). Returning to the haunt for the purpose of mooching seems to have been a trend that began early. The 1852 Bones Black Book, which is something like a club diary, wryly notes that "Ten famished Patriarchs favored us with their presence, drank our coffee, devoured our oysters, and departed as they came."

enclosed in black-edged envelopes bearing the black wax seal of the society with the letters *S.C.B.* (presumably Skull and Crossbones). Often the envelopes are labeled with a request that if the letter is not delivered by a certain date, it is to be returned to the society's post office box. The invitation to Convention sometimes includes a Latin pun on the word *bone*, such as *"Nisi in bonis amicitia esse non potest"* ("No friendship can exist except in good men," from Cicero); *"Grandiaque effossis mirabitur ossa sepulchris"* ("He will wonder at the huge bones when [their] tombs have been dug up," from Virgil); *"Quid dicam de ossibus? Nil nisi bonum"* ("What should I say about Bones? Nothing except good"); and in 1856, the year the tomb was built, *"Quid dicam de ossibus? O fortunati, quorum jam moenia surgunt!"* ("What should I say about Bones? [from Cicero] O fortunate ones, whose walls are already going up." [from Virgil]) Members who can't make it to Convention often mail in information about themselves, such as location, accomplishments, personal tidbits, and other Class Notes–like information. That way, when an alumnus stops by the tomb during the year, he can look up other members to see what they have been doing.

Dinners are relatively lavish affairs consisting of several courses: soup, salad, entrée (roast beef, for instance, or whole lobsters), side dishes, and elaborate desserts baked by the two cooks, often followed by a round of cigars. "It's like a nice restaurant," a Bonesman told me. Dinner is presented by two servants, usually African Americans who are filched from the residential-college dining halls. Ice cream, which is always available by the tub in a downstairs freezer, is a particularly frequent feature. Alcohol, however, is not. According to Skull and Bones tradition, no member can drink alcohol within the tomb; instead, members make do with milk, soda, and juice. (Apparently, Eulogia's presence alone serves as a social lubricant.)* "It was a hard-and-fast rule designed to make sure people were levelheaded," one patriarch explained. But the

---

*This rule forced diehard drinkers to pursue that type of revelry outside of the tomb. One high school student in the 1960s, a future Bonesman, recalled spotting George W.

society has been known to savor wine on special occasions. In 1836, at the annual Christmas function, the society sealed two bottles of Madeira to be saved for the hundredth anniversary of the society. Meanwhile, the room in which Skull and Bones met was undergoing extensive renovations, which were completed in February. According to the "Bible of Patriarch Dwight" (a history of the society written by Yale president Timothy Dwight), after the club had finished its regular debate in its newly enhanced Temple, the knights found themselves to be unusually thirsty. Thus "it was resolved that this being an occasion so extraordinary and one which ought not to pass unhonored, and the building of the Temple being an event of importance to justify any sacrifice of principle or custom, the members do immediately proceed to uncork the bottles sealed for the hundreth [sic] anniversary, and transfer the contents of the same to the inward man." A knight named William Maxwell Evarts, a future U.S. attorney general and secretary of state and the founder of the *Lit.*, rationalized the premature opening of the bottles by defining the word *anniversary* "taken as is supposed from an unpublished dictionary, vis—that it means any great occasion [and therefore it is justified,] as every moment in the existence of the *Eulogian Club* is evidently a great occasion."

While most other societies invite non-Yale guests to speak to the membership in the tombs, Bones allows only its own members, except for the servants, within its walls. The guests often speak about their lives and the ways Skull and Bones has shaped them. Even for the more renowned members, the after-dinner presentations often take advantage of the audience's secrecy oaths. According to the 1968 yearbook, "McGeorge Bundy [recently] dropped by his spawning-ground, Skull and Bones. It was said that Bundy, making use of the famed privacy,

Bush during a visit to Yale. "I must have seen George W. five times that weekend, totally, completely drunk," the Bonesman laughed. "On a Sunday morning at five A.M., I saw him raving drunk, holding on to the back of a garbage truck in a three-piece suit, singing and carrying on and helping the garbage guys put the garbage in the truck. He was known in those days as an affable drunk."

spoke in complete candor on leading political figures as well as frankly discussing foreign policy developments." In the 1970s, Tex McCrary spoke often about how he had been the person who set up the American home in Moscow for the famous Nixon–Khrushchev "kitchen debate." In 1998, as evidenced in part by his signature on the guest register, the post-commencement dinner speaker was George Herbert Walker Bush.

Thursday sessions are relatively relaxed. Often after dinner — the frequency depends on the athleticism and frivolity of the group — the seniors play "boodleball." The knights clear the dining room, or Boodle, of its furniture so that they have a sixty-foot-long arena flanked by the two large fireplaces. With the fireplaces as goals and a half-deflated ball — pretty much any ball will do as long as it is half-deflated, I was told — the knights play an aggressive soccer–hockey hybrid that has left members bleeding on the floor. "It's very physical and real intense, but it never crosses a line in terms of violence," an avid boodleballer explained to me. Boodleball is so popular that when ten members of a club met up at a Yale reunion in 1981, they stopped by the tomb late at night to play "a brutal game of boodleball" — and sneaked their wives and girl-friends in to watch.

At 7:55 (VIII S.B.T.) — later if there has been a speaker — the Uncle Toby for the evening rings a bell fifteen times to summon the knights to the official session. When the knights are gathered together, the Secretary of the Eulogian Club drapes a robe around Uncle Toby, who opens the gold cabinet containing the engraving of Eulogia, to whom Archibald MacLeish referred in his 1959 letter as "the noumenous [sic] lady in the frame." Skull and Bones is deferential to Eulogia; at functions, a speaker addresses the membership by beginning, "Most Sacred Goddess Eulogia, Uncle Toby, and Knights of Eulogia." Uncle Toby sets the grandfather clock to VIII and the session officially begins. When the knights are seated, they sing two opening songs, or, in Skull and Bones parlance, "sacred anthems," before an activity called the Hearing of Excuses, during which the knights are assessed fines for crimes such as tardiness or absence, forgetting song lyrics, or using a non-Bones name in the tomb or a Bones name outside it. If a knight refuses to pay a fine, the Little Devil is authorized to seize an article of his clothing.

The sacred anthems represent an important part of the Bones experience. Scattered throughout each session's program, the songs are meant to convey different moods for each activity. During the closing sacred anthem in the Inner Temple, for example, when the knights are probably relieved that the serious part of the evening has ended, they muss each other's hair in what they colloquially refer to as "the dandruff dance." Other anthems range from the silly to the sentimental-bordering-on-sappy, with the society's two principal songs sung to the old melodies "Kiemeo" and "Rosin the Bow."

Some of the more memorable lyrics from three songs include

Cremo cramo hiro dare.
Hi melo mee arms me pomme diddle.
Nap dang pizzle wing linkmem rigdam,
Rigdam polly mitte crameo.

* * *

We catch the fire of love they feel
For those bright days of yore.
When weekly they met Pat O'Neill
And Madame Pompadour.

* * *

The Skull it is the mind,
The Bone it is the muscle.
And these I leave behind
To Major General Russell.

Some of the songs, a Bonesman sheepishly admitted to me, "are pumped with a little testosterone, but it's testosterone of the late nineteenth century. It's never belligerent."

The debate portion of the evening usually follows the speaker or the meal. Discussions, which can be frivolous or grave, last roughly ninety minutes, though some heated exchanges, including one over two knights who took their girlfriends on a tour of the tomb in the early 1980s, have sparked fierce arguments that lasted the rest of the evening. To begin the debate, Uncle Toby, robed again by the S.E.C., rings the bell in the Inner Temple fifteen times. On a table in front of Uncle Toby, who sits on a chair on the Inner Temple's platform, lies the five-minute sandglass and the Yorick, the skull divided into compartments from which the initiates drink "blood." In the back compartment, each member places a question written on a slip of paper; the front compartment contains papers printed with each knight's name. Uncle Toby draws both a question for the topic of the debate and the name of a Bonesman who will speak about the topic until the sands in the glass run out. Uncle Toby continues drawing names of speakers until each member present has offered an opinion. (It is through these debates and the autobiography sessions that Bonesmen come to know their brothers thoroughly. On the strength of 1948 Bonesman George Bush's debating performance in this arena, Bonesman and former Ohio congressman Thomas Ludlow "Lud" Ashley reportedly asked him upon his appointment as United Nations ambassador: "George, what the fuck do you know about foreign affairs?") During the debate, Uncle Toby takes notes that will be assembled at the end of the year into the club's Black Book. The accuracy and thoroughness of the Black Book notes depend on the dedication of that week's Uncle Toby, but regardless, a Bonesman remembered fondly, "They were great—we can go in there and read debates from the Civil War."

After a recess during which activities vary, the knights sing a sacred anthem in room 323, the Outer Temple, and Uncle Toby again dons the robe and strikes the bell fifteen times to signal a new activity. At this point during the first meeting in the fall, all knights participate in the "vacation experiences" discussion, which is something like an oral "What I Did on My Summer Vacation." Beginning with the next meeting, each knight spends a Sunday session standing in front of the painting of a woman that Bones calls "Connubial Bliss," where he delivers his sexual history. ("Connubial Bliss" is a term that knights have also used to refer to any woman.) The anthem introducing the activity, which begins "The young May moon is beaming with love" and ends "So let's steal a few hours from the night, my love," is "kind of sweet," one Bonesman said. The room is lit only by a fireplace and the doors are closed, leaving the knights sitting on plush couches in a quiet, cozy setting meant to be conducive to the most intimate of chats. The speeches can take several hours, but despite their graphic nature, do not necessarily concentrate solely on sex. "After the first one or two times," a young Bonesman clarified, "it's like guys listing their conquests, and that gets old because there's just not that much to talk about." As a result, the CBs evolve into a discussion as much about relationships as physical exploits. It is an activity that some members dread and some await with delicious anticipation—a knight named Yorick of the club of 1917 wrote to a friend that the CB was "a wonderful sensation." Another Bonesman said to me that the CB "could be in as comic or sincere a fashion as you wanted it to be. It was entirely up to you how much you revealed about yourself." And the reason that "people really unloaded," a patriarch has said, was that "the one thing we all agreed on was that whatever was said in that room would never leave that room."

Some Bonesmen insisted that the experience, frequently misconstrued by the public as some strange and salacious Gothic ritual, is not unique to the society. "The sexual history was strange, but it's the kind of stuff a lot of guys just do with their teammates in a less revealing way," said a Bonesman in his late thirties. "It was a really interesting thing to do. There was nothing perverse or surreal or prurient—just a kind of open exchange. It's like TV's Ricki Lake—there's now a national mania for purging thoughts at large. This is a way of doing it in a very private, nonsensationalist way that benefits the people who are listening and the people who are telling."

By mid-autumn, after each member has presented a CB, the time slot shifts to "Life Histories," during which Bonesmen spend their allotted period—or more; these autobiographies can take up more than one session—discussing their lives. Usually, knights stick with a time range of one and a half to three hours to deliver their autobiographies. The Life Histories are hardly easy. "You have to think about how to describe to fourteen other people what your life is like and you cannot gloss over it," an RTA board member said. "There is a degree of self-assessment and personal honesty." But depending on the club, members can also get away with whatever degree of honesty they want to exhibit. A patriarch who graduated in the 1970s told me, "If someone told of an 'Ozzie and Harriet' life without obvious discrepancies, it was not in vogue in those years to challenge people in that respect. But when you opened yourself up, if you put on the table dilemmas you had, people picked up on that and talked about them. We saw a lot of emotional outcomes. It made quite an impression." The intimacy of the environment leads some Bonesmen to reveal more than they want to: with fourteen pairs of eyes boring into the presenter, it isn't always easy to keep up a guard. "It's a much smaller group, so there's no place to hide," one Bonesman has said. "You've got to deal." While most Yale societies revolve around the "autos" in their attempts to model themselves after Bones, Bones places the most significance on this oral introspective. "The most beneficial thing of all is the skills that are developed in communicating ideas to the people around you," a mathematician Bonesman said. "There were lots of different ideas expressed. Being there enabled me to appreciate multiple points of view." An actor Bonesman added, "Rather than talking through scripts, you see people with their guard down. Guys would talk ad nauseam about their lives, experiences, and opinions, and come to understand, themselves, how they came to be that way." The Bonesmen also say the experience, like the CB, is merely an enhanced, intensified version of an activity that occurs in everyday life. A Bonesman in his thirties explained, "It's a human bonding experience. You can do it on a train with a stranger, you get something out of it. You do it in a society with strangers, you get something out of it."

While current events are important, they are peripheral to the true purpose of society discussions. "The secret-society experience shuts out some of the noise but not the essence of what's going on outside," a Bonesman from the mid-1960s told me. "You talk about what's going on in the world and put it in a personal context. It's as much a part of the internal experience as the external." In the early seventies, Bones provided its knights "with a wide window on who were the people at Yale and what was going on in their lives," said a Bonesman who graduated then. "There was a great deal of shocking information. There were several people who were gay and talked quite movingly about it. That was new for many of us. You learn humility and tolerance because you can't just walk away if you're going there two nights a week and spending so much time with these people. If you have some kind of conscious or unconscious yearning to open up, it's a great opportunity to do so." Clubs in the late 1980s spent the vast majority of their time discussing whether the society should accept women; they had, said one member, "no time to deal with anything else."

During the presentation, other members can ask questions or request elaboration on certain points, particularly if a knight hasn't described something as thoroughly as his clubmates would like. This activity is also accompanied by "criticisms," which consist of members' candid and sometimes brutal analysis of the speaker's account of himself. On one occasion, for example, an elderly patriarch led several knights to interrogate a knight giving his Life History because he felt that the knight was omitting a conflict from his junior high school days and therefore holding out on his fellow members. "There is a sense of heightened objectivity about one's self when you hear that many people tell you what they think of you," an elderly patriarch said. When I asked him whether there was additionally a sense of hurt, he replied, "That's always a risk." A patriarch in his mid-sixties told me he still has the comments his clubmates gave him. He sorts through the small scraps of paper every couple of years, he said, because "they were a touchstone. I wanted to save them because they were an important part of my youth. I find I'm not too different than I was then, which is kind of reassuring. I'm still the person I was when I was with them."

In the early twentieth century, a knight received his criticism before he delivered his Life History, presumably so he could address his newly revealed character flaws during his discussion (and fix them before graduating into the barbarian world). In the mid-1900s, a criticism was given to one of Skull and Bones' better-known members, to whom I will refer only as Merlin, his society name. In the letter, the assigned Bonesman stated that Merlin's most egregious flaw was that he was oversophisticated to the point that he had detached himself from the world with such a coolness that he had lost his boyish enthusiasm. While his social polish was enviable, his critic wrote, Merlin needed to let himself experience emotional highs and lows rather than look upon the world with a constantly bemused nonchalance. The critic speculated that Merlin's defect was due to an easy life of luxury in which his wealth made him insensitive, uncaring, and perhaps a bit naive.

While programs inevitably vary according to club, Bonesmen stray from the schedule of activities only at certain preapproved sessions. During the Thursday session before winter vacation, dubbed "the Skull and Bones Christmas," knights perform skits at a party. For six weeks or more during the second semester, Bonesmen devote sessions almost exclusively to the election of new members, a process during which groups, as in any society, can become fractious, friendships erode, and loyalties divide because of strong preferences for successors.

After the final activity of the evening, regardless of whether it is a CB, Life History, party, or election, the Bonesmen, still gathered around a table, sing two songs. During the first one, they beat an accompanying rhythm on the table with bones while Uncle Toby stands underneath the bell. During the second song, the knights walk around the table. After the anthems, Uncle Toby calls for three cheers for each absent member, three cheers for the patriarchs, and three cheers for the tomb. Finally, he strikes the bell three times, twice, then twice again as the knights beat the bones on the table and shout "Three!" "Two!"

"Two!" It is not uncommon for meetings to last until two or three in the morning. In the society's earliest years, members were supposed to go directly to bed after meetings without speaking to anyone, even their roommates; apparently during some years toothbrushes were provided so that members wouldn't have to run into barbarians in the bathroom. Today the knights may exit the tomb silently, but will also often reconvene in small groups at bars, where they won't avoid speaking to their barbarian friends.

During sessions, the knights memorialize their time in the tomb by keeping a scrapbook and a Black Book. The scrapbook, which is candid and uncensored, is like an informal yearbook, the blank, brown pages of which the knights fill any way they please. "People write in them and paste pictures. I drew caricatures of the fourteen other guys," said a patriarch who is now a professor. "Some of the older scrapbooks are pretty puerile, like Playboy bunnies are pasted in with a picture of one of the guys next to them. The Black Books are much more serious."

Every ten years or so, all patriarchs receive in the mail two bound books: one titled "Living Members" and the other titled "Deceased Members," both of which catalogue the society membership to date. Once in a long while, a patriarch, presumably with a grant from the society, will write a Bones Bible, which chronicles the society's history up to that point. (Timothy Dwight wrote the first Bones Bible in 1863 to commemorate the thirtieth anniversary of the "Foundation of our American Chapter." It would not be out of character for the next Bones Bible to be published and presented during Convention in 2007, the society's 175th anniversary.) Before the end of the year, each knight receives a small album containing a group picture, a photograph of the outside of the tomb, and a picture of each individual knight with an accompanying autograph (of the Bones name only).

Unlike members of other societies, Bonesmen pay no dues. But every year, all patriarchs receive a letter from the society treasurer that requests them to make a "voluntary contribution." One early-twentieth-century form-letter solicitation was phrased this way:

MY DEAR SIR: —

  YOU ARE REQUESTED TO MAKE A VOLUNTARY CLUB CONTRIBUTION TO
THE RUSSELL TRUST ASSOCIATION OF NEW HAVEN FOR THE YEAR 1921.

  YOUR LAST DONATION WAS $10

  FAITHFULLY YOURS.

[NAME]

TREASURER

By the late 1990s, Bones had in this manner amassed an endowment of
$3 million, the second-highest amount of any of Yale's secret societies.[*]
In 1997, the society's tax filing (under RTA Incorporated) stated that the
year's net assets were $4,260,597; in 1998, the figure shrank slightly to
$4,115,360. The society's stated total revenue for 1997 was $738,212 and
in 1998, $759,061. In 1997, the society received $164,529 in donations; in
1998, the contributions shrank to $116,256.

---

[*]A document titled "Annual Budget of Club's Expenditures," likely from the 1920s or
1930s, gives an idea of how Bones once spent its budget:

Annual Budget of Club's Expenditures

#Food Bill—Quality Grocery Store:

	Thursday and Saturday dinners and Thursday late S.B.T.	
	7 months @ $190.00 per month	$1330.00
	1 month (May–June) 2 Clubs	380.00
#Ice Cream—8 months @ $7.00 per month		56.00
#Cigars and cigarettes—8 months @ 21.00		168.00
#R.T.A. Bill—(wood, light, gas, repairs, and John and Pierre)		600.00
#Photograph albums		176.00
Pictures at Pach's:	225 single pictures for album @ 1.00	225.00
	15 Group @ $6.00	90.00
	15 Temple @ $6.00	90.00
	80 Single pictures for back of album @ $1.00	80.00
	1 Group for Temple @ $4.00	4.00
	15 Crates for expressing @ $1.00	15.00
		504.—

In the 1990s, Marina Moscovici was paid two or three thousand dollars each for restoring small paintings and up to seven thousand each for larger paintings in the tomb. But the process stretched over a period of six years — not because Moscovici had to manage her time, but rather because Skull and Bones needed to manage its budget. "The whole place is more about the prestige of who they are, not what they have," Moscovici told me. "It's not a big money club; it's more of a connection club." In recent years, the society has had to spend a significant amount of money to fix the roof, which had been leaking.

One major difference between Skull and Bones and the other secret societies is that Bones does not use its wealth and connections to help the community. Instead, it "is more or less designed to serve its members, to varying degrees," said a member from the late 1980s. "It's a pretty self-serving organization, not in a dark or evil way, but the whole point is for it to be it and not to be it to anyone else." Scroll and Key, by contrast, provides thousands of dollars in grants and summer fellowships to Yale, the Yale University Press, and nonmember Yale students each year, has raised thousands of dollars for charities and community

Badges for next Club — 15 @ $9.75	146.25
2 Scrap Books — Volume I & II @ $15.00	30.00
Black Book	20.00
Christmas presents — John & Pierre — $15.00 and $10.00 respectively	25.00
2 tickets Harvard football game — John	10.00
Tips at D.I.[Deer Island] — Fall and Spring - $5.00 per person for 3	30.00
Miscellaneous — (Paste, pads, ink, paints, Christmas decorations, etc.)	20.00
Insertion Yale Banner and Pot Pourri	30.00
Stay @ D.I. 1 week @ 5.00 x 15 x 2 yrs	1050
	4575.25

Notes: —

      # Figures are approximate and represent average over period of several months.
      R.T.A. item is for year and likewise approximate.
      Pach's charges are exorbitant.

programs, and has provided loans to Yale organizations such as the *Yale Record,* a campus publication, and WYBC, the campus radio station. The Russell Trust Association's money, however, "goes to the upkeep of the building, taxes, and the island," a patriarch said. "No one gets any money. The only person we knew of who got money was somebody who in our year had some terrible drug debts, so he came in, stole a rug, and sold it." As for the alleged graduation gift of $15,000, a Bonesman from George W. Bush's 1968 class told me: "I'm still waiting for mine."

Besides its wealth, another prevalent rumor is that Skull and Bones is an anti-Semitic organization. I found no indisputable evidence that Bones as an institution has at any time preached anti-Semitism, but there is ample proof that some of the society's members as individuals loathed Jews. In 1922, Robert Nelson Corwin (Bones 1887), the chairman of Yale's board of admissions from 1919 to 1933, wrote a letter to Yale dean Frederick Jones (Bones 1884) that advocated the institution of a quota on Jewish enrollment; the analysis was titled "Memorandum on the Problems Arising from the Increase in the Enrollment of Students of Jewish Birth in the University." Jones agreed, and the quota was set. Farwell Knapp (Bones 1916) held a similar view. After visiting Jones in November 1922, Knapp wrote in his diary:

> I know he hates Jews, tho I think he is generally impartial. But not always, I am glad to say. For instance, when I was in college, Jews held 80% or so of all important Scholarships, tho the Jews were but an insignificant fraction of the college enrollment. Since then, Jones, with [Yale president Arthur] Hadley's [Bones 1876] acquiescence, has quietly tried to oust them, so that today not one important scholarship is held by a Jew. I dislike Jews, so I am in favor of this sort of discrimination. . . . Men are not equal, and disagreeable or otherwise disqualified ones had best be frankly kept out.

Six months later, Knapp's feelings had intensified: "My general trend of thought may be summed up as follows: complete and whole-hearted sympathy with the French occupation of the Ruhr; feel that the ultimate solving of the Jewish problem lies with the Ku Klux Klan, think they're pretty good."

The juvenile behavior that outsiders have speculated goes on in the tomb is not entirely absent, but it isn't a regularly scheduled part of the program. As one patriarch explained, in Skull and Bones historically "some guys have done some hellacious things because when you get a group of guys together they do hellacious things." A patriarch who graduated in the middle of the twentieth century affirmed, "There is a great sense of humor associated with Bones that is quite contrary to the society's appearance." A 1970s Bonesman added, "There was all sorts of sophomoric fun to be had if you wanted it."

If there is no torrid hazing, no masturbation, and no money, a disappointed watchhound might be reluctantly inclined to surmise that there are no true secrets in the society. The watchhound would be slightly wrong. Skull and Bones does have at least one skeleton in its closet, although it is fairly small and has by now crumbled mostly into sand. But it is a good illustration of the attitude within the tomb, particularly the sense of entitlement that these society members have with respect to the rest of the world.

There is a reason that for many years, whenever an item of value or sentimental significance disappeared from the Yale campus, the community just naturally figured it had gone to Skull and Bones: Skull and Bones in most cases had indeed taken that item. Because its building is inaccessible to nonmembers, including the barbarian police, Skull and Bones treats its tomb like a trophy case. In the nineteenth century, Bonesmen (who call their purloined treasures "gifts of tribute to the Goddess") stuck to minor items that were important in Yale's history, such as the Old College gong from the treasurer's office, the Old College drum, a small church bell from East Haven, an Old College flag, the "Old College punch bowl and ladle," and pins of every Yale secret society. The card table in the Inner Temple is supposedly the "Old College table" on which John C. Calhoun would play.

Other alleged Bones thefts have been more controversial. In the 1980s, when Ned Anderson, a former chairman of the San Carlos Apache tribe in Arizona, was in the process of trying to find the remains of the Apache chief Geronimo where he was supposed to be buried at Fort Sill in Oklahoma, he received a letter from someone who claimed to be a member of Skull and Bones. "What you're seeking," the letter read, "is not over at Fort Sill. It is in New Haven, Connecticut, on the Yale University campus. If you are interested in pursuing the matter further, I will make photographs available to you." When Anderson wrote that he was interested, the Bonesman sent him a photograph of the Bones tomb and a photograph of a glass display case containing bones, stirrups, a horse bit, and what the informant said was the skull of Geronimo. The Bonesman also included a purported Skull and Bones document that told the story of how George W. Bush's grandfather Prescott Bush and a band of fellow patriarchs stole the skull of Geronimo in 1918 from Fort Sill and stowed it in the tomb:

From the war days also sprang the mad expedition from the School of Fire at Fort Sill, Oklahoma, that brought to the T its most spectacular "crook," the skull of Geronimo the terrible, the Indian Chief who had taken forty-nine white scalps. An expedition in late May, 1918, by members of four Clubs, Xit D.114, Barebones, Caliban and Dingbat, D.115, S'Mike D.116, and Hellbender D.117, planned with great caution since in the words of one of them: "Six army captains robbing a grave wouldn't look good in the papers." The stirring climax was recorded by Hellbender in the Black Book of D.117: ". . . The ring of pick on stone and thud of earth on earth alone disturbs the peace of the prairie. An axe pried open the iron door of the tomb, and Pat Bush entered and started to dig. We dug in turn, each on relief taking a turn on the road as guards. . . . Finally Pat Ellery James turned up a bridle, soon a saddle horn and rotten leathers followed, then wood and then, at the exact bottom of the small round hole, Pat James dug deep and pried out the trophy itself. . . . We quickly closed the grave, shut the door and sped home to Pat Mallon's room, where we cleaned the Bones. Pat Mallon sat on the floor liberally applying carbolic acid. The Skull was fairly clean, having only some flesh inside and a little hair. I showered and hit the hay . . . a happy man. . . .

Anderson and his attorney returned to Fort Sill, where they discovered through research that those personal items had indeed been taken from the grave. At the Bonesman's invitation, Anderson and his lawyer visited him in New Haven, where he took them on a tour of the campus to point out key sites that were relevant to the Geronimo theft. "He was so worried about his safety that he walked sixty feet ahead of us, and when he wanted us to look at something, he would give us a cue—he'd turn around and gesture as if he were pointing a gun," Anderson told me. "He said there had been 'incidents,' and that people had been rummaging through his trash. Eventually he went on the run."

Anderson and his attorney set up a meeting with Bonesman Jonathan Bush, brother of then vice president George Bush. They met on a Thursday in a New York City high-rise for no more than an hour. Anderson showed Bush the photographs and asked that Geronimo's skull be returned to its intended resting place with the tribe in Arizona. "At first he seemed nice, like he was genuinely interested in helping with the cause," Anderson said to me. Bush told Anderson, "I know what you came for and I'm going to see to it that you will get what you want and be satisfied." He told Anderson to call him the following day. The next day, Anderson said, he tried calling several times but could not reach anybody until a receptionist finally told him that Bush had gone golfing for the afternoon and could not be reached. Anderson and his lawyer returned home to Arizona.

Eleven days later, the duo returned to New York for a meeting with Bush, Skull and Bones counsel Endicott Peabody Davison (Bones 1945 and a partner in Winthrop, Stimson, Putnam & Roberts from 1959 to 1980), and a young Bones knight. "The young guy started to talk in favor of us and Endicott told him to shut up. When Endicott scolded him, the guy cowered. Then Endicott did all the talking," Anderson told me. "He said the skull we were interested in was right there on the conference table." On the table was a display case, identical to that which Anderson had seen in the photograph, complete with the authentic stirrups and horse bit. But the skull looked different.

"We had it analyzed," Davison said, gesturing to the skull. "We found out it's not Geronimo's skull, but the skull of a ten-year-old boy."

The Bonesmen then tried to persuade Anderson to sign a document stipulating that the society did not have Geronimo's skull, that he would take home the display case, and that he would never talk about the matter again. Anderson refused.

When Anderson returned home to Arizona, he asked Senator John McCain to intervene by contacting George H. W. Bush, who was due to visit Arizona, and asking him for help. McCain told Anderson that Bush would not return his call. Today the display case remains in the tomb, with a skull—perhaps the skull from the meeting, perhaps not—that Skull and Bones members told me they still call Geronimo.

Similarly, a group in 1987 charged that Bones had paid $25,000 to an American soldier in the 1920s to steal the skull of Pancho Villa. Bones retorted that not only did the society never have the skull, but that the stingy alumni would never have given up $25,000 in the first place.

The least publicized, but most accurate, claim of theft by Skull and Bones is over the gravestone of Elihu Yale. Unless the large stone in the tomb is a stunningly accurate replica that society members paid for with time and money they likely would not have spent, the encased tombstone, labeled "Tablet from the Grave of Elihu Yale Taken from Wrexham Churchyard" and set on a black mantel, is real. In 2000, when I reported the whereabouts of this relic, I was interviewed by the BBC Wales. After the interview aired, I heard from Wrexham, Wales, residents about the tablet. "Elihu Yale has a lot of ties to Wrexham," Reg Herbert, then the editor-in-chief of the *Wrexham Evening Leader*, said to me. "The stone is very important to us. If they don't give it back, we might as well come steal the torch off the Statue of Liberty."

Skull and Bones does not just condone stealing, it actively encourages it. One October in the 1970s, Yale professor Gaddis Smith, then the master of Pierson College, received a telephone call at 3:00 A.M. from the campus police. One of his students had been arrested by the New Haven Police Department and placed in jail. The officers said they would release the student on Smith's recognizance. Smith went to the jail. The student and two friends had broken into the Berkeley College dining hall and removed a portrait of former Yale president Charles Seymour. When the police caught them they split the three up and interrogated them. "What'd you do that for?" Smith asked his student. The students, it turned out, were Bones knights, and Seymour a 1908 Bonesman.

"I'm in Bones," the senior told Smith. "This is part of our initiation. We have to 'crook' something. The tomb is full of things, with plaques reading 'crooked by' and then a name. Even George Bush, the director of the CIA, has a plaque in there—'crooked by George Bush, 1948.'"

The Bones knights had "talked about what to crook to outdo the other clubs," one of them told me. "We were going to put the painting in our dining room." Three knights were selected to perform the crook, including Gog, "because he'd never done anything even remotely questionable in his life." Gog broke down and confessed to the police.

When Smith found out that the Berkeley College master wanted to press criminal charges, he called the university treasurer, who was a lawyer as well as the Bones alumni liaison.

"You've got two boys in big trouble. Breaking and entering, and theft. That was a twenty-thousand-dollar portrait, and they're looking at ten to twenty," Smith said. "If your society were to invite a representative of the university into the tomb to take an inventory of everything that does not belong to you, then the charges will go away."

"Nothing presently of value is in the building," the liaison replied.

A day later, a plaster-of-Paris model of Abraham Pierson, which had been missing from the Fellows Room in Pierson College, showed up, swathed in blankets, at Smith's door. The students were never charged.

For Bonesmen, "crooking" doesn't exactly feel like stealing. With a kleptomaniacal thrill, the knights rationalize that anything they take they are taking as a conquest for the society. Crooking is a lighthearted activity that is viewed within the society as just another Skull and Bones tradition, in tribute to the goddess who inspires them, as implied in a draft of an 1843 Bonesman's poem about the society:

The "Temple"—now so rich and rare
Was never furnished fully
Until they consecrated there
The Club of the College Bully.
Sweet bully, sin has fled like dew
At the Faculty's parching tones, boys—
Let it rest in peace till the Order anew
Is endowed by the Skull and Bones boys.

The drum, that whilom used to raise
The calliathump alarum—
And if the tutors should come to gaze
With wildest notes to scare 'em
Though in the hands of the Poet & Fellows—it was
Each tutor dejectedly owns, boys,
That he didn't know where the Devil it is
"Let's ask the Skull and Bones boys."

The old card table, too, is here
Of relics much the oldest.
For seventy years 'twas handed down
To him who played the boldest.
Though marred and bruised by many a thrump
The college its loss bemoans, boys
Our club is sure of the ace of trumps
Hurrah for the Skull and Bones boys.
Ri-de-fol-di-rol-rol. . . .

The Soul is too Ethereal,
Too viewless, light and airy.
Its home is not on the Earth at all
Of day it soon grows weary.
The flesh with the Devil is aye in league
His sway it too often owns, boys—
Then let it go—who cares a fig
For aught but the Skull & Bones boys?
Ri-fol-di-rol-de

☠   ☠   ☠

Beginning early in the second semester, after each knight has delivered his Life History, most Skull and Bones sessions are devoted to electing the next year's club. The arduous process is a matter of continuously narrowing down the most promising students of the junior class until fifteen people can more or less agree on a group. The knights must come up with a list of about twenty-one candidates, in case half a dozen of their first-choice candidates turn them down. Qualifications have changed for elections to Skull and Bones and the other secret societies in recent years. Rather than reward merit, the societies now often lean toward rewarding ethnicity, which turns the groups into overly politically correct hyperventilators and the candidates into token quota taps. In a recent Wolf's Head election, according to the *New Republic*, a Korean American student "threw a tantrum," sobbed, and stalked out of a meeting because he wanted his slot to go to another Korean rather than to an individual of different Asian heritage. Then a Chicano member threw a similar fit. Skull and Bones likewise chases down minority candidates—the juniors who, rather than sit at the top of their class, instead fill certain society niches. The woman who is also gay and outspoken, and preferably Native American, is likely to be considered. The white male scholar, unless he is truly Old Blue, is not.

Generally, the best prospects for Bones have traditionally been the students who are most likely to bring honor and prestige to the society, in whatever aspects of campus and national life are in vogue at the time. In the mid-1800s, for example, when scholarship was valued, Bones tapped scholars: between 1861 and 1894 only eight valedictorians were not tapped for a senior society. When Yale undergraduates' interest in scholarship waned between 1894 and 1902, no valedictorians were tapped. In the mid-twentieth century, Bones grabbed more honor society members (Torch and Aurelian societies) than its rivals did. Until the 1960s, Skull and Bones tapped mostly fraternity and prep school men; the rationale, a Bonesman from the early 1960s told me, was that if a student came from one of the nation's top five private schools, "the kid's got to be good." A position as a class officer or class committee man, or membership in a religious organization such as Dwight Hall or the Undergraduate Deacons was also a preferred qualification. Bones nearly always used to tap the editors of the *Lit.* and the *Yale Daily News.* But by the late twentieth century, few undergraduates cared about the literary magazine, and the *Daily News* editors-in-chief from the classes of 1997 and 1998 were not tapped for any secret societies at all. This snub is actually not so surprising. The top editor position on a major publication was a much more powerful position in the nineteenth century than in recent years. At that time, a likely reason Skull and Bones tapped editors was so the society could control the campus press. An 1873 editorial of the anti-society Yale publication the *Iconoclast* reported, "The college press is closed to those who dare to openly mention 'Bones.' "

Although they no longer reflexively look to campus publications when tapping, Bones itself has had an enormous influence on American journalism. Two of the country's top news magazines were founded by Bonesmen. Henry Luce and Briton Hadden, both Bones 1920, reportedly came up with the idea for *Time* in the tomb, which still may hold the minutes and memos regarding the founding of the magazine. Averell Harriman (Bones 1913) founded a publication called *Today* that merged with another publication in 1937 to become *Newsweek.* A few years later, when *Newsweek* questioned the efficiency of the daylight bombing of Germany, Robert A. Lovett (Bones 1918), then assistant to Secretary of

War Henry Stimson, wrote to Harriman in London to ask for help. Harriman instructed his brother Roland (Bones 1917) to "strong arm" *Newsweek*'s directors into going along with an editorial policy discouraging that and similar lines of questioning.

During the election sessions, the knights convene in the Inner Temple and hash out their feelings about particular juniors. Each member chooses somebody to replace himself, formally nominates the junior, then stands up in front of the group and explains why this candidate should succeed him. If a candidate receives two negative votes ("blackballs"), he will not become a Bonesman. If he receives just one, the society may in some cases call forward the anonymous blackballer in order to present his case to the quorum. Once a candidate has been elected, his name is deposited in a silver skull. "What I find interesting," a Bonesman who graduated in the early 1970s said to me, "is that in many, many respects what happens in there is the flip side of the lore, which has diminished in the past twenty years. It was in many respects a great leveling of people regardless of their family or individual accomplishments. There was this sense that everyone in the building was equal." Of course, in order to be considered an equal, one had to first gain entrance into the society, which was not a possibility for women until 1991, when it was one of only two remaining single-sex secret societies at Yale.

Bones' historical misogyny is hardly hidden. The refusal to recognize women as deserving of knighthood, the reified attention to "Connubial Bliss," both as an activity and as a name for the other gender, some adornments in the tomb, including a picture titled *The Taming of the Shrew* and a painted portrayal of a woman's nether regions that allegedly used to hang in the bathroom — all of these have fostered and perpetuated an atmosphere that could inarguably be construed as sexist. Some of the alumni, one Bonesman said, view women as "people you see on weekends in party dresses." Marina Moscovici recalled with amusement that before 1991, members had to sneak her in through the side door of the building on weekends — and that it was "a big deal that the society had even chosen a woman as [an art] restorer." Today, some

Bonesmen still say they regret that the society opened its doors to the other gender. "The experience was so special that I never felt it should be changed in any way. I was very much against admitting women," a Bonesman who graduated in the early 1940s told me.

But not long after Yale became a coeducational institution and the knights became accustomed to studying alongside female students, the idea of admitting women began cropping up in scattered debates inside the tomb. The Bones knights of 1971, known in the society for years afterward as the "bad club," formally proposed making the society coeducational. Philosophically, the bad club was fairly evenly split, but one faction of the group made a strong enough case to the rest of the knights that the club unanimously agreed upon electing three women among the next fifteen members. "A lot of the guys knew the women and agreed they were exceptional," said a member who elected a woman as his direct successor. "We had already spoken to the women to make sure they knew what they were in for as the first women—and they were prepared to be the Jackie Robinson of Skull and Bones."

When the society's alumni heard that the bad club planned to tap women, they were in an uproar. They demanded a meeting with the club to discuss the situation. The patriarchs held court in a private room at an expensive French restaurant on the Upper East Side of New York. The bad club piled into a light green VW microbus headed into the city. "We had the long hair, the beards, and when we opened the door to the microbus, smoke came billowing out; it was a classic 1971 scene, like that scene in *Fast Times at Ridgemont High*," a bad-club member told me. When the club arrived at the restaurant, they were shown to their assigned seats: spread out about the room among fifty alumni so that there were no more than two knights to a table. "They deliberately split us up. We were definitely outnumbered," the bad-club member said. "We were brought down to New York so they could slap us around." The club was startled to see some of the society's more prominent members at the meeting, including McGeorge Bundy, Jonathan Bush, Tex McCrary, and R. Inslee Clark, Jr. After cocktails and dinner, a knight who is now an actor in Los Angeles delivered an eloquent speech about why his group had come to the decision to elect women. Sometime during that speech, McGeorge Bundy elbowed the patriarch next to him and loudly joked, "So Aunt Jemima's coming to dinner?" The patriarchs laughed. When the actor ended his speech by stating that nothing went on in the tomb that women couldn't have been a part of, Jonathan Bush "shot up out of his chair like he had a Roman candle up his butt," said a participant in that meeting. Bush retorted, "Then you guys use the place wrong." The knights were left wondering, as one of them told me, "What the hell did they used to *do* in there?"

Then the patriarchs said their piece: They paid the bills, thus the club was theirs, therefore there would be no women in Skull and Bones. Various alumni stood up and said that the bad club "just didn't get it" and that they did not understand "what the place was all about." The only patriarch to support the bad club was Inslee Clark, the Yale admissions director from 1965 to 1970 who had led Yale to accept more minorities, public school students, and, eventually, women. But when Clark went so far as to state that tapping women could actually benefit the society, the alumni were upset. "He defended us, saying it was a great idea, and he took a lot of heat for that," the bad-club member said. "There was a lot of macho posturing, like women couldn't be rough and tough enough to play boodleball." Finally, the patriarchs issued an ultimatum: If the club of 1971 insisted on tapping women for the 1972 club, the alumni would seal the tomb and close it down for one year. The alternative was for the bad club to stay in the restaurant with the alumni and, together with them, choose the fifteen men to be tapped. Eight of the knights walked out. The remaining seven elected the men of the 1972 club.

Even as late as 1983, knights were generally adamant about keeping Bones a single-sex entity. When an older alumnus returned to the tomb then, he asked the knights whether talk about admitting women had resumed. "There is no talk," they replied, "and there will probably never be." In 1986, knights again unsuccessfully tried to persuade the alumni to accept female members.

Until 1991, the closest a woman could come to Skull and Bones — besides art restoration work — was to marry a Bonesman; she could then undergo the Skull and Bones wedding ceremony, which involves rites that essentially initiate a bride into the Bones family. Sometimes the aura of Skull and Bones came into play even when choosing a wife in the first place. In a diary entry from August 1922, Farwell Knapp (Bones 1916) agonized over proposing to a girlfriend who might not be up to the society's standards:

Hester is right, though, about the quality of the wives of the club. They get along well enough with their respective husbands: and, perhaps, from certain viewpoints are up to them. But, on the whole, I think not. The club is generally supposed to be — and is — composed of the best men of the class. Everyone has a high regard for them, so far as I am aware; and as cold and impartial an analysis I am capable of shows them to be high class stuff. I don't think their wives are. Hester is the only exception: and she is rare and unique. . . . She would be and is recognized to be a star by everyone that knows her. So I'm glad Kin has acquired what is reported to be another star.

Stewart and Walker and I remain, and (according to Hes) on us rests the solemn duty of pulling up the average. What Stewie will do even God doesn't know: and no one of our friends can figure out what sort of a woman will suit either Walker or myself. . . . Supposing I picked Hen Bayne — that would not raise the average to the casual observer, who would regard her as pleasant enough, but certainly no star. . . . But I feel no duty to marry the World's Greatest Woman just to raise the average of the club: and, anyway, one can't marry to satisfy one's friend. If my wife satisfies me, to Hell with them. . . . Damn! I wish I could stop this arguing with myself.

Knapp married Hen Bayne on June 23, 1923, when he wrote in his journal about the Bones wedding ceremony:

Wedding Day.

> And then I gathered up all the GB's present—more than twenty—an
> unusually large number—and we took Hen way upstairs to the uncle's
> room, and had a Bones wedding—a good one—and Hen sat in the
> midst and just drank it down and reveled in it—as I knew she would.
> Rat and Phil and Cliff sat together on a bed, through it, sort of holding
> hands and crying a little—it meant so much to them, and hit them so
> exactly right. (When Rat came up to me in the reception line his eyes
> were full, and he couldn't say anything. We just wrung each other's
> hand, silently.)

Knapp included in his journal a letter about the ceremony he received
from 1916 clubmate H. Phelps Putnam:

> The wedding wasn't as bad as you thought it would be—was it now? I
> liked it—I thought it was one of the best weddings. And I particularly
> liked the B____ part—Hen was so exactly right for that, and showed
> that she felt exactly right, that it was most pleasing—and there are so
> damned few girls who can get through that business correctly.

Generally, a Bonesman invites his fourteen clubmates and a smatter-
ing of patriarchs to his wedding. At the wedding, or if the circumstances
are too inconvenient, at some other time during the weekend's festivities,
the patriarchs gather in a circle in a different room, apart from the rest of
the partygoers, and, at a precise moment, beckon to the bride and groom
to enter the circle arm in arm and stand in the middle while the group
sings. This private ceremony, not surprisingly, does not always go over
well with the rest of the wedding party. "My parents were so mad," a
Bones bride from the sixties told me. "The whole time I was thinking,
'Please just get this over with.'" Until approximately 1963, Skull and
Bones delivered to each new married couple a tall, beautiful grandfather clock purchased with funds donated by the other fourteen

clubmates, but apparently the gifts eventually became too pricey, or perhaps too many Bonesmen were having too many marriages. ("Ours was more of a grandmother clock. At least it chimed," the 1960s bride said.)

One woman, the sister of a Bones bride, told me how she managed to watch an entire Skull and Bones wedding ceremony in the 1960s. A group of about twenty Bonesmen took the bride and groom into a barn at the other end of the complex where the festivities were held. "Everyone was to be excluded—but I wasn't in the mood to be excluded," the woman told me, so she hid in the loft of the barn. During the ceremony, which was officiated by a patriarch in his mid-eighties, the Bonesmen wore black, hooded robes and intoned chants in strange languages. As the sister peered down at the ceremony, her mouth agape, the men waved an object that resembled a baton over a coffin and spoke about ghosts. "It was weird, weird, weird. It was ritualistic—almost pagan. They went through this whole thing about how if any of them ever were to get in trouble, they would come to the rescue of their Skull and Bones compatriots, including financially. There was an emphasis on those pledges forever to help out your brother," she said. "I remember thinking then that it reminded me of the ceremony when you step up from Brownie to Girl Scout, which happens in, oh, about second grade. But I was also slightly scared at the time because I was thinking that these guys—and there were older people there, too—looked really serious." The sister was apparently not scared into silence, however. Near the completion of the ceremony, she told me, the ludicrousness of what she was watching finally got to her. "At the end, I couldn't take it anymore, I was laughing so hard. I stood up and cried, 'You people are full of shit!'" Shocked, the Bonesmen gaped at her. Five or six of them ran up the stairs to the loft, as one of them growled, "You are never to speak of this to anyone." When the woman responded, "Are you threatening me?" the Bonesmen didn't answer. "I was a bit intimidated," she said to me now, cackling, "but if that's what they do in Skull and Bones, all those leaders of the free world, then we're in deep trouble. I'm sixty-two years old and I don't think in my entire life I have ever been so stunned like that. It was all just too bizarre."

In a series of events that made national headlines, the Bones class of 1991 eventually tapped female juniors. "Being a part of Bones is often an embarrassment, a source of ridicule and occasionally a good way to lose a friend. Very rarely is Bones still seen as an honor, and never is it seen to represent the mainstream of Yale," the 1991 club explained in a six-page single-spaced letter to the patriarchs that expressed frustration over the Bones reputation for being "flagrantly discriminatory and bigoted." The patriarchs, unmoved, changed the locks of the tomb and threatened to shut down the society in order "to prevent or discourage unauthorized efforts to change the society's traditions"; the society would not tolerate the inclusion of women, despite its reverence for a goddess as muse. After the seniors contacted prominent lawyers and threatened to sue Bones for breach of contract, the patriarchs offered a "separate but equal" compromise: the seniors could tap ten women and ten men. The coed club would be able to dine together, but when it came time for the intimate activities — the Life Histories and the CBs — the group would segregate into separate-sex groups. The seniors rejected the offer because they felt that the women would be made to feel second-rate.

In 1991, after approximately eight hundred living members voted by mail, Bones narrowly endorsed the admission of women. But in early September, the day before the women were to be initiated, a faction led by patriarch William F. Buckley (1950) obtained from New Haven Superior Court Judge Donald Celotto a court order that temporarily blocked the 1991 club from initiating the nine men and six women it had tapped; as a result, the ceremony was canceled. The plaintiffs claimed that admitting women would lead to "date rape" in the "medium-term future" and that before women could be admitted to the society, a change in society bylaws was necessary. Bones held a second vote on October 24. More than 425 members came to the tomb and hundreds more voted by proxy; the votes tallied 368 to 320 in favor that women should be elected to the society. The women were initiated on Sunday, October 27.

Senators David Boren and John Kerry later disclosed that they voted for the admittance of women. George Bush and George W. Bush have never confessed how they voted, though George W. might have provided a clue when in 1994 he told PBS producer Lynn Novick, a woman who graduated from Yale in 1983, that Yale "went downhill since they admitted women." During his 1988 presidential campaign, George Bush admitted he was not necessarily inclined to let women into the society.*

Today, some Skull and Bones elders have disassociated themselves from the society because of the 1991 vote, not just because women were admitted, but rather because of how they were admitted. The 1991 club "lied," said a 1950s Bones patriarch, one of the men who sued to stop the vote. "They told us they would canvas the membership with open minds and hold meetings around the country. And that they hadn't yet made up their minds. But that was a salesmanship job—they didn't attempt to elicit our opinion and they already knew what they were going to do. Skull and Bones is not what it used to be." Other patriarchs put on a pleasant face when they discuss the admission of women. A Russell Trust Association board member insisted to me that "Bones has changed to continue to reflect the increasing diversity of the Yale student body—it has been as diverse as Yale." When asked whether Bones changed when it admitted women, he replied, "From close observation, not at all. Twentysomethings today have a far greater concept of the opposite sex as something besides as potential target. It was a change for

---

*Another clue might be found in the strenuous lobbying of Jonathan Bush against allowing women in the society. During the summer of 1991, a patriarch who had led the "bad club" received a personal phone call from Bush. The patriarch's girlfriend, who was aware of the situation, answered the phone. When the caller said, "This is Jonathan Bush," the girlfriend responded, "Oh, is this about 'the issue'?" Bush hung up on her. "That's what they called it—'the issue,'" the patriarch said to me. "When he called back later, I answered the phone. He said, 'I'm calling to say that I hope you're going to vote against letting women in.' I laughed and said, 'Obviously you don't remember who I am. I was in the group that first proposed electing women, so I very much hope we do let women in.' Then he hung up on me."

the better. There are far fewer concerns about the ability to maintain friendships and not get caught up in boy–girl games. Every club is a little different because clubs never fully reconstitute or perpetuate themselves. Connubial Bliss is still part of the discussion, but it is certainly less ribald than it was in my day, though perhaps more relevant."

Chapter Six

THE NETWORK

During George W. Bush's first political campaign, a run for Congress in 1978, people began to insinuate that his and his family's involvement in such organizations as Skull and Bones, the CIA, and the Trilateral Commission had tainted his qualifications. *First Son,* Bill Minutaglio's biography of Bush, recalls one afternoon debate moderated by radio talk-show host Mel Turner.

Turner, speaking for a good chunk of West Texas, wanted to know if the young Bush was a tool of some shadow government; it was the same thing people had confronted his father with when they had called him a "tool of the eastern kingmakers":

"Are you involved in, or do you know anybody involved in, one-world government or the Trilateral Commission?"

Bush, who had been telling people he was tired of being hammered for having "connections" through his father to the eastern establishment, was fuming. "I won't be persuaded by anyone, including my father," he said, with a biting tone in his voice.

On the way out of the restaurant, Bush was still livid. He refused to shake hands with Turner. "You asshole," Turner heard him hiss as he walked by.

Democrat Kent Hance, who followed up on the accusations of elitism by publicly describing Bush as "riding his daddy's coattails," trounced the Bonesman. The charges of belonging to a powerful network of elite societies, theories that in his autobiography, *A Charge to Keep,* George W. Bush calls "the kind of connect-the-random-dots charges that are virtually impossible to refute," had frustrated his grandfather and at times rendered part of his father's supposedly stellar résumé a disadvantage. In a 1966 interview with the *Yale Daily News,* Senator Prescott Bush bristled at the idea that the Senate was controlled by members of an "establishment" group. Fay Vincent told me that when he made a consolation call to George Bush after he lost the 1980 Republican presidential nomination to Ronald Reagan, the weary candidate sighed. "Fay, let me tell you something. If you ever decide to run for office, don't forget that coming from Andover, Yale, Skull and Bones, and the Trilateral Commission is a big handicap. People don't know what they are, so they don't know where you're coming from. It's really a big, big problem." A 1960s Bonesman who is close to the Bush family concurred. "The family is very tired of [the conspiracy theories]," he told me, "but they view it as one of those things that happen in politics— things get invented about you."

Perhaps, then, it was George Bush who encouraged his son to be so unmistakably vocal about expressing his distance from and disdain for the elite Northeastern connections that shaped his family's political dynasty. After graduation in 1968, George W. did not return to Yale until 1991, for his father's honorary-degree ceremony, and even then grumbled because he felt the university had taken too long to confer the degree. George W.'s biting dismissals have been particularly aimed at Yale: he has sneered at the "intellectual snobbery" of his alma mater, a place that he has said epitomizes "a certain East Coast attitude" and an "intellectual arrogance" he finds unappealing. He has said that "people at Yale felt so intellectually superior and so righteous" and that he wanted to get "away from the snobs," far from Yale. When he finally agreed to speak at Yale in 2001, he used the podium as an opportunity to make fun of his Yale education.

"The biggest benefit to Skull and Bones," a Bonesman who graduated in the 1980s told me, "is the networking. In the rest of the world you get to know people through accident or through choice. In Bones you meet people whom you otherwise wouldn't get to meet. It's a forced setup among a group of high achievers, even the legacies." This "forced setup" is clearly effective. The list of prominent members of Skull and Bones is staggering, particularly given that, with only fifteen new members initiated each year, there are only approximately eight hundred living members at any one time. It would seem to be no small coincidence that a tiny college club has somehow managed to spawn three presidents of the United States. (Indeed, every president who attended Yale as an undergraduate was a member of Skull and Bones.) And recent events would suggest that as the society nears its two hundredth anniversary, this number could easily grow: as of this writing, the 2004 campaign could possibly become the first Bones versus Bones presidential race: incumbent George W. Bush, Skull and Bones 1968, against Senator John Kerry, Skull and Bones 1966.

"It is extraordinary how the leadership of Yale right up to the middle of the twentieth century was so dominated by Skull and Bones," Professor Gaddis Smith said to me. Bones protected its own. In 1873, for example, two students, a Bones knight and a neutral, were in danger of expulsion for failing the same exams. The neutral was suspended for a term and could not retake his exams until the next term. The Bonesman continued his studies and was able to retake his exams within six weeks. According to one publication, a professor who was a Skull and Bones man justified the discrepancy by saying that the second student was "a special case." This type of episode led the *Iconoclast,* a nineteenth-century Yale publication, to editorialize: "We believe that Skull and Bones, directly and indirectly, is the bane of Yale College." In 1928, when the disciplining of Yale students was still handled under the honor system by a student council, six of the eight senior-class representatives on the council, including the chairman, were Bonesmen. On several occasions, the council was informed of another Bonesman who was suspected of cheating on tests. The council did nothing. When, finally, a delegation of the cheater's classmates approached the council for an explanation, the Bonesmen said that they simply preferred not to rule on that particular classmate. The next year, Yale discarded the honor system.

When *U.S. News & World Report* asked George Herbert Walker Bush in 1989 why he had chosen to attend Yale, he replied, "My family had a major Yale tradition, many of my uncles, an older brother and my dad having gone there. Many of my friends were attending, too." He might as well have been speaking about Skull and Bones. His father, Senator Prescott Bush, brother Jonathan Bush, uncles John Walker and George Herbert Walker III, great-uncle George Herbert Walker, Jr., cousin Ray Walker, and several close family friends had pledged allegiance to 322. The connections these relatives provided not only extended George Bush's channels, but also made it possible for his son to join the network himself—a network that will likely add another Bush, George W. Bush's daughter Barbara, in April 2003.

Prescott's own Bones connections had themselves been fruitful. The investment banking house of W. A. Harriman & Company was run by W. Averell Harriman (Bones 1913), Roland Harriman (Bones 1917), and Prescott's father-in-law, George Herbert Walker, who wasn't a Bonesman himself but had a Bones son, George Herbert Walker, Jr. (Bones 1927) and eventually a Bones grandson, George Herbert Walker III (Bones 1953). The Harrimans hired Prescott at age thirty-one, at what was then the largest private bank in the United States, not long after he had gotten his first job after college from another Bonesman, Wallace Simmons (1890), who owned Simmons Hardware. Prescott often returned to the Skull and Bones tomb for alumni functions and Thursday night dinners; one Bonesman recalled that during the 1958–59 academic year, Bush visited the tomb at least five times.

Averell Harriman, whose illustrious career would later include positions such as governor of New York and ambassador to the Soviet Union during World War II, was tapped first for his Bones club. "It gave me purpose," he said nearly three-quarters of a century later. "I scoffed at

Harvard's Porcellian Club. It was too smug. But to get into Bones, you had to do something for Yale." Harriman took his Bones vows seriously. In their 1986 book *The Wise Men: Six Friends and the World They Made,* Walter Isaacson and Evan Thomas reported:

> Harriman regularly went back to the tomb on High Street, once even lamenting that his duties as chief negotiator at the Paris Peace Talks on the Vietnam War prevented him from attending a reunion. So complete was his trust in Bones's code of secrecy that in conversations at annual dinners he spoke openly about national security affairs. He refused, however, to tell his family anything about Bones. Soon after she became Harriman's third wife in 1971, Pamela Churchill Harriman received an odd letter addressing her by a name spelled in hieroglyphics. "Oh, that's Bones," Harriman said. "I must tell you about that sometime. Uh, I mean I can't tell you about that." When Harriman carried secret dispatches between London and Moscow during World War II, he chose as the combination on his diplomatic case the numerals 322.

In fact, the Harriman family had long prospered with help from Bones ties. Stuyvesant Fish (Bones 1905) helped Harriman's father get his start in the big leagues of railroading. In 1904, E. H. Harriman (who would have two sons in Bones) promised to raise campaign money for Theodore Roosevelt if, in return, Roosevelt made Senator Chauncey Depew (Bones 1856), a railroading supporter, the U.S. ambassador to France. After Harriman raised the money, Roosevelt reneged on his promise. Harriman eventually tried to reconcile with Roosevelt by sending lawyer Maxwell Evarts (Bones 1884) as an emissary to smooth things over. As governor of New York in the 1950s, Averell Harriman hired Jonathan Bingham (Bones 1936) as his secretary; Bingham, who stayed with him for four years, would later become a U.S. congressman, state department official, and United Nations diplomat.

The Harrimans formed W. A. Harriman & Company with financial help from Bonesmen such as Percy Rockefeller (Bones 1900), whom

Averell Harriman also persuaded to contribute to many other of his ventures, including approximately $10,000 to his brother-in-law's airplane manufacturing company in 1929. The Harrimans hired several Yale graduates, such as Walter Camp, Jr., son of Bonesman Walter Camp (1880). When Averell and Roland formed the bank Harriman Brothers and Company in 1927, they lent Knight Woolley (Bones 1917) $400,000 so that he could become a partner, and then put him in charge. "Here's four million," Averell said to Woolley. "Go ahead and run the bank."

Even the idea of merging W. A. Harriman and Brown Brothers first brewed between Skull and Bones clubmates as early as 1920. Harriman Brothers managing partner Knight Woolley and W. A. Harriman vice president Prescott Bush, the Harrimans' two top partners, had been Bones clubmates with Roland Harriman. Brown Brothers partners Robert A. Lovett (Bones 1918, one of the men tapped at the naval station in West Palm Beach) and Ellery James (Bones 1917) were also Bonesmen from roughly that time. In 1930, the idea to merge resurfaced as W. A. Harriman's Woolley and Bush and the Brown Brothers' James played cards on a train on their way back from a Yale class reunion. Within two weeks, the two companies had agreed on the partnership, though there was one matter left unresolved: the name of the new company. Averell Harriman refused to keep the name Brown Brothers and Company, while Brown Brothers senior partner Thatcher Brown rejected "Harriman and Brown Brothers." The men formed a committee out of longtime friends of both families and asked them to vote on a name, but the committee was split. The committee's chairman finally decided on the name Brown Brothers Harriman and Company; the chairman, Frederick Allen, was Bones 1900. Even in 1972, nine of the twenty-six Brown Brothers Harriman partners were Bonesmen.[*]

---

[*]Many other Bonesmen formed similar partnerships in various areas of society; for example, William H. Donaldson, future chairman of the New York Stock Exchange, and Dan W. Lufkin, both members of the Bones club of 1953, co-founded Donaldson Lufkin & Jenrette, the most successful start-up firm on Wall Street in the 1960s.

Before George Bush even arrived at Yale, his family's Bones connections seem to have heavily influenced his life. On September 2, 1944, Lieutenant Bush and his flight crew were instructed to take out a radio installation in Chi Chi Jima, from which the Japanese were reporting the routes of the American bombers they spotted. William Gardner "Ted" White (Bones 1942), who was a gunnery officer with no naval aviation training, pleaded to Bush to let him come along as an observer. Bush (and, subsequently, his commander) granted White permission to fly with him, replacing Leo Nadeau, the regular turret gunner. Halfway through Bush's sixty-degree dive toward the radio station, the Japanese shot down Bush's TBM Avenger plane. Bush launched the bombs that took out the radio installation and parachuted to safety before the plane crashed. But White and another crewman, radioman John Delaney, went down with the plane. Since then, Nadeau, the regular gunner, has fretted that because he had been more familiar with the plane than Lieutenant White, if he had been on the plane he might have been able to lead Delaney and himself to safety.

About three years later, Bush told this story to a captive Bones audience as he delivered his Life History. "I wish I hadn't let him go," Bush reportedly said that night. Fellow 1948 Bonesman Lud Ashley has recalled that Bush revealed during that night that he "was heartbroken. He had gone over it in his mind 100,000 times and concluded he couldn't have done anything. . . . He didn't feel guilty about anything that happened on the plane. . . . But the incident was a source of real grief to him. . . . It tore him up, real anguish," Ashley said. "It was so fresh in his mind. He had a real friendship with this man. . . . He described the quiet kind of hysteria being in the front of the plane, not seeing the two in the back, the smoke, losing control of the plane, the anguish as you lose altitude and don't see motion, nothing, no effort to eject [by the two crewmen], then the horrible moment when you go yourself or you don't go."

At Yale, Prescott's son George was given the high honor of being the last tap for Skull and Bones, a tap that he by all accounts deserved: not just a legacy, he was a Phi Beta Kappa student and captain of the baseball team. Eventually, his new Bones connections would also become personal. Alexander Ellis, Jr. (Bones 1944), future insurance executive and roommate of future senator John H. Chafee (Bones 1947), would marry Bush's sister Nancy (Bush, Chafee, and future senator and U.S. Court of Appeals judge James L. Buckley [Bones 1944] would serve as ushers at the wedding).

After he graduated from college in 1948, George Bush had several employment options. Brown Brothers Harriman broke its own long-standing rule against nepotism—Prescott was still a partner—to offer Bush a position. But he declined. He also had the option to work for his uncle George Herbert Walker, Jr. (Bones 1927), at GH Walker & Co. Investments in St. Louis. Instead, he turned to another Bonesman, Neil Mallon (Bones 1917), whom, at Prescott's suggestion, Roland Harriman had placed as the president of Dresser Industries, an oil company that did business in the Southwest. That year, Mallon hired Bush as the company's only trainee, promising him, "You'll have a chance to run it someday." When Bush left the company two and a half years later, Mallon tutored Bush on how to finance an independent oil company. Bush was so devoted to his mentor that he eventually named one of his sons Neil Mallon Bush.

In 1950, Bush left Dresser Industries to form the Bush-Overbey Oil Development Co., with $350,000 of initial capital raised by his Bones uncle George Herbert Walker, Jr. Prescott Bush put up $50,000. Eugene Meyer, the publisher of the *Washington Post* and one of Prescott's Brown Brothers Harriman clients, contributed $100,000, half in his name and half in the name of his son-in-law, Phil Graham. Several other Bonesmen, including Lud Ashley, invested money in Bush-Overbey. Later, when Bush ran Zapata Oil company, he hired Robert H. Gow (Bones 1955), who eventually became president of Zapata after Bush left. Bush persuaded several Bonesmen to invest in Zapata, including at least one who invested $40,000 and eventually sold his shares for almost a 300 percent profit, and another who made enough of a profit to put a down payment on a house. "Family, Yale, country, our group, these were the driving forces," a member of Bush's 1948 Bones club explained to reporter Bob Woodward. Bush "works at it . . . they are one extended family."

After Bush's loss to Ralph Yarborough in the 1964 senatorial race, William F. Buckley (Bones 1950) — reportedly tapped by future Boston Celtics star Tony Lavelli, who broke a string of athletic taps after he was tapped by Bush — invited Bush to help regroup the Republican Party by participating in a symposium sponsored by Buckley's *National Review*. The symposium helped revitalize Bush's political career. In 1987, Bush agreed to participate in a debate among GOP presidential candidates to be moderated by Buckley. Buckley later came to Bush's aid again in 1989, when President Bush tried in vain to push John Tower through the nominations process for secretary of defense. "I want to thank you for all you did over the last month or so in behalf of my nomination of John Tower to be Secretary of Defense," Bush wrote Buckley in March of that year. "I am convinced we did the right thing by standing behind this nomination. We were fighting to protect a President's right to have his own team. . . . Again, thank you for your diligent efforts. It's nice to know you were there when we needed your support."

Another Bonesman with whom Bush has had a loyal relationship is Lud Ashley. Bush often turned to Ashley for counsel, including before he accepted the chairmanship of the Republican National Committee in 1973 and again during the years when they both were members of the House of Representatives, Bush as a Republican from Texas and Ashley a Democrat from Ohio. During Bush's presidency, many groups publicly questioned the ethics of his relationship with Ashley, who, after he retired from Congress, became the president of the Association of Bank Holding Companies, an organization that aggressively lobbied for Bush's banking deregulation bill — a bill that Ashley, the top Washington lobbyist for the banking industry, had helped to write. "It is almost unprecedented that the head of a narrow private-interest lobby directly and immediately influences presidential policy to the direct financial benefit of the group's members," Kenneth Guenther, executive vice president of the Independent Bankers Association of America, said at the time.

Beginning in 1989, Ashley played a pivotal role in assisting Bush's son Neil, who was enmeshed in an ugly savings and loan scandal. Federal regulators claimed that Neil, who was a paid director of the Silverado Savings & Loan in Denver between 1985 and 1988, engaged in a conflict of interest by approving $132 million in loans from Silverado to two of his business partners from his Denver oil company, JNB Exploration Inc. One regulator claimed that Reagan–Bush administration officials had asked him to postpone the seizure of Silverado until after the 1988 presidential election; this information was passed on to the FBI. In December 1989, Neil told federal regulators that Ashley had gotten in touch with him to help at "Dad's request." After that session, Ashley insisted Neil's statement had been incorrect. "I called Neil. Neil needed help," Ashley said to the media. "I said that I was available for advice and counsel, and I thought he was going to need some." But a letter George Bush wrote to Ashley that month suggests otherwise. "I would appreciate any help you could give Neil," Bush wrote. "He tells me he never had any insider dealings."

At George Bush's request, Ashley coached Neil before he testified in front of federal investigators and the House Banking Committee, a group with which Ashley was intimately familiar, given his position. Ashley also helped Neil's lawyer devise political and legal strategies. As a result of Ashley's aid, the Office of Thrift Supervision imposed the lightest possible punishment: Neil was prohibited from serving as a director of a financial institution—with some exceptions—and he had to pay only $50,000 of the $49.5 million the directors of Silverado had to give to the Federal Deposit Insurance Corporation to settle a subsequent lawsuit. Meanwhile, Ashley set up and managed a legal defense fund with contributions that covered Neil's $250,000 in legal fees. Ashley also helped to settle a $200 million negligence suit against Neil and other Silverado directors and saved Neil from paying any significant out-of-pocket costs.

George Bush kept up his side of the relationship as well. In

December 1988, the president-elect named Ashley, along with former senator Paul Laxalt, a Nevada Republican, to the National Economic Commission, a high-level panel studying the deficit problem. Then, with twelve days left in his presidency, Bush gave Ashley, by then a Camp David regular, a recess appointment on the Postal Service Board of Governors, although a federal judge later declared it invalid. Bush's move enraged the Senate Democratic leadership, who argued that it represented an abuse of the president's power to make appointments while Congress is in brief recess.

Other examples of Bones intersecting with Bush's life abound. As another member of Bush's Bones club has said, "In Skull and Bones we all stand together, fifteen brothers under the skin. [It is] the greatest allegiance in the world." During Bush's tenure as ambassador to China, he broached the idea of a presidential campaign with a Bonesman who visited him in Beijing. "I am going to run for president," Bush reportedly told the Bonesman, who inquired, "For what company?" Bush laughed. "The United States." In 1979, at a $100-per-plate dinner in Rhode Island, presidential contender Bush addressed more than two hundred guests, including John H. Chafee, by then in the Senate, who attended despite the fact that he was leading rival Senator Howard Baker's presidential campaign at the time. Sometimes, Bones seemed to be everywhere: In 1976, 1981, and 1985, Bush was sworn in as director of the CIA and as vice president by Supreme Court Justice Potter Stewart (Bones 1937), who frequently attended Bush family barbecues.

On February 21, 1981, one month after Bush was sworn in as vice president, the twelve living Bonesmen from his 1948 club, their wives, and the widows of two of the clubmates had a reunion in Washington that included a Saturday night dinner at Bush's new mansion. That evening, among other activities, Jack Caulkins read a poem he had composed, consisting of a stanza about each member, including Bush, "Old Poppy, our own V.P." On Sunday, the Bonesmen and their wives took a tour of the Oval Office, Bush's office, and the Capitol. On a Saturday night in October 1985, when Vice President Bush was at a political low — or "getting the crap kicked out of him," in Lud Ashley's words — Ashley threw a dinner party for Bush and four other 1948 Bonesmen in order to boost the vice president's morale. Ashley, Thomas W. Moseley, Jack Caulkins, Samuel Walker, Jr., Bush, and their wives gathered at Ashley's northwest Washington home. At some point during the evening, the party morphed into a Skull and Bones session. As Ashley recounted to Bob Woodward, "Moseley, a true believer in the magic that is woven by these relationships . . . stands up and says, 'Let's repair to the inner sanctum.' Bush was all for it and said, 'Why not, why not?' Everyone else seemed to want to do it, so I acquiesced." Ashley told Woodward that Bush seemed eager to unload the worries that weighed on him. "Bush rejoiced. He was almost the first one to go into the den, the library I have there. He welcomed the questions."

During the session, Bush talked about how surprised he was at the media's attacks on him. He told his clubmates how he felt stuck in the "gridlock" of the Office of the Vice President and shared his concerns about running for president. Bush, Woodward wrote, told the group that he was determined to run, "that he knew how hard this would be, and that he would soon establish his own political identity."

Fellow Bonesmen didn't just boost morale, they also raised significant funds for Bush's presidential bids. Nineteen forty-eight clubmates George H. Pfau, Jr., Jack Caulkins, and William Judkins Clark all pitched in, with Clark raising at least $400,000 in campaign contributions. In 1992, the Bush campaign named Frederick W. Smith (Bones 1966), the founder of Federal Express, to its Business and Industry Leadership Council, which consisted of one hundred executives who were garnering business support for Bush's reelection; Smith hosted fund-raisers for Bush.

The favors, of course, went both ways. In 1990, Bush, as president, had given Smith and FedEx the country's most prestigious quality award: the Malcolm Baldrige Quality Award, named after the son of a 1918 Bonesman, one of Bush's closest advisers and commerce secretary in the Reagan–Bush administration. In 1991, President Bush appointed

Pfau, a senior vice president at Paine Webber, to be a director of the Securities Investor Protection Corporation. (Bush had been the best man at Pfau's first wedding, and in 1975, when Pfau married again, Bush hosted him and his wife in China for their honeymoon.) Bush's favors didn't end with his own classmates. He named Richard Anthony Moore (Bones 1936), one of his campaign advisers, as ambassador to Ireland and Paul Lambert (Bones 1950), who had no diplomatic experience but had served as chairman of Bush's National Finance Commission in 1988, as ambassador to Ecuador. Bush appointed David George Ball (Bones 1960) an assistant secretary of labor. Christopher Buckley (Bones 1975) was Bush's speechwriter from 1981 to 1983, and Raymond Price (Bones 1951), who had worked on Prescott Bush's 1950 Senate campaign, was a Bush campaign speechwriter who was called out of retirement to draft Bush's 1992 Republican National Convention address. James T. Hemphill (Bones 1959) joined Bush's Department of the Interior in 1991. David Grimes (Bones 1948) represented Bush on a number of State Department trips to Bulgaria. Bush dispatched Thomas W. Moseley (Bones 1948) as part of a delegation to Uruguay (Moseley was also rewarded with an overnight stay at the White House). Edward McNally (Bones 1979) was the speechwriter responsible for Bush's Desert Storm and Berlin Wall speeches and the attention-getting speech on feminism that Barbara Bush delivered at Wellesley College (McNally also worked on Bush's 1980 campaign).

Soon after his inauguration, Bush also named Edwin L. Dale, Jr. (Bones 1945), a *New York Times* reporter who had been Baldrige's counselor in the Department of Commerce, as the counselor and director of external affairs in the Office of Management and Budget, where he was a senior adviser to Bush's budget director. In 1990, Bush appointed Barry Zorthian (Bones 1941), a former vice president of Time Inc. and a spokesman for the U.S. embassy in Saigon during the Vietnam War, to the Board for International Broadcasting. As her chief of staff, Barbara Bush hired Susan Porter Rose, the wife of Jonathan Chapman Rose (Bones 1963), an assistant attorney general in the Reagan–Bush administration. Bush invited several Bonesmen to White House state dinners, including Pfau to Yemen, Zorthian to Mexico, William H. Donaldson (Bones 1953) to Germany, and Richard E. Jenkins (Bones 1948) to Czechoslovakia. The Reagan–Bush administration had also appointed Winston Lord (Bones 1959) ambassador to China and James L. Buckley (Bones 1944), who had aided Bush's 1980 presidential campaign, to the U.S. Court of Appeals, D.C. Circuit, while Charles S. Whitehouse (Bones 1944) served as assistant secretary of defense for special operations and low-intensity conflict. Furthermore, according to a recovered White House e-mail, the Reagan–Bush administration seriously considered naming Democrat David Acheson (Bones 1943) as U.S. negotiator at the arms-reduction talks with the Soviet Union in Geneva.

It would also be possible to trace Bush's presidential activities and find some patterns wherein Bones-related officials actively supported their Bones president. For example, in 1989, the Export-Import Bank did not want to extend credit to Iraq for the benefit of Saddam Hussein. Bush, however, was determined to push through credits. By the time the foreign aid appropriation bill reached the Senate floor in September 1989 with a provision for a barrier against Iraq, Republican senator John Heinz of Pennsylvania, the son of a Bonesman, had obtained an amendment stating that President Bush could waive the restriction on Export-Import Bank credits if he found that the provision's "application is not in the national interest." On January 17, 1990, President Bush issued a formal public waiver order invoking that amendment.* George Bush, charged Reagan speechwriter John Podhoretz, "turned American foreign and defense policy into a boys' club."

---

*The Export-Import Bank and Hussein had been a Bones-related issue earlier in Bush's tenure as well. The Reagan–Bush administration appointed William H. Draper III (Bones 1950), who had been a member of the Bush Financial Committee for the 1980 presidential campaign, as chairman of the Export-Import Bank. At the time, Bush supported efforts to assist Iraq against Iran. He favored a plan to help Saddam Hussein build a pipeline to Jordan in order to circumvent Iran's blockade of Persian Gulf ports. Bush's instructions, presumably from Secretary of State George Shultz and the National

Whereas George Bush returned to the Bones tomb as recently as 1998 for the annual commencement week alumni party, Bonesmen cannot recall ever seeing George W. Bush back at High Street. Even in 2001, George W. feigned detachment from the society. When asked about it by ABC News, he responded, "Does it still exist? The thing is so secret that I'm not even sure it still exists."

Certainly, George W. Bush never amassed the conglomerate of friends his father collected, though he inherited many of his father's cronies. (As Ann Richards has said of W., "He's missin' his Herbert.") Thus his dependence on Bonesmen has been all the more noticeable, as he has deeply benefited from both his own and his father's Skull and Bones connections. Some of those links have been personal. Despite George W. Bush's repeated attempts to distance himself publicly from this elite group, he has kept in close contact with his Bones clubmates. In 1969, he flew his own plane to the Wisconsin wedding of Brit Kolar (Bones 1968)—and showed up wearing his flight suit. Fellow 1968 Bonesmen attended Bush's 1977 wedding.

But there have been other benefits. The Bush family Bones network could very well have been one of the reasons George W. Bush, by all accounts an unqualified student who did not like to learn, got into Yale in the first place. As a lackadaisical student at Phillips Academy in Andover, Massachusetts, where his crowning achievement was to elect himself High Commissioner of Stickball, George W. ranked 114th in a class of 238. His grades were mediocre at best—he has said he was afraid he would flunk out—his athletic skills were unremarkable, and his musical talents consisted of participating in a rock-and-roll band as a clapper. Undoubtedly, he was popular, but popularity does not get students into Yale; neither do SAT scores of 566 (verbal) and 640

Security Planning Group, were to persuade Draper to get the bank to reverse its refusal to finance the pipeline. In June 1984, Bush called and Draper convinced the bank to agree to fund a $484 million loan, though the pipeline was never actually constructed because of insurance problems. (Also, in 1982 and 1983, Winston Lord [Bones 1959] was first vice president, vice chairman, and then a director of the Export-Import Bank.)

(math). When he was admitted to Yale, he was not the only one who was surprised.

For an underqualified matriculant who has repeatedly claimed that he has never received any "special treatment" because of his surname, Bush's coup is all the more perplexing because of the shift in Yale admissions policies during the sixties. In 1962–63, President A. Whitney Griswold had revised admissions standards and increased academic requirements. During the period when Bush applied to Yale, admissions officers were in the process of deemphasizing preparatory schools and legacies in favor of academics; this shift culminated in 1965 (just after Bush had matriculated), when R. Inslee Clark, Jr., a Bonesman who was on the admissions staff when Bush applied, underscored the reduction in Andover admittances. "I said, in effect, Yale can do a lot better than the bottom quarter at Andover," the former dean of admissions told the Yale alumni magazine in December 1999. "We're looking for the top kids at Andover. If you haven't performed well at Andover, what makes us think you're going to perform well at Yale?"

But while Bush clearly was not one of the top students at Andover, he was the descendant of two of Skull and Bones' favorite sons. And in 1963–64, the academic year during which Bush was accepted into Yale, the Yale Committee of Admissions and Freshman Scholarships, which reviewed admissions policies, had ten members, one a Bonesman and one, the committee chairman, the namesake son of a Bonesman. The Office of Admissions and Freshman Scholarships, which directly chose Bush's freshman class, consisted of seven members. At least three were members of Skull and Bones.*

---

*Despite the oddity of Bush's acceptance into Yale—and that he fared so poorly in academics once he got there—the fact that the school is on his résumé is now used to combat charges that he is an intellectual lightweight. In December 1999, Republican National Committee chair Jim Nicholson defended Bush's intelligence only by saying, "You've got a guy that went to Yale and Harvard, two of the finest educational institutions in America, very difficult to get [into]." Not so difficult, apparently, for a member of the Skull and Bones family.

Skull and Bones has had a history of offering invitations to the same types of people every year; as a result, many Yalies deride the organization for tapping "tokens." In 1968, these stereotypes were as distinct as ever. The 1968 yearbook observed:

> If the society had a good year, this is what the "ideal" group will consist of: a football captain; a Chairman of the *Yale Daily News*; a conspicuous radical; a Whiffenpoof; a swimming captain; a notorious drunk with a 94 average; a film-maker; a political columnist; a religious group leader; a Chairman of the Lit; a foreigner; a ladies' man with two motorcycles; an ex-service man; a negro, if there are enough to go around; a guy nobody else in the group had heard of, ever.

George W. Bush, it is noticeable, fell into none of these categories. He was not even a campus leader in the political sense; a fellow Bonesman from the class of 1968 has said of him, "He had good useful opinions, but there were others in the class who came across as born leaders." Bush was generally regarded as a legacy tap. His brethren, by contrast, slipped easily into the desired slots: among them, Olympic gold medalist swimmer Don Schollander; future Harvard Medical School surgeon Gregory Gallico; Rhodes scholar Robert D. McCallum, Jr.; Robert Birge, the pitch of the Whiffenpoofs; Donald Etra, an Orthodox Jew; Jordanian Muhammed Saleh, a future Timex Corporation executive; National Institute of Mental Health deputy director Rex Cowdry; and black soccer captain Roy Austin.

When *Time*'s Walter Isaacson asked George W. Bush whether he had had any qualms about joining Bones, Bush replied, "No qualms at all. I was honored. I was fairly nonchalant. I didn't view it as a great heritage thing. I didn't take it all that seriously." (Bush did, however, reportedly spend a weekend driving through New York and New Jersey to try to find a tattoo parlor that would brand him with the Skull and Bones logo.) Of Bush's initiation, a patriarch participant told me, "All I will say about it is that he caught on pretty quickly and I was pleased with his response." While in Bones, George W. Bush spent a lot of time in the tomb, but he didn't impress upon his clubmates any presidential sort of aura. At least one of his clubmates said, "It's absolutely surprising to me that he would want to run for president." When George Herbert Walker Bush gave his Life History, he focused on his military service — most Life Histories of that year centered around the military — his love for public service, and his married life with Barbara, but also looked ahead, one of Bush's 1948 clubmates told me. "He was talking about the future, first about his family and then about being able to have an impact in public service and giving back." While many of the 1968 knights similarly spoke about the Vietnam War, a fairly closemouthed 1968 Bonesman agreed to tell me that George W. Bush, by contrast, spent most of his presentations in the tomb speaking about his father — reportedly in "almost God-like terms." Being in Bones, one of Bush's 1968 clubmates has said, made George W. feel even closer to the line of ancestors who had been in Bones before him — "it just kind of crystallized his value system."

The 1960s were a strange time for Bones, which struggled to find its identity on a campus that increasingly shunned the idea of small, elite groups, including fraternities. "Bones had a loss of esteem in the sixties," a 1960 Bonesman said. The 1968 club was heavily affected by the era — a time framed by assassinations. It was, said another Bonesman who graduated in the mid-1960s, "still a cusp era in Bones, before social awareness and activism became a focus for students. My group was like the people in the fifties, so there was an extent to which George W.'s group was really part of the new campus focus and consciousness." On June 5, 1968, George W. Bush and his Bones club went to Deer Island for one final jaunt before graduation. In the car on the way there, the group heard on the radio that Bobby Kennedy had been shot. Shocked, they nonetheless stayed at the island — where they had no telephone access — to bond for three or four days. At least one Bonesman took a boat to the Alexandria Bay Saloon to watch taped rebroadcasts of the assassination on the nearest television to Deer Island. "The events of the Kennedy assassination and the Martin Luther King death were pulling asunder the fabric of what had been a much better world at least politically and socially back in 1963, and there was deterioration from 1963 to 1968," one of those Bonesmen has said. As for Bush, the Bonesman added, "I don't think he would despair for his own safety as much as he would despair for his father's."

When in 1971 Bush was rejected by the University of Texas Law School, he did not have the wealth of job opportunities that had been available to his father. Because President Nixon had appointed George Bush ambassador to the United Nations, George and Barbara had moved to New York. Alone in Texas, George W. did precisely the opposite of what one would expect from a man who says he has never relied on his elite Northeastern establishment connections: he called a Bonesman, years after other Bonesmen had given his father and his grandfather their first jobs out of college. Robert H. Gow (Bones 1955), who was close friends with Bush's cousin Ray Walker (Bones 1955), told the *Washington Post* that his company had not been looking for anyone at the time, but Gow still hired Bush as a management trainee at the Houston-based agricultural company Stratford of Texas. Despite the favor, Bush didn't stay long—shortly thereafter he went on to Harvard Business School and worked on a handful of campaigns.

But in 1977, when Bush formed his first company, an oil company he called Arbusto Energy Inc. (*arbusto* is Spanish for "bush"), he once again sought the help of Skull and Bones. Relying on his uncle Jonathan Bush (Bones 1953), who ran the New York investment firm J. Bush & Company, George W. quickly lined up $565,000 from twenty-eight investors. One of them put together $172,550: California venture capitalist William H. Draper III (Bones 1950).

Not even George W.'s baseball deal, perhaps the one mark in his career that he is generally believed to have achieved on his own, without his father's connections, is devoid of Skull and Bones ties. In 1989, Bill DeWitt, who recruited George W. to purchase the Texas Rangers, lined up four Ohio investors to help. One of them, Dudley S. Taft, the president of Taft Broadcasting, was the grandnephew of the other Skull and Bones U.S. president and a member of the one family with more Bones members than the Bushes.* Bush brought on investment banker Richard Rainwater, who assembled a group of small investors that included Edward S. Lampert (Bones 1984), now a professional investor and multimillionaire in Greenwich, Connecticut.

Nor are Bonesmen (and kin such as Dudley Taft, who gave $25,000 to Bush's "State Victory Fund") absent from lists of donors to George W. Bush's political campaigns. The wife of Frederick W. Smith (Bones 1966) chaired a $100,000-goal fund-raiser for Bush in Tennessee. In October 2000, Stephen Adams (Bones 1959), who owned Adams Outdoor Advertising Agency, spent $1 million on billboard ads for Bush; the ads ran in key states such as Illinois, Michigan, Minnesota, Pennsylvania, North Carolina, South Carolina, Virginia, and Wisconsin. "I just contributed because I liked him," Adams explained to me. But Adams said he had not met Bush in person. Although he claimed that Bush's Bones membership was only a "minor factor," Adams agreed that he had an affinity for all Bonesmen just because they are members of Skull and Bones and "shared that common experience."

At least nine Bonesmen and the son of a patriarch contributed more than $25,500 to Bush's 1998 gubernatorial campaign. At least fifty-eight Bonesmen—four from George Bush's 1948 club, six from George W. Bush's 1968 club, and seven from William F. Buckley's 1950 club—contributed at least $57,972 to Bush's presidential bid, though many of them tried to circumvent campaign finance rules and donate more than the legal limit. Others donated in their wives' names, which are not included in the aforementioned Bones total. And seven namesake sons of

*Other (non-Bones) Tafts have kept up Bush ties as well. Ohio Governor Bob Taft was the chairman of George W.'s presidential campaign in Ohio, where he went door to door for the candidate. In addition, George W. appointed William Howard Taft IV as legal adviser to Secretary of State Colin Powell. Taft also served as deputy U.S. representative to NATO under George W.'s father.

Bones members donated an additional $6,000. A 1959 Bonesman said to me he thought it "reasonable and logical" to contribute $322 to Bush's campaign in late November 2000, when his election was still undecided; a registered Independent, the Bonesman had also contributed $322 three times to George Herbert Walker Bush's presidential campaigns.

Loyal Bonesman George W. has returned the favors throughout. In 1984, he jetted to Nashville to accompany GOP Senate nominee and current Knoxville mayor Victor Ashe (Bones 1967)—who told me that Skull and Bones "is not something I can do interviews on"—on a seven-city tour. Bush spoke devotedly about his father to boost Ashe's GOP ties against an opponent who would later become more familiar: Al Gore. In 1992, when Bones son Fay Vincent was pressured to resign from his post as baseball commissioner, Bush, then a Rangers owner, stood up and delivered a lengthy—though ultimately fruitless—speech in favor of Vincent during a meeting of team owners.

Also like his father, George W. Bush has used his presidential power to reward his fellow Bonesmen. One of the first social gatherings (possibly the first gathering) George W. held at the White House after his inauguration was a reunion of his Skull and Bones clubmates. Some of his Bones cohorts would receive much more than a White House meeting, however. In February of 2003, the Senate approved Bush's nomination of William H. Donaldson (Bones 1953) as chairman of the Securities and Exchange Commission. In November 2001, Bush appointed Edward McNally (Bones 1979) general counsel of the new federal Office of Homeland Security and a senior associate counsel to the president for national security.

Frederick W. Smith (Bones 1966) was reportedly George W.'s top choice for secretary of defense until he withdrew from the running because of a heart problem. One of President Bush's first appointments was 1968 Bones clubmate Robert D. McCallum, Jr., to the $125,700-per-year position of assistant attorney general, civil division, the largest litigation component in the Justice Department. The division represents the federal government in significant domestic and foreign policy cases such as fraud, international trade, patents, bankruptcies, and foreign litigation, which can involve billions of dollars. Bush also nominated 1968 clubmate Roy Austin as ambassador to Trinidad and Tobago. His administration appointed Evan G. Galbraith (Bones 1950) as the secretary of defense's representative in Europe and as the defense adviser to the U.S. mission to NATO. In addition, Bush announced the appointment of Victor Ashe—who in April 2001 was one of four mayors to attend a private meeting with Bush in the Oval Office before Bush spoke to a group of thirty-five mayors—to the board of directors of the Federal National Mortgage Association (Fannie Mae), the country's largest source of financing for home mortgages. Prior to Ashe's appointment, a mayor had never been named to the board of directors, a position that is accompanied by a hefty compensation package including stock options, $1,000 for each of the seven annual meetings, and reimbursement for travel expenses.

☠   ☠   ☠

While the Bush family is certainly Skull and Bones' most powerful political dynasty, other prominent Bonesmen have also effectively taken advantage of the Bones network. The family of President William Howard Taft (Bones 1878), the only man who has ever been both president of the United States and chief justice of the United States, counts at least nine Bonesmen among its members, including Alphonso Taft, a member of the founding club in 1832–33. Between 1909 and 1913, William Howard Taft had two Bonesmen in his eleven-man cabinet: Henry L. Stimson (Bones 1888), secretary of war, and Franklin MacVeagh (Bones 1862), secretary of the treasury.

Henry Stimson was another prime example of a Bonesman who took his duty to promote other Bonesmen seriously. From the beginning, he had been impressed by the secret society as a Yale undergraduate because it offered the toughest competition at the university. He later admitted to his fiancée that "the idea of a struggle for prizes, so to speak, has always been one of the fundamental elements of my mind, and I can hardly conceive of what my feelings would be if I ever was put in a position or situation in life where there are no prizes to struggle for." Stimson called his time in Skull and Bones "the most important educational experience of my life." Therefore, he considered other men who had passed that test to be superior to products of other institutions. Biographer Godfrey Hodgson observed:

> He attended commencements and reunions at Andover, at Yale and at the Harvard Law School whenever he could, and was a loyal member of Skull and Bones, the secret Yale senior society of which many of his friends were also members. He was apt to attribute superior qualities to products of these institutions. On one occasion he was so impressed by the work of a new young lawyer at Winthrop, Stimson that he assumed the man had been educated at Andover and Yale, and it was with some difficulty that partners persuaded him that, in spite of the man's excellence, this was not the case.

Stimson married Mabel White, the daughter of a Bonesman.

Stimson, like George Bush and George W. Bush, had his career jump-started by Bonesmen. Stimson received his first job after law school from Sherman Evarts (Bones 1881), who ran a practice on Wall Street. Stimson grew bored and frustrated, however, defending the New York and Northern Railway Company against suits brought by passengers, so William C. Whitney (Bones 1863) pulled strings. He persuaded Elihu Root, a powerful lawyer and the leader of the New York bar, to hire Stimson (Whitney was Root's biggest client). In the early 1900s, when Stimson was U.S. attorney for the Southern District of New York, he hired Thomas D. Thacher (Bones 1904) as one of his assistants. In 1911, William Howard Taft appointed him his secretary of war. When Stimson came to Washington, he also brought with him as an assistant another lawyer from his firm, Arthur E. Palmer (Bones 1930). Then in 1929, Taft, as chief justice, swore Stimson in as Herbert Hoover's secretary of state. Soon afterward, Stimson hired Harvey H. Bundy (Bones 1909) as special assistant to the secretary of state. Bundy, who served in that capacity from 1931 to 1933, had been hired by Stimson after the two were introduced to each other by Bundy's clubmate Allen Klots (Bones 1909).

Klots, who had been Stimson's law partner at his New York law firm, Winthrop, Stimson, also served for a time as one of Stimson's special assistants in Washington. (Another of Stimson's law firm partners was Endicott Peabody Davison [Bones 1945], the Skull and Bones attorney who would meet with Apache chairman Ned Anderson.)

Stimson became Franklin D. Roosevelt's secretary of war in 1940. As his assistant secretaries, he hired Robert A. Lovett (Bones 1918) and Harvey Bundy; he rounded out his War Department with two barbarians, John J. McCloy and Judge Robert P. Patterson, as well as George L. Harrison (Bones 1910) as special assistant. Stimson had worked closely with Harrison during the economic crisis of 1931, when Harrison was president of the New York Federal Reserve Bank. In Stimson's memoir, coauthor McGeorge Bundy, Harvey's son and Bones 1940, observed: "If it had not been for the constant and intelligent co-operation which he had received from George L. Harrison . . . Stimson would have found it very difficult to play any useful role at all in financial matters." These five men formed Stimson's inner circle. "The plain fact is," Godfrey Hodgson wrote in 1990,

that, during a war for democracy conducted by a Democratic President—which was also, more than any previous foreign war in American history, a democratic war in the sense that millions of men from every corner of American life fought it together—the War Department was directed by a tiny clique of wealthy Republicans, and one that was almost as narrowly based, in social and educational terms, as a traditional British Tory Cabinet. It was certainly far narrower than Churchill's wartime Cabinet. For this striking class composition, Henry Stimson was very much responsible. As Harvey Bundy put it, "he told the President about it, but he had carte blanche from FDR, so we had the most united team in the War Department you've ever seen."

Stimson was also strongly influenced by Bonesman Averell Harriman, who was the ambassador to the Soviet Union from 1943 to

1946. Additionally, Stimson made use of the talents of Archibald MacLeish (Bones 1915). During World War II, Stimson wanted to maintain a healthy relationship with the media so that the Army's public relations department could keep the confidence of the people without leaking too much information. MacLeish, an assistant secretary of state from 1944 to 1945, was one of the government officials who kept the relationship smooth.

Along with their colleagues, it was this troop of Bonesmen— Stimson, Harrison, Lovett, Harriman, and Bundy—who essentially oversaw the construction and deployment of the atomic bomb. After one extensive conversation with Stimson about the bomb on March 5, 1944, Harvey Bundy wrote in his diary:

> We are up against some very big decisions. The time is approaching when we can no longer avoid them, and when events may force us into the public on the subject. Our thoughts went right down to the bottom of human nature, morals and government, and it is by far the most searching and important thing that I have had to do since I have been here in the office of Secretary of War because it touches matters which are deeper even than the principles of present government.

Stimson put Harrison in charge of the atomic bomb, and appointed him deputy chairman of the 1945 committee (of which Stimson himself was chair) that was to decide how the bomb—then known only by its code name S-I—should be used. Harrison sent a cable to Stimson that announced the first successful test of an atomic device in the New Mexico desert: "Child is born. Larger than expected. Its cries could be heard at my farm and the light in his eyes seen at yours." (Harvey Bundy later translated the cable in a 1957 issue of the *Atlantic Monthly:* "This meant that the explosion had been so terrific that if it had been set off in Washington the sound could have been heard at Upperville, Virginia, some forty miles away, and the light from the explosion seen at Stimson's farm on Long Island over 200 miles away.")

Even John J. McCloy, the barbarian who was Lovett's fellow assistant secretary of war, was exposed to Skull and Bones ethics. McCloy, who later became president of the World Bank, high commissioner for Germany, and chairman of both the Chase Bank and the Council on Foreign Relations, said during a meeting with Stimson, President Truman, and the joint chiefs about actions to take against Japan: "I think our moral position would be better if we gave them specific warning of the bomb." He recounted later: "As soon as I mentioned the word 'bomb'—the atomic bomb—even in that select circle, it was sort of a shock. You did not mention the bomb out loud. It was like mentioning Skull and Bones in polite society at Yale. It just wasn't done."

Before he retired, Henry Stimson arranged for his inner circle, including Bundy and Lovett, to receive Distinguished Service Medals, the citations for which he wrote himself. (Stimson also received one.) Later, as President Truman's undersecretary of state (he would eventually be Truman's secretary of defense), Lovett persuaded Truman to involve Averell Harriman in the administration; Truman subsequently appointed him special representative of the Economic Cooperation Administration. Soon after John F. Kennedy's inauguration, the president formed an exclusive committee of Soviet experts to brief him. Harriman, dismayed that he had been left off the list, called Bonesman McGeorge Bundy, Kennedy's national security adviser. Harriman was immediately invited to participate and was eventually named Kennedy's assistant secretary for Far Eastern affairs. When he left the position, he lobbied to have William Bundy (Bones 1939), McGeorge's brother, named his successor, but the administration did not want to remove Bundy from his position as assistant secretary of state.[*]

Members of Skull and Bones have also influenced American foreign policy through another government organization: the CIA. Robert

---

[*]Although Stimson had died in 1950, his ghost still held sway over the men. When McGeorge Bundy sought Lovett's advice during the Cuban missile crisis in 1962, Lovett gestured to a photograph of Stimson near Bundy's desk. "The best service we can perform for the president," said the older patriarch to the younger one, "is to try to approach this as Colonel Stimson would."

Lovett and McGeorge Bundy dealt often with CIA operatives. George Bush was CIA director. Averell Harriman was an active supporter of the CIA. "I know I speak for the entire Intelligence Community when I express my appreciation for your support for the mission of the CIA," Bush wrote to Harriman in 1976. William Bundy, William Sloane Coffin, Jr., F. Trubee Davison (Bones 1918), Richard Drain (Bones 1943), Evan Galbraith (affiliated through the Navy), Frederick W. Hilles (Bones 1922), George Holmes (Bones 1945), Samuel Walker, Jr., (Bones 1948), and Charles S. Whitehouse (Bones 1944) were among the Bones CIA operatives. These operatives regularly returned in large numbers to the tomb, where, I was told, "they would speak openly about things they shouldn't have spoken about."

The CIA was so fraught with Yale alumni — so many that other members of the agency would often feel uncomfortable and inferior around "the Yalies," as they called them — that even in remote outposts in Asia and Africa, British and American intelligence officers were known to conclude festive occasions with a rendition of "The Whiffenpoof Song." Yale alumnus Nathan Hale, whose statue stands on Old Campus as well as in front of CIA headquarters in Langley, Virginia, is generally considered "the first American spy." But while many of these Yale men had Bones ties, the CIA was not consistently run by Bonesmen. Tracy Barnes and Richard Bissel were two of the CIA's best agents, though they were major players in the disastrous Bay of Pigs invasion of 1961. Neither one was a Bones member, but both were close: Barnes was a member of Scroll and Key with Bones relatives, and Bones had tried to get Bissel, but he had boycotted Tap Day of 1931 by staying in his room instead of waiting in the courtyard. At five o'clock, a Bonesman nonetheless rapped on his door, barreled into his room, slapped Bissel on the back, and yelled, "Go to your room!" Bissel, who later regretted that he hadn't replied that he was actually already in his room, rejected the tap.*

---

*When Barnes was a freshman, during the Great Crash of 1929, his cousin Harry Payne Whitney (Bones 1894) sent him a check for $1 million with the message, "Mr. Whitney thought it might be useful." Barnes sent it back.

As Godfrey Hodgson noted, "In a very direct way, the men Colonel Stimson recruited and their friends became the nucleus of the foreign-policy establishment." And several other Bonesmen played peripheral but important roles during this "Establishment's" reign: Townsend Hoopes (Bones 1944) was assistant to the secretary of defense from 1948 to 1953. Dean Acheson, another instrumental figure, could also be linked to Bones. While Acheson himself was in Scroll and Key, his son David was a Bonesman (1943), and Bonesman William Bundy married Dean Acheson's daughter (William and McGeorge Bundy's sister Harriet also married a Bonesman). Furthermore, the "Establishment" members held similar beliefs. In *The Wise Men,* Walter Isaacson and Evan Thomas explain "some basic tenets these men shared, foremost among them an opposition to isolationism. They were . . . Atlanticists, an outlook that resulted in a certain willingness to make sweeping American commitments. They viewed America's leadership role, and their own, as part of a moral destiny." Not all of them were Bonesmen, but many of them had gone to Yale and, if they had not themselves belonged to secret societies, knew well what it meant to be part of a cloistered elite.

This elite was cohesive, but it was not always consistent. While its members may have been intimately involved with crucial military maneuvers in the twentieth century, Skull and Bones did not as a society conspire to deploy the atomic bomb and invade the Bay of Pigs. In fact, Robert Lovett objected to the plans for the invasion. McGeorge Bundy was accused of not doing more, as national security adviser, to improve communications between the CIA and the White House. Nor was it Skull and Bones that specifically instructed members to aid Adolf Hitler, though Hitler's financier stowed $3 million in the Union Banking Corporation, a bank that counted among its seven directors Prescott Bush. And Bonesmen sparred over Vietnam: Lovett called the war "one of the stupidest things we ever did." Moreover, Bonesmen publicly clashed over the issues. When in 1965 Archibald MacLeish questioned the morality of the Vietnam War, William Bundy fired back that in World War II the country had accepted "the responsibility of holding and using power."

Certainly, a relatively large number of Bonesmen have achieved influential positions that control foreign policy; several members have served on the Council on Foreign Relations, including Winston Lord, its president from 1977 to 1985. But Skull and Bones does not dictate a society-wide worldview to its members. It does not provide them automatically with the funds and framework with which they will be able to find their fortune and pursue positions of prominence. "Skull and Bones doesn't encourage certain political policies," a Bonesman told me. "The alumni overall are certainly conservative, but Skull and Bones is its own little world—and it's a weird little world, too."

The network is indeed in place, however, for those who wish to take advantage of it. With the magic words, "Do you know General Russell?" to determine whether a suspected Bonesman is a legitimate member, those who are willing to make the effort to ask fellow Bonesmen for favors, I was told, will more often than not get what they want. "On one level, you just trust people from Yale because you know they're smart, and if they're in Bones, that's even better. But it's also understood that you help a Bonesman who asks. There's a real sense of camaraderie that way," a patriarch who is a professor explained to me. "Especially with the older groups, if a Bonesman called you and said you have my word that this person is qualified to do this or that, people believed it. Those connections are there."

Along with those connections naturally comes the pressure of having to live up to a long line of Skull and Bones stalwarts. In the 1970s, when Yale president Kingman Brewster called Yale the breeding ground of "a thousand male leaders," the Bonesmen naturally considered themselves the top fifteen of those male leaders. "There's this whole idea that these are the fifteen most prominent people on campus and you're supposed to live up to that. It's not blatant, but you look around at who's been in there, and there's always an awareness of that," a Bonesman said. "It's a real unspoken thing—a sense of expectation on you. All these older, prominent guys show up to give you the sense that this is where Skull and Bones leads you. We were the first senior society and we're made very aware of the Tafts, Harrimans, Bundys, Buckleys. These guys still really buy the whole thing. They love the place." They also work in-tensely to make sure that a structure remains that can pave a path to some of the most prestigious platforms in the country—but it is available only to those members who, like the Bushes, specifically seek it out. "For some people," a patriarch explained to me, "Skull and Bones becomes the most important thing that ever happened to them, and they tend to stay involved."

Even the least committed Bonesman can still feel as if Skull and Bones connections offer him a trump card. When William Sloane Coffin, Jr., wanted to influence the Kennedy administration on desegre-gation, he called McGeorge Bundy, then President Kennedy's national security adviser, at the White House, collect from a public pay phone outside a grocery store. The switchboard operator immediately trans-ferred the call to Bundy's home. Despite Coffin's ambivalence toward the society, the prospect of its networks remained strong. "I had selected Bundy as he was a fellow member of Bones," Coffin wrote in his autobi-ography. "I didn't approve anymore of Yale's secret societies, but de-cided at this moment to capitalize on connections."

Chapter Seven

THE ORDER

These campus Elks, Masons, secret what-you-wills, that undertake to select men on a basis of personality and accomplishment, seem so hideously out-dated, so out of step with the very ideals of university life, that it is hard for us to believe in their existence today. It is hard for us to believe in them because fundamentally they and their impositions are unreal. The standards they set up create an artificial distinction between individuals. That a man can be kept by any obligations from talking to an intimate friend after a meeting is of course farcical; but in a more general sense the silent shrouding of secrecy about Societies is unreal because it is unbelievable that any one should not be entirely free to examine into and question all that he meets. We believe it definitely harmful for any one to grow into habits of unthinking acceptance. The importance of Senior Societies is accepted at Yale today; but there is no reason why that importance should go on forever. When the organizations have become a burden and a repressive force, it is time to end the play.

Yale's *Harkness Hoot* published this editorial in 1933, surely without even fathoming that the societies would still thrive nearly three-quarters of a century later, and the piece remains noteworthy not only because it reflects a still-enduring attitude that the secret societies manage to thwart, but also because it has a concept backwards. "It is hard for us to believe in them," it states, "because fundamentally they and their impositions are unreal." In fact, it is precisely because these secret societies project such unreal impositions that we believe in them in the first place.

In December 1997, I headed over to my own secret society's tomb for a Sunday night "session." Sunday night is alumni night for many of the societies—any graduate member is welcome to join the seniors for about two hours of cocktails, dinner, songs, and presentations, while Thursday nights are often reserved for the seniors only. This particular night was my society's annual Christmas party (nearly every society has one), complete with food, drink, and gifts more than a notch above the usual impressive fare. The New Haven sky was especially dark that evening, which was difficult for me because, as I had explicitly explained to the society members as soon as they tapped me, I have a genetic disorder that prevents me from having night vision. On my way into the tomb that night, I slammed my hand in the thick iron door because I could not see it swinging shut. Afterward, as I lay on a couch in the cocktail room, my face bone-white, while some of my concerned society clubmates kindly helped me ice my mangled fingers, I turned to the presiding alumni officer (class of 1955).

"Do you think it would be too much trouble," I gasped softly, still somewhat out of breath, "if we could place a tiny nightlight outside the tomb door so that I and the other members—such as the senior citizens and future members who might have poor night vision—would be able to see our way in?"

"No, that's not possible," he said, shaking his head emphatically. "That wouldn't be good for our image."

This popular secret society attitude begins to explain the Skull and Bones paradox mentioned in Chapter 2: The society has always demanded invisibility while simultaneously publicizing its supremacy. It is a paradox that dichotomizes swagger and silence, as epitomized by the way George W. Bush briefly mentions his Skull and Bones membership in his autobiography, *A Charge to Keep*. "My senior year I joined Skull and Bones, a secret society," Bush wrote, "so secret, I can't say anything more." As an anonymous society member charged in the *Harkness Hoot*, "What a Senior Society needs, essentially, is prestige and peace. It wants to be old beyond recollection. It wants its tomb or house to be recognized as what it is by all of Yale. It wants a roster of famous graduates. It wants the pick of the Junior class. And it wants to be let alone." But in order to gain the prestige, the roster, and the pick of the junior class, societies have to do more than put up a public front—they first have to make their members believe in the myth. They have to make the unreal seem plausible; they have to stoke their image so that we, in tinted spectacles, believe.

In the beginning, Skull and Bones took root at Yale because it was established during the university's pre-athletic age, when society membership had little competition as an exclusive pursuit. Also, unlike the men of the other class societies, Skull and Bones members were seniors who would graduate before they had the chance to leak secrets to other friends on campus. But since then, the growth of Skull and Bones as a corporation and as a formidable entity has an intricate background laced with the pursuit of image in mind.

A biographer of one of Bones' central figures, Henry Stimson, offered an effective explanation of why students were inspired to form societies at Yale. "Young men had to find some way to give body to that system of idealism that Santayana and others discovered to exist at New Haven," Elting Morison wrote.

There was not much in the classroom, on the evidence, to excite the mind, train it, bring it into useful support of healthy principle. With considerable ingenuity, therefore, the undergraduates turned elsewhere—to the feelings—to find a possible source of energy. They constructed in the senior societies, with admirable insight, a mechanism to mobilize the emotions of the selected few to their high purposes. . . . Such special election produces no doubt a sense of large responsibility; the compressions of the secret can generate great energy. At any rate, for

most of those engaged, it worked. Out of these agencies youthful powers were organized to fortify the love of life, the trust in success, the ra-
diant convictions and healthy ideals. As the English observer Graham
Wallas said, the experience within the senior societies at Yale, in this
time, convinced the members that it was a better thing to be and to do
than to seem to be and seem to do.

But what Morison was not able to clarify was *why* the experience
worked, why these high purposes could still inspire, why the undergraduates could be and do while seeming to be and seeming to do something else. "How this was done," Morison wondered, "how in nine
months, in weekly meetings, in secret places, whole lives were changed,
is past all discovery."

There is reason to everything Skull and Bones does; its headquarters, program, and rituals have all been carefully calibrated to cultivate its
power by essentially training its members. The presence of the tomb is
only the first step toward breeding new knights. It is introduced to the
second-semester juniors as their own private space, which they quickly
learn can serve as hideout, library, office, lounge, and café. It is hardly uncommon for new knights to spend practically the entire week after initiation in the tomb, where they explore the artifacts, raid the kitchen, write
term papers, and marvel at their exclusive access to this large property —
a new alternative to the usual dorm room/common room/restaurant/bar
options. The tomb also provides them with immediate inside jokes and
private spaces, such as room 322 and the garden, that they share only
with the other privileged members.

Eventually a member's self-perception is so intertwined with his
secret-society identity ("I am the Little Devil, the runt of my club; I
am a bit of a goof and collect all fines") that if he were to betray or leave
Skull and Bones, he would lose what has become a major part of the way
that he identifies himself. The same can be said for the secret society's language and for S.B.T.—Skull and Bones Time. Each serves as a factor that
sets the Bonesmen apart in their exclusive, elusive, illusory little world.

A large part of the traditions that help Bones to endure involves elitism. Certainly, not all Skull and Bones members are inherently elitist, though many of them do carry the Old Blue sense of entitlement. But it can be difficult not to get caught up in the egotistical affirmation of privilege and self-worth. Pre-initiation proceedings for my own society provide a good example of this subconscious sense of superiority. Soon after Tap Night, I received a strange, old-style-calligraphy-printed notice in an envelope with a wax seal bearing the society's insignia. The note instructed me to be at an out-of-the-way New Haven address at a particular time. When I arrived, the two other juniors there were just as confused as I was about why we were asked to meet at a building that was unlit, unlocked, and uninhabited (we later discovered it was across the street and just down the block from our tomb). After a while, a limousine pulled up and a man in a black suit gestured to us from the window. When we were seated and the car pulled away, the man sternly told us in an intimidating voice that we were strictly to say nothing. We complied (though I laughed a couple of times). The ride wound around unfamiliar suburban streets behind several other limousines for more than half an hour before dropping us off at a dark house. By the time we got out of the car, the guide had disappeared, the doors had locked behind us, and we were left in the spacious driveway as a part of a group of fourteen (one initiate was studying abroad) with no idea of what we were supposed to do next. Eventually, someone discovered an unlocked side door and the group of us filed inside.

There we found an elegantly furnished sitting room, in the middle of which was a square glass table with fourteen small goblets and fourteen tiny cards with Latin writing. A few members of the group were able to translate the first instruction—Drink—so we knocked back the concoction of what tasted like champagne and a few other liquors. Then we waited, thrilled but still occasionally poking the silence with a lame Alice joke. After some time, a door creaked open and an initially imposing well-dressed man came in and welcomed us to our secret society. (We would later learn that the man was a prominent Yale admissions officer, accomplished poet, and the society treasurer.) After a short but impressive speech, he led us to a room that upon our arrival lit up brightly to reveal dozens and dozens of beaming alumni, reveling in our election. They plied us with stories about our new home and the famous names on the membership roster, and insisted we partake of the enormous bounty of food and drink (underage drinking far from being a concern of the majority of the societies). In awe, we scattered solo about the room as if at a cocktail party, and listened as, individually or in small groups, nearly every alumnus in the room introduced himself (we did not need to reciprocate; they all seemed to know our names already) and told us some secret society tale.

After a couple of hours, the limousines again whisked us away, this time to a popular restaurant back on campus that the society had rented for the evening. There, the unlimited entrées and bottles dumbfounded us as we continued our celebration. At closing time, about eight of us, unwilling to let this strange night end, headed to Naples, a popular pizza-and-beer hangout. It was there that sometime late that evening, the group of us, mostly inebriated, huddled on the dance floor together like a scrum and whisper-chanted something that embarrasses me painfully now: something to the effect of "We're in, they're not; we're in, they're not" as we glanced around the packed place and our minds, swelling larger with each pounding beat of the club music, took in that all of those peers ate and drank and danced in ignorance of the new secrets that we and only we had been elected to preserve. A Bonesman from the 1970s agreed that our experiences in this vein had been similar. "The secrecy in many respects surrounding the society before I got in was for one purpose: to make the other people who didn't get in feel bad."

E. E. Aiken (Bones 1881), writing about secret societies in general (he did not name his own), noted in 1882:

> Secrecy may be used to create and strengthen friendship. The binding force of a common secret is a well-known fact; it rouses the instincts of fidelity and honor, and marks off its possessors as a circle by themselves,

more or less distinctly according to its nature. . . . The sharing of a secret makes a bond, but it is a very different one from that of a generous friendship. It is like the external force which holds two soldiers together in the ranks, while they may be hating each other in their hearts.

Many Bonesmen happily recalled for me that the best part of their experience in the society was their new intimate relationships with strangers. Skull and Bones "was a significant part of my senior year for none of the reasons that are generally assumed to be significant," a Bonesman from the early 1980s said. "For me, not being on a sports team or fraternity, it was really the only experience I've had of sitting in a room with a number of other people and exchanging thoughts, observations, and ideas with a group of people who had not necessarily been my friends. We exchanged personal discourse with these people, which was enlightening and sensitizing. I learned about people and defined who I was in relation to other people. That was the heart of the experience." Echoed a 1968 Bonesman, "It was an opportunity to build friendships with fourteen people whom I otherwise wouldn't have come across in college years at a depth that is difficult or impossible to achieve in the ordinary course of college life." A Bonesman in his sixties explained that the confessionals leave Bonesmen with the feeling that these strangers may know them better than the barbarians in their lives do. "We see each other once a year and the understanding of each other is still very much a part of the experience. It creates the capacity to maintain long-term relationships." Unprompted, a Bonesman from the 1960s quietly said to me, "I am a better person because of my year in Bones. No question about it."

The exercise that best represents this idea of self-betterment is the criticism, during which members blatantly and brutally tell each other how they are perceived. This process of reflection can be painful, but Skull and Bones considers it a necessary step in the development of a Knight of Eulogia. One longtime Yale administrator has admitted that his roommate fell into a severe depression after his Bones brothers re-

vealed to him that one of his great character flaws was laziness. A distinguished Yale professor has said that several students have had to seek
psychological help following their Skull and Bones criticism. A couple of
the secret societies modeled after Bones also force their members to
undergo this ego-beating; fittingly, they call the experience "Mirror
Images." (In Berzelius, for example, this activity, which is called
"Audits," requires each member to write a long letter—members have
been known to write twenty pages—to each of the fourteen other members in which he describes his true feelings.)

In truth, Skull and Bones itself is like a hall of mirrors. The society
has become so difficult to pin down for nearly two centuries because of
the countless contradictory reflections—ricocheting from Bonesmen,
patriarchs, Yale, and barbarians—that bounce against each other. But
the reflections begin from within. "It really is a place that is full of itself,"
a Bonesman said to me. "It loves its own hype. They *love* perpetuating
the mystique." Inside the tomb, the seniors desperately want to believe
that they are part of something larger than themselves. Sometime during their year as knights, they learn that, contrary to their beliefs before
they became neophytes, there is no money awaiting them at graduation,
no stake in the society's rumored large real estate spanning Connecticut,
and above all, no promises. There is only the network, which is powerful but intangible and available only to those who seek it out. Thus one
reason young members perpetuate the myth of Skull and Bones after
they have graduated and even after they have traveled far from the
Temple's suffocation may be that they are insecure about what the legendary society turned out to be. Their cognitive dissonance becomes
necessary in order to rationalize why they sacrificed every Thursday and
Sunday night of their final year in college—more nights if they had to
prepare essays or debate arguments in advance—to meet with a bunch
of strangers in a relatively windowless building when the reward to a
twenty-two-year-old in fact involves no money, dubious power, and diminished mystique. As one middle-aged Bonesman sighed, the society
"didn't do anything for me academically. It was harder to get my work

done because we were meeting two nights a week." Another Bonesman grumbled, "That was the most sleepless time I've ever had. By spring I was practically hallucinating."

Certainly, not every Bonesman is in thrall to the society. In 1873, one of the principal speakers at the Yale commencement alumni meeting was former U.S. attorney general William Maxwell Evarts, a Bonesman. Evarts railed against the secret societies because, unlike the older, open debating societies they had replaced, they bred, he claimed, only snobbishness. But Evarts was a glaring exception — even the exceedingly rare Bonesmen who dropped out of the organization during their senior year still often refuse to elaborate on their experience, however ephemeral. A man who dropped out in the late 1980s said to me that even though he was not a patriarch, "They would prefer that people don't talk, so I would not feel comfortable betraying them."

In fact, the society makes every effort to ensure that a Bonesman does not resign from the society. A member from the 1970s told me he had been upset when the Bones alumni would not let him tutor New Haven schoolchildren in the tomb's empty rooms when they were not in use. In October of his senior year, he came to the tomb for Thursday dinner straight from working with these students, who lived in a less than desirable neighborhood. "I come into the tomb and the two black guys who serve the food put a whole lobster down in front of me just because I show up," he said. "I left right then. I found the place elitist and offensive. The next day I took my Tiffany Skull and Bones pin, attached it to a letter, and pinned it to the front bulletin board. That's when they told me, 'You can't resign from Skull and Bones. You are a member for life.'" I asked him why a self-described rebel like him would have joined such an organization in the first place. "I grew up in a working-class family, so it was a big deal for me to even be at Yale," he explained. "And then to be tapped for Bones, well, the aura of that meant something to my family. It showed how far we had come."

The rumors and conspiracy theories about Skull and Bones, as described in the Introduction, are widespread and deep-rooted. Probably the most fascinating thing that I learned through my interviews with members of Skull and Bones is that the majority of those rumors were carefully planted by the Bonesmen themselves. The patriarchs are the publicists, leaking gossip to the columnists; they are the politicians, spinning stories as distractions; they are the magicians, directing patter to enhance the sleight of hand. By spreading rumors about their society, they create a cloak of mystery that both protects the privacy surrounding what they truly do and makes them feel as if they belong to something transcendent and omnipotent, when in truth the society is less than the sum of its parts. As one Bonesman said, "It's essential to have a certain amount of confusion and uncertainty about just what goes on because it actually protects what goes on inside. It's an effective smokescreen to protect that privacy." A Bonesman from the late 1950s was more blunt: "Rumors, true or untrue, heighten the mystery." The patriarchs blow up smokescreens that allow the barbarians outside to see within the mist whatever it is that they want their imagination to find. They lay the foundation for broad speculative postulations and then they encourage the conspiracy theories. And why wouldn't they? If people believe in something strongly enough, it becomes the truth to them. Skull and Bones is, at its core, equivalent to the Wizard of Oz, the puny but cunning man hidden behind a curtain of mystique, projecting images that inspire awe and terror in order to expand himself into something great and terrible. This is not to downplay the remarkable power of the Bones network or the impact that the network has had. But many of the secrets of Skull and Bones—the initiation ceremony, the membership rolls, the tomb's artifacts—may simply serve as skulduggery to mask the society's biggest mystery, or lack thereof.

         ⚐   ⚐   ⚐

It is possible, and arguably helpful, to treat Skull and Bones as a prism through which to view the facades of Yale and, more broadly, the elitist old-school power that so many people truly believe runs the country. Behind their veils, like Skull and Bones, these schools—Harvard, Yale,

Princeton, and a handful of others—focus much of their energies on sustaining their own mythic import. Yale is indeed the premier example. It is a school that, for instance, chose a particularly weathered quarry from which to fashion buildings in the early 1900s so that its gargoyle-stamped campus would look older than it is. Yale also patched many of its broken windows with molten metal lines, in medieval fashion, rather than simply replacing them, so that they would appear more ancient.

Of course, Yale is not alone in putting up such facades. Every institution of any kind plays the political game. Nor is Yale the only university with a society system, although Yale's system created "a moral pressure . . . probably unparalleled in any other university," as Edmund Wilson observed in 1923. Princeton has its eating clubs, which are mostly social in nature. Harvard has its Hasty Pudding Club, now famous for annually dressing its members in drag to bestow awards and kisses on good-humored Hollywood celebrities, and the Porcellian Club, the top-ranked "final club," founded in 1791 and known for choosing members based on bloodlines, not merit. Some upper-crusts considered Porcellian so important that they dropped out of Harvard when they were rejected. When Theodore Roosevelt told Kaiser Wilhelm about the engagement of his daughter Alice to Nicholas Longworth, the future House speaker, he added, "Nic and I are both in the Porc, you know." Franklin Roosevelt, denied club membership, said publicly that the snub was the worst rejection in his life. Other universities have exhibited what have been called "feeble imitators," including Columbia College's Axe and Coffin, University of Michigan's Owl and Padlock, Wesleyan's Skull and Serpent, Dartmouth's single-sex Sphinx, and Georgetown's controversial all-male Second Society of Stewards.

But institutions such as Yale, Harvard, and Princeton have their differences. When asked in 1968 why Yale societies maintain their mystery while societies at other colleges do not, Harvard professor of social relations David Riesman pointed to a distinctive "achievement orientation and competitiveness." He said that Yale was simply a more competitive place than Harvard and gave as an example a Yale student who had "heeled" the *Daily News,* lost, went out for football manager, lost, and finally became president of the Christian Association, a position that he used to attract the tap he desperately sought from Skull and Bones. "This kind of achievement orientation is only in recent decades entering Harvard," Riesman said, "which was always in a sense . . . Georgian rather than Masonic."

In 1893, William Lyon Phelps, who graduated from Yale in 1887, blamed the differences between Harvard and Yale solely on the society system, which created a kind of Catch-22: The societies caused Yale to be the way it was, which in turn maintained the atmosphere conducive to the societies' survival. "Harvard has nothing that is all at once so influential and so exclusively anti-democratic as our Senior Society system," Phelps wrote.

> Anyone who has watched how carefully the candidates begin to choose their companions in Sophomore year, how skillfully the Sunday afternoon walks on Whitney Avenue are manipulated, and how every precaution is taken to avoid being seen with "chumps," understands how undemocratic that life is. And this influence extends even long after graduation; for at all class gatherings society men unconsciously cohere.

Edmund Wilson wrote that at Yale

> the eccentric or non-competitive man who might be happy at Princeton or Harvard, is likely to be juggernauted by the machine and acquire little but an extreme bitterness. At Princeton, the energetic and earnest man, who would probably find grist for his mill at Yale, is in some danger of being debauched by triviality and idleness. . . . Harvard has a definite personality and stamps many of her students unmistakably. They are ironic like the Princetonians, but less provincial and boyish; they are sophisticated like the Yale men but less violent and less harsh.

It is this Yaleness, what Wilson calls the machine and what Phelps calls manipulation, that has endured as a characteristic unique to this New Haven campus. Yale graduate and scholar Thomas Bergin observed in 1982:

> At Cornell, casualness was the style; no one seemed to be in any hurry. At Yale, faculty and undergraduates alike are always in high gear, busy, competitive and zealous. The odd thing was that as much work seemed to get done in the one place as in the other. This led me to ponder the quintessence of Yalehood. The difference it seemed to me was that the old, puritanical imperatives of service, competition and awards still linger in New Haven.

Bergin remembered a conversation he had had with Bonesman Henry Luce (1920), whose attitude typified that of Skull and Bones. Luce asked Bergin what was the point of the underground secret societies that appeared on campus in the mid-twentieth century. "I replied," Bergin wrote, "that the undergraduates recognized the desirability of the intimate association offered by the traditional senior secret societies, but many felt that they were too blatantly 'prestigious.' Luce responded, 'What the hell is wrong with prestige?' His was, I think, the authentic voice of old Yale."

As Scroll and Key grew from Skull and Bones, Skull and Bones from Phi Beta Kappa, and even Princeton from Yale, and Yale from Harvard, each group of men broke off from a larger group because, accustomed to recognition and authority, they formed a smaller, exclusive group that would better serve those purposes. This fragmentation addresses a dissatisfaction with access to prestige: if the pool is too large, narrow it down and publicize the exclusivity of the newer, tiny pool. Brown University used a similar method to ascend in the public eye to the upper echelons of the Ivies during the 1980s. By rejecting applicants who would not be rejected at other elite institutions—those with 1600 SAT scores, for example—it successfully improved its image by suggesting that even those students wholly accustomed to recognition weren't necessarily good enough for Brown. Some of the wealthiest and most well connected individuals in the country operate on a similar policy by going on retreats with people of similar stature. In 1999, the *New Yorker*'s Ken Auletta described the annual five-day Sun Valley, Idaho, camp conducted by the investment firm Allen & Company. Among the "campers" were Paul Allen and Bill Gates of Microsoft, C. Michael Armstrong of AT&T, Jeffrey Berg of International Creative Management, Jeffrey Bezos of Amazon.com, Michael Bloomberg of Bloomberg L.P., Warren E. Buffett of Berkshire Hathaway, Stephen Case of America Online, Michael Dell of Dell Computer Corporation, Barry Diller of USA Networks, William T. Esrey of Sprint, Donald and Katharine Graham of the Washington Post Company, Andrew S. Grove of Intel, Christie Hefner of Playboy Enterprises, John S. Hendricks of Discovery Communications, Nobuyuki Idei of Sony, Steven Jobs of Apple Computer and Pixar Animation Studios, Robert L. Johnson of BET Holdings, Mel Karmazin of CBS, Jeffrey Katzenberg of Dreamworks SKG, Geraldine Laybourne of Oxygen Media, John C. Malone of the Liberty Media Group, Thomas Middelhoff of Bertelsmann AG, Jorma Ollila of Nokia, Sumner Redstone of Viacom, Oprah Winfrey of the Harpo Entertainment Group, Robert Wright of NBC, and Jerry Yang of Yahoo. Half the point was being invited, the other half gloating about who was not invited.

It is fitting that Skull and Bones' building is unmarked and relatively windowless. The tomb's obscure facade prevents clarity between inside and outside the society. The Bonesmen cannot see the outside world without first looking through the Bones-constructed prism; at the same time, the outside world cannot see into Bones headquarters—instead, barbarians can only project their own imagery onto the blank, brown walls of the tomb. Which they do. Often. At great length. The attention paid to Skull and Bones is cultlike, and it has grown exponentially in recent years because of the Bush dynasty and the expansion of the Internet, which has provided a most convenient medium through which to discuss and expound on conspiratorial ties. Skull and Bones is not a legend just to those who live it. To barbarians also, it is more than merely an institution; it is a concept onto which people project the images necessary for them to be able to make sense of the world. However sinister the notion of an all-powerful secret society might be, the existence of a Skull and Bones also brings us some measure of relief. The secret society allows us to believe that things don't just happen: genocide isn't just caused by one crazy individual, presidents aren't just assassinated, family political dynasties aren't just born. Even chaos, the society's conspiracy theories tell us, has causality. The secret society—like the power of the elitist, old-school colleges, the small groups of mogul networks, and the political dynasties—survives because people like to believe that seemingly random events are orchestrated by someone or something in control. "We've all done a good job of keeping the quintessential mystery alive," one patriarch said to me, "because people don't believe this is all we do." Perhaps one of the reasons people are so fascinated with conspiracy theories, particularly the far-reaching networks associated with secret societies and old-school power, is that they need causality in much the same way as they need a God. People's need for the Skull and Bones conspiracies to elucidate an underlying order is similar to the need for religion to explain death and purpose. Underground control suggests order and order implies reason. Explanations, however implausible, are somehow reassuring.

If the Wizard of Oz can represent Skull and Bones, then one must point out that, for a while, Oz *needed* its Wizard to provide balance and a constant current of reassurance. Likewise, the power of organizations such as Yale and its secret societies is similarly found in the facades in which people leap to believe. This is not to say that outsiders want or need a Skull and Bones, or that it belongs in twenty-first-century America. But it exists in part because we believe it is too powerful to tear down. It is hardly revelatory to note that the United States places appearance on a pedestal, or that this devotion expands progressively with technological advance. It is also worth mentioning that Oz was not without his power. He had used his smarts to his advantage, and if much of his strength came from a facade, that facade came from him. Connections are power. It means something to have access to the sort of network a member of Skull and Bones can tap or, for that matter, the networks shared by graduates—society members or not—from any of these elite schools. The 2000 presidential election, for example, featured three Yale men (two of them secret society members and one likely related to members) and a Harvard man. More than three hundred years after the founding of those schools, their continued prominence in a nation of fads and franchises speaks again both to the power of images and the imagery of power.

Lord Chesterfield wrote, "A proper secrecy is the only mystery of able men; mystery is the only secrecy of weak and cunning ones." The assertion that Skull and Bones both boasts a proper secrecy and skulks behind cunning mystery is not a matter of trying to have it both ways. Skull and Bones surely has its secrets. But these are the secrets of an organization that traffics in intangibles. The secrets of Skull and Bones are found in the Black Books that reveal the innermost thoughts of a Civil War soldier, the fiery debates about the differences between genders, and the reactions to college students who chronicle for a group of wide-eyed strangers their lifelong psychosexual histories. The secrets are found in the long essays of character critique that can bruise even the most well-honed ego. The secrets are found in the whispers between seniors in the garden concocting postgraduation plans. And the secrets are found in the correspondence between a president and a man he will appoint to a position of prominence solely because he knows that his hire has been privy to the secrets, too.

Whether the legend of Skull and Bones reflects a sinister veracity or a prismatic distortion depends almost entirely on one's desired perception. The great conspiracy surrounding the society is one of half-truths and our own willing complicity. And its secret, great and terrible, is that Skull and Bones, unreal, has mastered both.

ACKNOWLEDGMENTS

This book, frankly, was great fun to write. It might have been less so, if not for the following people's assistance. Most of all I thank my parents, siblings, and grandparents for their unwavering encouragement. My love and gratitude are too deep to express on a public page.

Thanks also to Ellie and Vicki for continually boosting my excitement about my writing, and for inspiring me regularly with their own. Furthermore, life would be boring—and not nearly as cheerful—without Dave, Amy, Nick, Rachel, Melanie, and Andrea.

Professionally and personally, I am tremendously grateful to Jane Mayer for her editorial guidance and for constantly brightening my day. Jeff Goldberg, Sy Hersh, Joe Klein, Nick Lemann, Elsa Walsh, and Kevin Buckley have also provided invaluable support, advice, and amusement. Thank you to Cullen Murphy, who edited my original article on Skull and Bones for the *Atlantic Monthly* and did a brilliant job of it. And thanks to David Remnick of the *New Yorker*, who enthusiastically sponsored my original research on this subject. I'm also grateful to Jeanie Pyun, who taught me more with her magazine edits than she realizes.

I would like to thank the staff of Yale University's Manuscripts and Archives Library for their indefatigable energy and willingness to help, particularly Renee Cawley, Nancy Lyon, Bill Massa, Judith Schiff, Sandra Staton, and Chris White. Thanks, as well, to Norman Eule and Andy Pike for their time and counsel.

I knew that working with Geoff Shandler would ensure that this book would be intelligent, but it was not until I saw the effects of his red pencil that I truly understood what a phenomenal editor he is. I cannot thank him enough. I also greatly appreciate the efforts of Dena Koklanaris and Elizabeth Nagle. Finally, Paula Balzer of Sarah Lazin Books, agent and friend, has been terrific in both roles.

BIBLIOGRAPHY OF SELECTED TEXT SOURCES

Abramson, Rudy. *Spanning the Century: The Life of W. Averell Harriman 1891–1986*. New York: Morrow, 1992.

Aiken, E. E. *The Secret Society System*. New Haven, Conn.: Tuttle, Morehouse & Taylor, 1882.

American Enterprise Institute for Public Policy Research. *A Conversation with George Bush (October 19, 1979)*. Washington, D.C., 1980.

Anderson, Dave. "Why Plato Is in This Hall of Fame." *New York Times*, June 28, 1999.

Andrews, John William. *History of the Founding of Wolf's Head*. Lancaster, Pa.: Lancaster Press, 1934.

Angell, James Rowland. "Address to the Graduating Class." *Yale Daily News*, July 6, 1934.

———. "Spiritual Progress in Government." *Yale Daily News*, July 5, 1935.

Aronson, Steven M. L. "Tex Rex: Journalist and Political Advisor John Reagen 'Tex' McCrary." *Town & Country*, August 1993.

Asbury, Edith Evans. "Taft Letter in Cache of 50 Tell of Early Struggles." *New York Times*, November 2, 1980.

"Ashe Praises Bush Plan." *Knoxville News-Sentinel*, February 28, 2001.

Associated Press. "Skull-Bones Club Finally Will Admit Women," *Los Angeles Times*, October 26, 1991.

Associated Press. "Winston Lord Is Named as Envoy," *New York Times*, July 23, 1985.

Auletta, Ken. "What I Did at Summer Camp." *New Yorker*, July 26, 1999.

Bagg, Lyman Hotchkiss. *Four Years at Yale (By a Graduate of '69)*. New Haven: Charles C. Chattfield, 1871.

Bailey, William S. "Minutes of the Fifty-Third General Meeting of The Elihu Club," November 20, 1920. Manuscript and Archives, Yale University.

Baker, David J. "A Serious Number: 30 Decades of Distinguished Graduates." *Yale Alumni Magazine: The University at 300,* March 2001.

Barilleaux, Ryan J., and Mary E. Stuckey, editors. *Leadership and the Bush Presidency: Prudence or Drift in an Era of Change?* Westport, Conn.: Praeger, 1992.

Benét, Stephen Vincent. "Poem Written for the Hundredth Anniversary of the Kingsley Trust Association." Read June 9, 1942.

Bergin, Thomas. "My Native Country." In *My Harvard, My Yale,* edited by Diana Dubois. New York: Random House, 1982.

Berzelius News Letter 3, no. 2 (April 1921).

Berzelius papers, 1923–1927. Manuscript and Archives, Yale University.

Blanton, Tom, ed. *White House E-mail: The Top Secret Computer Messages the Reagan/Bush White House Tried to Destroy.* New York: New Press, 1995.

"Bones of Contention: Gosh, Biff! Tarnation! A Move Toward Equality at Yale's Skull and Bones Puts Elite Ivy Alums in a Tizzy!" *People,* May 6, 1991.

"Briefs 0100315204." *Knoxville News-Sentinel,* April 6, 2001.

Brosnan, James W. "Bush Honors Fed Ex as Quality Pacesetter; Smith Has Eyes on Japan Prize." *Commercial Appeal,* December 14, 1990.

Buckley, William F. *Saving the Queen.* New York: Doubleday, 1976.

Buckley, William F., Jr., *God and Man at Yale.* Chicago: Regnery, 1951.

Bundy, McGeorge. "For the Defense." *Yale Literary Magazine,* February 1939.

Bush, Barbara. *Barbara Bush: A Memoir.* New York: Scribner, 1994.

Bush, George. *All the Best, George Bush: My Life in Letters and Other Writings.* New York: Scribner, 1999.

Bush, George, with Victor Gold. *Looking Forward: An Autobiography.* New York: Doubleday, 1987.

Bush, George W. *A Charge to Keep.* New York: Morrow, 1999.

"Bush: Underestimate Him at Your Own Risk?" *Hotline,* December 9, 1999.

Cannon, Carl M. "Faith of Our Fathers." *National Journal,* July 21, 2001.

Chernoff, Joel. "Standoff Ends; Ball Approval for DOL Post." *Pensions & Investment Age,* October 30, 1989.

Childs, Richard S. "The Elks in Our Midst." *Harkness Hoot*, April–May 1931.

Clayton, John. "Tony Lavelli: One in a Million." *Union Leader*, January 14, 1998.

Coffin, William Sloane, Jr. *Once to Every Man*. New York: Athenaeum, 1978.

"Commencement Address at Yale University in New Haven, Connecticut; George W. Bush; Transcript." Weekly Compilation of Presidential Documents. May 28, 2001.

Conconi, Chuck. "Personalities." *Washington Post*, March 1, 1991.

"The Constitution of the Elihu Club." June 1912. Manuscript and Archives, Yale University.

Cross, Wilbur L. *Connecticut Yankee: An Autobiography*. New Haven, Conn.: Yale University Press, 1943.

Crutsinger, Martin. "Former Ohio Congressman Named to Deficit Commission." Associated Press, December 20, 1988.

Davis, Lanny J., and G. Barry Golson. "Secret Societies." *Yale Banner*, 1968.

"Deer Island" brochure.

Deer Island Club. 1908. Manuscript and Archives, Yale University.

Devroy, Ann. "Recent Policy Shifts Follow Bush Pattern." *Chicago Sun-Times*, January 15, 1992.

Dexter, Franklin Bowditch. *Documentary History of Yale University 1701–1745*. New York: Arno Press & the *New York Times*, 1969.

"Digest of Other White House Announcements." *Public Papers of the Presidents*, January 30, 1989; August 10, 1990; August 31, 1990.

Dowd, Maureen. "Biography of a Candidate: Man in the News: Making and Remaking a Political Identity: George Herbert Walker Bush." *New York Times*, August 20, 1992.

———. "Liberties: The Age of Mars." *New York Times*, January 3, 2001.

Dries, Bill. "Bush Fund-Raiser to Host Ex-First Lady." *Commercial Appeal*, February 12, 2000.

Dubois, Diana, ed. *My Harvard, My Yale*. New York: Random House, 1982.

Duffy, Michael, and Dan Goodgame. *Marching in Place: The Status Quo Presidency of George Bush*. New York: Simon & Schuster, 1992.

Dunlap, David. "Yale Society Resists Peek into Its Crypt." *New York Times*, November 4, 1988.

Dwight, Timothy. *Memories of Yale Life and Men*. New York: Dodd, Mead, 1903.

"Editorials: Senior Societies." *Harkness Hoot,* May 1933.

"Education: The Steady Hand." *Time,* June 11, 1951.

"Endicott Peabody Davison, 73, A Former Fund-Raiser for Yale." *New York Times,* August 5, 1996.

English, Bella. " 'Skull' Club Has Rocks in Its Head." *Boston Globe,* April 22, 1991.

"Evan G. Galbraith Appointed as Representative to Europe." *FDCH Federal Department and Agency Documents,* September 7, 2001.

"Ex-Rep. Jonathan Bingham, 72, Dies." *New York Times,* July 4, 1986.

Fellman, Bruce. "Tercentennial Talent." *Yale Alumni Magazine,* Summer 2001.

Fitzgibbons, Ruth Miller. "George Bush, Too." *D Magazine,* April 1992.

Foer, Franklin. "Tomb of Their Own: What's Really Wrong with Skull and Bones." *New Republic,* April 17–24, 2000.

French, Robert Dudley. *The Memorial Quadrangle: A Book About Yale.* New Haven, Conn.: Yale University Press, 1929.

"Freshman Rules in 1764." *Yale Daily News,* October 19, 1934.

Fritz, Sara. "Bush Kin: Trading on the Name?" *Los Angeles Times,* May 10, 1992.

"George Bush: The Hot Property in Presidential Politics." *Washington Post,* January 27, 1980.

Gerstenzang, James, and Douglas Jehl. "In the End, Bush Was Out of Touch with Everyday America." *Los Angeles Times,* November 5, 1992.

Giamatti, A. Bartlett. *History of Scroll and Key 1942–1972.* Published by the society, 1978.

A Graduate of the Seventies. "Discussion of 'Tap Day.' Some History Recalled in Answer to the Leader in the June 'Lit.' " *Yale Alumni Weekly,* June 24, 1905.

Graubard, Steven. *Mr. Bush's War: Adventures in the Politics of Illusion.* New York: Hill and Wang, 1992.

Green, Fitzhugh. *George Bush: An Intimate Portrait.* New York: Hippocrene, 1989.

Grove, Lloyd, with Beth Berselli. "The Reliable Source." *Washington Post,* April 19, 2000.

Gruber, William. "On Business: Contract Exchange Weighed by Court." *Chicago Tribune,* July 19, 1995.

Harfield, Henry D. "A Freshman's Prayer on Thursday Night." *Harkness Hoot,* May 1934.

Hatfield, J. H. *Fortunate Son: George W. Bush and the Making of an American President.* New York: St. Martin's, 1999.

Havemeyer, Loomis. *Go to Your Room.* New Haven, Conn.: Yale University, 1960.

Hedges, Stephen J., and Brian Duffy. "Iraqgate." *U.S. News & World Report,* May 18, 1992.

Hodgson, Godfrey. *The Colonel: The Life and Wars of Henry Stimson, 1867–1950.* New York: Knopf, 1990.

Holahan, David. "The Bad News Bones." *Northeast Magazine,* May 29, 1988.

Houston, Paul. "Investigators Offer Political, Security Expertise." *Los Angeles Times,* November 27, 1986.

Howland, Henry E. "Undergraduate Life at Yale." *Scribner's,* July 1897.

Iconoclast. New Haven, Conn., October 13, 1873.

Isaacson, Walter. "My Heritage Is Part of Who I Am" (interview with George W. Bush). *Time,* August 7, 2000.

Isaacson, Walter, and Evan Thomas. *The Wise Men: Six Friends and the World They Made.* New York: Simon & Schuster, 1986.

Ivins, Molly, and Lou DuBose. *Shrub: The Short but Happy Political Life of George W. Bush.* New York: Random House, 2000.

Janofsky, Michael. "The Road Less Traveled to the Oval Office." *New York Times,* August 6, 2000.

Jennings, Peter, anchor, and Dan Harris, reporter. "Yale's Elite Secret Society: The Skull and Bones." ABC News *World News Tonight,* April 23, 2001.

"John Madden, 69, Banking Exec." *Newsday,* February 12, 1988.

Johnson, Owen. *Stover at Yale.* Edition prepared for the inauguration of the Yale Bookstore. New Haven, Conn.: Yale Bookstore, 1997. First edition, 1912.

"The Judges Who Could Hear Microsoft's Appeal." *Seattle Times,* June 8, 2000.

Kabaservice, Geoffrey. "The Birth of a New Institution." *Yale Alumni Magazine,* December 1999.

Keen, Judy. "Family, Friends, Staff Fill Bush's Overnight List." *USA Today*, May 17, 2001.

Kelley, Brooks Mather. *Yale: A History*. New Haven: Yale University Press, 1974.

Kellogg, H. L. *College Secret Societies: Their Customs, Character, and the Efforts for Their Suppression*. Chicago: Ezra A. Cook, 1874.

Kilian, Pamela. *Barbara Bush: A Biography*. New York: St. Martin's, 1992.

Knapp, Farwell. *Farwell Knapp Journal: Love Story of a Stoic Philosopher*. Unpublished manuscript, Beinecke Library, Yale University.

"Knoxville Mayor Ashe Named to Fannie Mae Board; First Mayor to Serve on Board." *U.S. Newswire*, July 18, 2001.

Kranish, Michael. "An American Dynasty." *Boston Globe*, April 23, 2001.

Lauter, David. "Rea's Tenacity Shows Why Some Government Programs Never Die." *Los Angeles Times*, October 1, 1989.

Lever, Janet, and Pepper Schwartz. *Women at Yale: Liberating a College Campus*. Indianapolis: Bobbs-Merrill, 1971.

Lewis, Paul. "Charles S. Whitehouse, 79, Diplomat and C.I.A. Official." *New York Times*, July 1, 2001.

Little Devil of D'121. *Continuation of the History of Our Order for the Century Celebration, 11, June 1933*.

"Local Lawyer Appointed to 2 D.C. posts." *Chicago Sun-Times*, November 27, 2001.

Luce, Henry. [Apology.] *Yale Daily News*, May 17, 1919.

Mack, Maynard. *A History of Scroll and Key*. Printed for the society, 1942.

Marrs, Jim. *Rule by Secrecy: The Hidden History That Connects the Trilateral Commission, the Freemasons, and the Great Pyramids*. New York: HarperCollins, 2000.

Martin, Douglas. "William P. Bundy, 83, Dies; Advised 3 Presidents on American Policy." *New York Times*, October 7, 2000.

Matalin, Mary, and James Carville. *All's Fair: Love, War, and Running for President*. New York: Random House, 1994.

Mayer, Jane. "School Ties: Can Yale Bring Back Bush?" *New Yorker*, April 23 & 30, 2001.

Mayer, Jane, and Alexandra Robbins. "Dept. of Aptitude: How George W. Made the Grade." *New Yorker*, November 8, 1999.

McAllister, Bill. "Bush's Recess Appointment Voided; Position on Postal

Service Board Was Not Vacant, Judge Rules." *Washington Post,* July 26, 1993.

———. "Justice Dept. Asks Delay in Ruling on Recess Appointee; Administration Wants Opportunity for Senate to Confirm Clinton's Choice for Postal Board." *Washington Post,* July 20, 1993.

———. "Recess Appointments: A Disputed Matter of Timing." *Washington Post,* July 19, 1993.

McFadden, Robert D. "Amory Bradford, 85." *New York Times,* September 6, 1998.

A Member. "Senior Societies and the Lord Jehovah." *Harkness Hoot,* May 1933.

"Memorial Mass for Diplomat." *Irish Times,* February 3, 1995.

Mendell, Clarence W. "Social System in the College." *Fifty Years of Yale News: A Symposium on Yale Development to Commemorate the Fiftieth Anniversary of the Founding of the Yale Daily News.* New Haven, Conn.: Yale Daily News, 1928.

Mervin, David. *George Bush and the Guardianship Presidency.* New York: St. Martin's, 1996.

Messud, Claire. "Bones of a Conspiracy." *Observer Life,* July 31, 1994.

Meyer, Peter. *The Yale Murder.* New York: Empire Books, 1982.

Minutaglio, Bill. *First Son: George W. Bush and the Bush Family Dynasty.* New York: Times Books, 1999.

"Minutes of the Fifty-Third General Meeting of the Elihu Club." New Haven, November 20, 1920.

Mitchell, Elizabeth. *W: Revenge of the Bush Dynasty.* New York: Hyperion, 2000.

Montgomery, Scott. "Taft Goes Door-to-Door for Bush Votes." *Dayton Daily News,* March 6, 2000.

Moore, Paul, Jr. "A Touch of Laughter." In *My Harvard, My Yale,* edited by Diana Dubois. New York: Random House, 1982.

Morison, Elting E. *Turmoil and Tradition: A Study of the Life and Times of Henry L. Stimson.* Boston: Houghton Mifflin, 1960.

Nettleton, George Henry. "On Realities." *Yale Literary Magazine,* February 1896.

Noah, Timothy. "Skull & Bones Initiation Rites Revealed!" *Slate,* April 18, 2001.

O'Connor, Rose Ellen. "Bush Names Gaddi Vasquez to U.S. Delegation Attending Inauguration in Uruguay." *Los Angeles Times,* February 24, 1990.

Oder, Norman. "Senior Societies: Changes Came Slowly Despite Some Criticism." *Yale Daily News,* April 13, 1982.

———. "Senior Societies: Coeducation Brought Change; Importance Now Downplayed." *Yale Daily News,* April 14, 1982.

———. "Senior Societies over the Years: A Long History of Influence at Yale." *Yale Daily News,* April 12, 1982.

Order of the File and Claw. *The Fall of Skull and Bones: Compiled from the Minutes of the 76th Regular Meeting of the Order of the File and Claw.* New Haven, Conn.: The Order, 1876.

Oren, Dan A. *Joining the Club: A History of Jews and Yale.* New Haven, Conn.: Yale University Press, 1985.

Oviatt, Edwin. *The Beginnings of Yale, 1701–1726.* New York: Arno Press & The New York Times, 1969.

Oviatt, Edwin S. "On Shams." *Yale Literary Magazine,* January 1896.

Parmet, Herbert S. *George Bush: The Life of a Lone Star Yankee.* New York: Scribner, 1997.

Payne, Charles. "Descent to the Tombs." *Harkness Hoot,* April–May 1931.

"Peculiar Institutions." *Elihu Bulletin,* June 1968.

People [George H. Pfau]. *Los Angeles Times,* January 8, 1991.

Phelps, William Lyon. "The Average Harvard Undergraduate." *Yale Courant,* June 10, 1893.

Pierson, George Wilson. *Yale College: An Educational History 1871–1921.* New Haven, Conn.: Yale University Press, 1952.

———. *Yale: The University College 1921–1937.* New Haven, Conn.: Yale University Press, 1955.

Podhoretz, John. *Hell of a Ride: Backstage at the White House Follies 1989–1993.* New York: Simon & Schuster, 1993.

Powelson, Richard. "Appointment to Fannie Mae Windfall for Ashe." *Knoxville News-Sentinel,* July 17, 2001.

———. "Baxter Enjoys Wide Support for TVA Slot; Chairmanship Selection Uncertain." *Knoxville News-Sentinel,* July 12, 2001.

"Quotable." *Roll Call,* September 8, 1994.

Radcliffe, Donnie. "Watchdog at the East Wing Gate: Susan Porter Rose, Guard of the First Lady's Realm." *Washington Post,* November 19, 1991.

———. "Welcome to the Bushes: The First Family's Friends Stay Overnight at the White House." *Saturday Evening Post,* November 1989.

Radcliffe, Donnie, and Roxanne Roberts. "Of Oil & Good Omens: At the White House, North Yemen and Texas Mingle." *Washington Post,* January 25, 1990.

———. "Vaclav Havel, Getting Down to Business: At the White House Dinner, Czechoslovak's Labor of Love." *Washington Post,* October 23, 1991.

Radcliffe, Donnie, and Jacqueline Trescott. "Panama and the President's Dinner; At Fete for Mexico's Salinas, Disappointment over Failed Coup." *Washington Post,* October 4, 1989.

The Record of the Celebration of the Two Hundredth Anniversary of the Founding of Yale College, Held at Yale University, in New Haven, Connecticut, October the Twentieth to October the Twenty-Third, A.D. Nineteen Hundred and One. New Haven, Conn.: Yale University, 1902.

Rehm, Barbara A., and Robert M. Garsson. "College Chum Snares Bush for Meeting." *American Banker,* September 10, 1990.

"Respice: A Look Back at Higher Education: Yale University History." *Matrix,* June 1, 2001.

Rhodes, Richard. "Shell Games." In *My Harvard, My Yale,* edited by Diana Dubois. New York: Random House, 1982.

Ridley, Matt. *Warts and All: The Men Who Would Be Bush.* New York: Viking, 1989.

"Rites Held for David Grimes, Omaha Native, Financial CEO," *Omaha World-Herald,* January 19, 1999.

Robbins, Alexandra. "George W., Knight of Eulogia." *Atlantic Monthly,* May 2000.

Roberts, Roxanne, and Laura Blumenfeld. "The Bushes' Spring Soiree: Keeping It Light at the Dinner for Germany's President." *Washington Post,* April 30, 1992.

Robinson, Lucius Franklin. "Air Jeremiah." 1843. In Beinecke Library, Yale University.

Romano, Lois, and George Lardner, Jr. "At Height of Vietnam, Graduate Picks Guard: With Deferment Over, Pilot Training Begins." *Washington Post,* July 28, 1999.

———. "Following His Father's Path—Step by Step by Step." *Washington Post,* July 27, 1999.

————. "The Life of George W. Bush: The Turning Point: After Coming Up Dry, Financial Rescues." *Washington Post,* July 30, 1999.

Rosebaum, Ron. "At Skull and Bones, Bush's Secret Club Initiates 'Ream' Gore." *New York Observer,* April 23, 2001.

————. "An Elegy for Mumbo Jumbo." *Esquire,* September, 1977.

Santayana, George. "A Glimpse of Yale." *Harvard Monthly,* December 1892.

Schiff, Judith Ann. "Wilbur L. Cross: From Scholar to Governor." *Yale Alumni Magazine,* April 2000.

"Senate Approves Appelate Nominee." *Washington Post,* June 27, 1985.

"Senate Confirms 30 Bush Nominees." *Bulletin's Frontrunner,* September 27, 2001.

"Senate Panel Approves 1st Judicial Picks." *Chicago Tribune,* July 20, 2001.

"Senior Society Elections Given to College Juniors." *Yale Daily News,* May 16, 1919.

Sheeline, William E. "Who Needs the Stock Exchange?" *Fortune,* November 19, 1990.

Sheler, Jeffrey L. "Yale's Most Famous Graduate." *U.S. News & World Report,* October 16, 1989.

"Short Takes." *Commercial Appeal,* October 1, 1992.

Singer, Mark. "La Cabeza de Villa." *New Yorker,* November 27, 1989.

"Skull and Spare Ribs." *Economist,* November 2, 1991.

Smith, Jean Edward. *George Bush's War.* New York: Holt, 1992.

Smyth, Nathan Ayer. "Junior Prize Oration: The Democratic Idea in College Life." *Yale Literary Magazine,* April 1896.

"The Society System of Yale College." *New Englander,* May 1884.

Specter, Michael. "Skull and Bones at Yale: First No Women, Now No Club." *Washington Post,* April 15, 1991.

Staples, Brent. "Wrestling with the Legacy of Slavery at Yale." *New York Times,* August 14, 2001.

Sterne, Laurence. *Tristram Shandy.* Edited by Howard Anderson. New York: Norton, 1980.

Stimson, Henry L., and McGeorge Bundy. *On Active Service in Peace and War.* New York: Harper & Brothers, 1948.

Stokes, Anson Phelps. *Memorials of Eminent Yale Men: A Bibliographical Study of Student Life and University Influences During the Eighteenth and Nineteenth Centuries*. Vol. 1, Religion and Letters. New Haven, Conn.: Yale University Press, 1914.

Stone, Peter H. "Ashley and the President: Ties That Bind." *Legal Times,* July 8, 1991.

Sutton, Antony. *America's Secret Establishment: An Introduction to the Order of Skull & Bones.* Billings, Mont.: Liberty House Press, 1986.

Swisher, Kara. "At Skull & Bones, Yalies with Dirty Faces: For the Secret Society, a Portrait Restoration Project." *Washington Post,* May 8, 1989.

Taft, William Howard. "Some Recollections of My Days at Yale." In *Fifty Years of Yale News: A Symposium of Yale Development to Commemorate the Fiftieth Anniversary of the Founding of the Yale Daily News.* New Haven, Conn.: Yale Daily News, 1928.

"Taft's Cousin Named Powell's Legal Advisor." *Columbus Dispatch,* February 17, 2001.

"Tampa Today." *St. Petersburg Times,* January 31, 1995.

Tapper, Jake. "Judging W's Heart." *Salon,* November 1, 2000.

Tarpley, Webster Griffin, and Anton Chaitkin. *George Bush: The Unauthorized Biography.* Washington, D.C.: Executive Intelligence Review, 1992.

Thomas, Evan. *The Very Best Men: Four Who Dared: The Early Years of the CIA.* New York: Touchstone, 1995.

Thorpe, Helen. "Go East, Young Man." *Texas Monthly,* June 1999.

Threadgill, Susan. "Who's Who." *Washington Monthly,* January/February 2000.

Tiefer, Charles. *The Semi-Sovereign Presidency: The Bush Administration's Strategy for Governing Without Congress.* Boulder, Colo.: Westview Press, 1994.

Tolchin, Martin. "Washington at Work: From Yale Days to Bank Lobbyist, a Friend and Adviser to the Bushes." *New York Times,* July 19, 1991.

"Transport Briefs." *Journal of Commerce,* December 15, 1995.

Travis, Neal. "A Blow to Our Defense." *Commercial Appeal,* January 2, 2001.

UPI News at a Glance, December 20, 1988.

Victor, Kirk, and Elisabeth Frater. "Justice Department Profiles." *National Journal,* June 23, 2001.

Wallis, James H. "The 'Lit.' Leader." *Yale Alumni Weekly,* June 24, 1905.

Warch, Richard. *School of the Prophets: Yale College, 1701–1740.* New Haven, Conn.: Yale University Press, 1973.

Welch, Lewis Sheldon, and Camp, Walter. *Yale, Her Campus, Class-rooms, and Athletics.* Boston: L. C. Page, 1899.

"Who's Been Blue." *Yale Alumni Magazine: The University at 300,* March 2001.

W.H.S. Catalogue. New Haven, Conn.: Yale University, 1926.

Wilson, Edmund. "Harvard, Princeton, and Yale." *Forum,* September 1923.

Winks, Robin W. *Cloak & Gown: Scholars in the Secret War, 1939–1961.* New York: Morrow, 1987.

Wisby, Gary. "Party Under the Pyramids." *Chicago Sun-Times,* August 8, 1999.

Witherspoon, Alexander. *The Club: Its First One Hundred and Twenty-Five Years.* New Haven: Van Dyck Printing Co., 1962 (printed for the members of the Club).

Wolcott, Holly J. "Signs Erected by Ventura Businessman Push Bush." *Los Angeles Times,* November 6, 2000.

"Women in the Crypt? Old Bonesmen Say No." *New York Times,* April 18, 1991.

Woodward, Bob. "To Bones Men, Bush Is a Solid 'Moderate.'" Series: "George Bush: Man and Politician." *Washington Post,* August 7, 1988.

Woodward, Bob, and Walter Pincus. "Bush Opened Up to Secret Yale Society: Turning Points in a Life Built on Alliances." Series: "George Bush: Man and Politician." *Washington Post,* August 7, 1988.

www.library.yale.edu/archives300/exhibits/building/part5/ResColl.htm

www.opensecrets.org

www.politicalgraveyard.com

www.yalealumnimagazine.com/issues/01_03/seal.html

Yale Banner. New Haven, Conn., November 3, 1842.

"Yale Group Remains All-Male—For Now." *Chicago Tribune,* September 8, 1991.

"Yale Plans to Fire Professor in Child Porn Case." *Hartford Courant,* March 19, 2001.

INDEX

"Abode of Bliss," 98
abuse of lowerclassmen, 25–28, 56
Acheson, David, 174, 188
Acheson, Dean, 61, 188
achievement orientation, 41–42, 44–45, 202–03
Adams Outdoor Advertising Agency, 180
Adams, Stephen, 180
Aerial Coast Patrol Unit No. 1, 108
Aiken, E. E., 196
alcohol, 65–66, 94, 130–31, 195, 196
Allen, Frederick, 166
Alpha Delta Phi, 58, 59, 84
Alpha Kappa, 57
Alpha Sigma Phi, 57
Anderson, Ned, 144–46
Andover, 48, 162, 175–76, 183
Angell, James Rowland, 41
"Annual Convention of the Order," 129–30, 139
Anti-Masons, 81
anti-Semitism, 142–43
Arbusto Energy, Inc., 179
armor, 86, 96

arms-reduction talks, 174
Ashcroft, John, 10
Ashe, Victor, 181, 182
Ashley, Thomas Ludlow, 134, 167, 168, 169–71, 172
Association of Bank Holding Companies, 169
Atlantic Monthly, 9, 103, 185
atomic bomb, 185–86
"Audits," 198
Aurelian, 72, 150
Austin, Roy, 177, 181
autobiographies, *see* Life Histories
Axe and Coffin, 201

"bad club," 152–53, 158
Baker, Howard, 171
Baldrige, Malcolm, 172
Baldwin, Simeon, 39
Ball, David George, 173
Bankers Trust, 125
banking deregulation bill, 169
Barnard, F. A. P., 37
Barnes, Tracy, 187
bathroom procedure, 116–17

Bay of Pigs invasion, 7, 187, 188
Beethoven Society, 37
Benét, Stephen Vincent, 74
Bergin, Thomas, 39, 203
Berzelius, 64–65, 71, 109
Beta Chi, 57
Bingham, Jonathan, 165
Birge, Robert, 177
Bissel, Richard, 187
blackballs, 57, 151
Black Books, 115, 122, 129, 134, 139, 141, 206
Blake, William, 88
"blood," 8, 98, 120
Blum, John, 123–24
Boaz, 126
bomb, *see* atomic bomb
Bones Bible, 122, 139
Bones whore, 5, 119
Boodle, 85, 90, 91, 132
boodleball, 132, 153
Book and Snake, 64–65, 71, 73, 74, 109
Boren, David, 124, 158
Brainerd, David, 22
branding, 57, 177
Brewster, Kingman Jr., 107, 189
Brodhead, Richard, 72
Brotherhood of Death, 3
Brothers in Unity, 36, 38, 80, 90
Brown Brothers, 166
Brown Brothers Harriman, 6, 166, 168
Brown, Thatcher, 166
Brown University, 203–04
B.S.C., 116
Buchanan, Pat, 10

Buckley, Christopher, 173
Buckley, James L., 168, 174
Buckley, William F., 41, 123, 127, 131–32, 157, 169, 180, 190
Bull and Stones, 62, 90
bulletin board, 86–87
Bully Club, 35, 148
Bundy, Harvey H., 183, 184, 190
Bundy, McGeorge, 53, 127, 131–32, 152, 184, 186, 187, 188, 190
Bundy, William, 127, 186, 187, 188, 189, 190
Bungalow, 96
Burial of Euclid, 15, 31–33
Burr, Aaron, 22
Bush, Barbara, 164
Bush, Barbara Pierce, 126, 173, 178, 179
Bush, George Herbert Walker, 13, 14, 89, 90, 115, 123, 124, 126, 132, 134, 145, 146, 147, 158, 161–62, 164, 166–75, 178, 179, 180, 181, 187
Bush, George W., 15, 18, 124, 126, 130–31, 142, 158, 161–62, 163, 175–82, 190, 192–93
Bush, Jeb, 10
Bush, Jonathan, 145, 152, 158, 164, 179
Bush, Neil, 168, 170
Bush-Overbey Oil Development, 168
Bush, Prescott, 126, 144–45, 162, 164, 166, 167, 168, 173, 188

Calcium Light Night, 59
calendar, 128–29
Calhoun, John C., 143
Calliope, 36, 90
Camp David, 171

Camp, Walter, 166
Camp, Walter Jr., 166
campaigns, 161–62
Caulkins, Jack, 171–72
Celotto, Donald, 157
Central Intelligence Agency, 6, 147, 161, 171, 187, 188
Chafee, John H., 168, 171
Chauncey, Henry, 74
cheating, 163–64
Cheney, Dick, 18
Cheney, Russell, 86
Chi Chi Jima, 167
Chi Delta Theta, 37–38
Christmas party, 138, 192
Clap, Thomas, 20, 22, 35, 93
Clark, R. Inslee Jr., 152, 176
Clark, William Judkins, 172
class rank, 23–24, 28–29, 33
Club, The, 39–40
Cochleaureati, 29, 58
code, 95
Coffin, Henry Sloane, 127
coffins, 56, 57, 115, 119, 156
Coffin, William Sloane Jr., 127, 187, 190
College Bully, 34–35, 148
Collegiate School of Connecticut, 19
Commissary, 128
community service, 141–42
Congregationalism, 19, 20
Connubial Bliss, 120, 134–35, 136, 151, 157, 159, 206
Cornell University, 203
Corporal Trim, 95, 128
Corwin, Robert Nelson, 142
costumes, 90, 117, 119

Council on Foreign Relations, 7, 186, 189
Court of Areopagus, 28
courtship, 72
courtyard, 98–99
Cowdry, Rex, 177
criticisms, 137–38, 197–98
crooking, 142, 143–49
Cross, John Walter, 86
Cross, Wilbur, 21
Crotonia, 35
Cuban missile crisis, 186
Cushing, Harvey, 39, 61

Dale, Edwin L. Jr., 173
"dandruff dance," 133
date rape, 7, 157
Davis, Lanny, 107, 111
Davison, Endicott Peabody, 145–46, 184
Davison, F. Trubee, 108, 187
Dead Week, 96
dean's office, 71–72
death imagery, 87, 88–89
debates, 133–34, 152
Deer Island, 5, 94–98, 141, 142, 178–79
Deer Island Club, 97, 98
degradation, 24
Delaney, John, 167
Delta Beta Xi, 57
Delta Kappa, 54
Delta Kappa Epsilon, 57, 58, 59
Demosthenes, 84, 86, 91
Department of the Interior, 173
Depew, Chauncey, 165
Depew, Ganson, 86

Desmos, 72
DeVane, William Clyde, 111
"Devil," 117, 120–21
DeWitt, Bill, 179
Dexter, Franklin, 51
Dickinson, Jonathan, 22
Diggers, *see* Spade and Grave
Distinguished Service Medals, 186
dome, 87, 91
Donaldson, Lufkin & Jenrette, 166
Donaldson, William H., 166, 174, 181
donations, 85, 95, 97–98, 139–40
donations, campaign, 180–81
Doodleburger challenge, 30
doorbell, 93
Dowd, Maureen, 10
Drain, Richard, 187
Draper, William H. III, 174–75, 179
Dresser Industries, 168
dropouts, 199
Dummer, Jeremiah, 19, 20
Dwight, Timothy, 21, 50–51, 83, 131, 139

eating clubs, 201
Economic Cooperation
    Administration, 186
Edwards, Jonathan, 22
elections, 80, 149–54, 157–58, 193
elections, presidential, 4, 18, 163, 206
Elihu Club, 72, 73, 74, 109
Ellis, Alexander Jr., 168
Ellis, Nancy, 168
"Establishment," 184, 188–89
Eta Phi, 57
Etra, Donald, 177
Eulogia, 4, 84–85, 92, 120, 132, 143

Evarts, Maxwell, 165
Evarts, Sherman, 183
Evarts, William Maxwell, 131, 199
Export-Import Bank, 174–75
expulsion, 22, 81

Farrar, John, 127
Farrar, Straus & Giroux, 7, 127
favoritism, faculty, 150–51, 163–64
Federal Express, 172
Federal National Mortgage
    Association, 182
Federal Reserve, 6
the Fence, 30–31, 57
finances, 5, 73–74, 85, 97, 139–42,
    198–99
financial aid, 64
fines, 80, 132–33, 194
Firefly Room, 119, 121–22
fireplaces, 90, 132
Fish, Stuyvesant, 165
Ford, Henry II, 65
Foster, Eleazar Kingsbury, 82
Freemasons, 80
freshman societies, 53, 54–57

Galbraith, Evan G., 181, 187
Gallico, Gregory, 177
Gamma Nu, 54
Gamma Tau, *see* Gin and Tonic
garden, 98–99, 194, 206
Gergen, David, 13
Germanic influence, 3, 82–83, 84
Geronimo, 7, 14, 144–46
GH Walker & Co. Investments, 168
Giamatti, A. Bartlett, 61
Gibbs, Josiah Willard, 39

Gill, Brendan, 127
Gilman, Daniel Coit, 83, 85
Gin and Tonic, 72
goblets, 91, 195
goddess, *see* Eulogia
Gog, 125–26
Gore, Al, 181
Gow, Robert H., 168, 179
Graham, Phil, 168
grandfather clock, 5, 91–92, 128, 156
grave robbing, 7, 144–45
gravestones, 88, 146–47
Great Awakening, 21–22
Great Conic Sections Rebellion, 80–81
Greenberg, Steve, 124
Grey Friars, *see* Wolf's Head
Grimes, David, 173
Griswold, A. Whitney, 176
guest register, 129, 132
"Guns," 73

Hadden, Briton, 127, 150
Hadley, Arthur, 48, 58, 142
Hale, Nathan, 36, 187
Hamlet, 61, 120
Hance, Kent, 161
Harkness, Edward, 42, 63
Harriman, Averell, 127, 150, 164–66, 184–85, 186, 187, 190
Harriman Brothers and Company, 166
Harriman, E. H., 165
Harriman, Pamela Churchill, 165
Harriman, Roland, 151, 164, 168
Harrison, George L., 184–85

Harvard, 17, 18, 19, 22, 23, 27, 42, 43, 123, 176, 201–02, 203, 206
Hasty Pudding Club, 201
hazing, 24–28
Hearing of Excuses, 132–33
Hé Boulé, 57
Heinz, John, 174
Hemphill, James T., 173
Hersey, John, 127
Hexahedron Club, 37
Hilles, Frederick W., 187
Hitler, Adolf, 5, 6, 83, 188
hoax, 103
Holden, Reuben, 127
Holmes, George, 187
homosexuality, 137
honor societies, 72, 150, *see* Phi Beta Kappa
Hoopes, Townsend, 188
Hoover, Herbert, 183
House Banking Committee, 170
Hussein, Saddam, 174

Illuminati, 3
image, 192–93, 198, 204–05
Inner Temple, 87, 91–92, 118–19, 133, 134
"intellectual snobbery," 162
intermarriage, 4
inter-society council, 74
Interview Presentation Outline, 113–14
Iraq, 174–75
island, *see* Deer Island

James, Ellery, 144–45, 166
Jenkins, Richard E., 174

Jennings, Peter, 102
JNB Exploration, 170
Johns Hopkins University, 85
Johnson, Owen, *see Stover at Yale*
Jones, Frederick, 60, 142
journalists and Skull and Bones, 7, 9,
    10, 123, 127, 150–51
J. P. Morgan, 6, 109
Junior Exhibition, 29
junior societies, 53, 58–60
Justice Department, 181

Kaiser, Robert, 72, 112–13
Kappa Psi, 57
Kappa Sigma Epsilon, 54
Kappa Sigma Theta, 57
Kennedy, John F., 186, 190
Kennedy, Robert, 178
Kerry, John, 85, 112–13, 158, 163
keys, 92–93
Kingsley, James L., 37
Klots, Allen, 183
Knapp, Farwell, 142–43, 154–55
knights in armor, 86
Kolar, Brit, 175
Ku Klux Klan, 143

Lambert, Paul, 173
Lampert, Edward S., 180
Lapham, Lewis, 125
Lasaga, Antonio, 16
Lavelli, Tony, 169
Laxalt, Paul, 170
Ledges, 96
legacies, 163, 164, 167, 175, 176–77
Levin, Richard, 18
libraries, 37, 90

Lieberman, Joseph, 18, 72
Life Histories, 135–36, 137–38, 157,
    167
Linonia, 35, 36, 38, 80, 85, 90
literary societies, *see* Linonia,
    Brothers in Unity, Calliope *and*
    Crotonia
Little Devil, 119, 121, 126, 133, 194
Long Devil, 126
Longworth, Nicholas, 201
Lord, Winston, 174, 175, 189
Louis XV, 92
Lovett, Robert A., 108, 150–51, 166,
    184, 186, 187, 188
Luce, Henry, 109–10, 127, 150, 203
Lufkin, Dan W., 166
Lycurgan Society, 37
lyrics, sacred anthem, 133

MacArthur, Douglas, 63
Mace and Chain, 73
machine gun, 87
MacLeish, Archibald, 118, 127, 129,
    132, 185, 188–89
MacVeagh, Franklin, 182
Madame de Pompadour, 92, 120, 133
mafia, 4, 8
Magog, 125
Malcolm Baldrige Quality Award, 172
Mallon, Neil, 126, 145, 168
Manuscript, 72, 74
masturbation, 5, 115
Mather, Cotton, 19
Mather, Increase, 19
Matthiessen, F. O., 126
McCallum, Robert D. Jr., 177, 181
McCloy, John J., 184

McCrary, Tex, 125, 132, 152
McCullough, David, 127
McNally, Edward, 173, 181
meals, 85, 95, 128–29, 130–31, 199
Mellon, Paul, 61
membership catalogues, 90, 139
Meyer, Eugene, 168
"Mirror Images," 198
misogyny, 7, 151–52, 157–58
Moore, Richard Anthony, 173
Moral Society, 37
Morgan Stanley Dean Witter, 6
Morton, Thurston, 63
Mory's, 48
Moscovici, Marina, 88, 89, 141, 151
Moseley, Thomas W., 172, 173
mummy, 87
murder, 8
muskets, 87

Nadeau, Leo, 167
Naked Party, 73
names, 125–27
National Economic Commission, 170–71
National Institute of Mental Health, 177
National Review, 169
NATO, 180, 182
Naval Aviation Unit, 108
Nazi influence, 5, 6
nepotism, 168
Newsweek, 7, 150
Newton, Isaac, 19
New World Order, 4
New York Federal Reserve Bank, 184
New York Times, 7, 8, 10, 109

Nicholson, Jim, 176
Northern Railway Company, 183
nudity, 5, 115

Office of Homeland Security, 181
Office of Management and Budget, 173
Office of the Vice President, 171
offices, 90
opium, 3
Outer Temple, 92, 134
Outlook, 96
Order of the File and Claw, 93–94
Owl and Padlock, 201

packing, 69–70
paintings, 86, 88, 89–90
Palmer, Arthur E., 184
Pancho Villa, 7, 146
Paris Peace Talks, 165
patriarchs, relationship with knights, 129–30, 131–32, 152–53, 155–56, 157–59, 189
Patterson, Robert P., 184
peanut bum, 55
Pfau, George H. Jr., 172–73
Phi Beta Kappa, 3, 37, 68, 80, 81–82, 90, 203
Philagorian Society, 38
Philencration Society, 37
Phi Theta Psi, 57
photographs, 86, 91, 92, 140, 144
pins, 6, 55, 62, 67–68, 90, 91, 107, 122, 199
pirates, 4, 67, 79
Playboy bunnies, 139
Podhoretz, John, 174

Pogue, John, 72
Pope, 119, 120, 121
Porcellian Club, 123, 164, 201
pornography, 16
Porter, Cole, 61
Postal Service Board of Governors, 171
Powell, Colin, 180
pressure to achieve, 89, 189–90
Price, Raymond, 173
Princeton, 22, 201–02, 203
Psi Upsilon, 58, 59
Pundits, 34
Putnam, H. Phelps, 155
puzzles, 93

"queering," 65–66

raids, 80, 82, 93–94
Rainwater, Richard, 180
rejection, 49, 58, 70, 104, 107
religion, 17, 19, 20–22, 63, 80, 84–85, 205
Republican National Committee, 169, 176
residential college system, 42–44, 71
retreats, 96
Ring and Candle, 73
Rockefeller family, 6
Rockefeller, Percy, 165
Roosevelt, Franklin D., 184, 201
Roosevelt, Theodore, 123, 165, 201
Root, Elihu, 183
Rose, Jonathan Chapman, 173
Rose, Susan Porter, 173
Rosenbaum, Ron, 7, 101–03
Rubin, Robert, 13
rules, 61, 67–68, 73, 123–25, 139

Russell and Company, 3
Russell Trust Association, 6, 85, 87, 97, 128, 129, 140, 142, 158
Russell, William H., 3, 39, 82, 87, 133, 189

sacred anthems, see songs
St. Anthony Hall, 72
St. Elmo, 72
Saleh, Muhammed, 177
sand, 17–18
sandglass, 91, 134
Santayana, George, 16–17, 193
Saturday Morning Club, 40
Saybrook Platform, 20
S.B.T., 87, 128, 194
Schollander, Don, 126, 177
scrapbooks, 122, 139, 141
Scroll and Key, 38, 45, 53, 60–61, 62, 65–67, 69, 73, 74, 107–09, 141–42, 187, 188, 203
S.E.C., 90, 118, 128, 132, 134
Second Society of Stewards, 201
Securities Investor Protection Corporation, 172
servants, 85, 95, 130, 131, 199
sex, 125–26, see sexual histories
sexual histories, 4, 134, 135, 157, 159, 206
Seymour, Charles, 127, 147
shakers, 116, 119
Sheffield Scientific School, 64–65, 71, 72
Sigma Delta, 54
Silliman, Benjamin, 64, 118
Silverado Savings & Loan, 170
Simmons, Wallace, 164
The Simpsons, 8

Sizer, Theodore, 43
skeletons, 56, 86, 87–88, 92, 119, 143
Skull and Serpent, 201
The Skulls, 8, 72, 94
slavery, 7
Smith, Frederick W., 172, 180, 181
Smith, Gaddis, 147–48
Smyth, Nathan, 66–67
songs, 57–58, 62, 67, 90, 95, 133, 134, 138–39
sophomore societies, 53, 57–58
Spade and Grave, 61, 90
speakers, 131–32
Sphinx, 201
Spock, Benjamin, 61
Stagg, Amos Alonzo, 126
Star and Dart, 61
Steele, Richard, 19
Stewart, Donald Ogden, 127
Stewart, Potter, 127, 171
Stiles, Ezra, 92
Stimson, Henry, 151, 182–86, 188, 193
Stokes, Anson Phelps, 74, 127
Stone, Oliver, 13
Stonecutters, 8–9
Stone House, 95, 96
Stover at Yale, 44, 52, 104–06, 125
Stratford of Texas, 179
subordination, class, 24–28
sulfur, 116–17
Sword and Gate, 73
swords, 31, 92, 117

Taft, Alphonso, 3, 82, 182
Taft, Dudley S., 179, 180
Taft, Robert, 126
Taft, William Howard, 3, 8, 9, 39, 90, 95, 126, 182, 183, 190

Taft, William Howard IV, 180
Talbott, Strobe, 72
Tang Cup, 13
Tap Day, 68–72, 104–07, 110–11, 187
tattoo, 177
Texas Rangers, 179–80, 181
Thacher, Thomas, 47, 63
Thacher, Thomas D., 183
thefts, *see* crooking
Thorne, David, 85
"thousand male leaders," 189
threats, 9, 156
"322," 3, 7, 84–85, 90, 91, 95, 123, 165, 180–81, 194
Time, 7, 150
Time Inc., 109, 127, 173
Timex Corporation, 177
tobacco, 30, 90
tokens, 149–50
Torch, 72, 150
Tower, John, 169
towers, 98, 110, 111
traditionalism, 23, 27, 30, 33–34, 40, 42, 44–45, 124–25
treasurer, *see* Commissary
Tribunal Panel, 16
Trilateral Commission, 7
Trillin, Calvin, 61
Tristram Shandy, 21, 86, 128
Trudeau, Garry, 13, 61
Truman, Harry S., 186
Turner, Mel, 161

Uncle Toby, 21, 93, 113, 116, 117, 118, 120, 121, 127–28, 132, 134, 138–39
underground societies, 72–73, 98, 203
underground tunnels, 14, 45

Union Banking Corporation, 188
U.S. Court of Appeals, 174

valedictorians, 3, 28, 33, 150
vandalism, 62
Van de Velde, James, 16
Vassar, 73, 123
vault, 92
Vincent, Fay, 124, 162, 181
violence, 26–27, 56, 62

W. A. Harriman & Company, 164, 165–66
Waite, Morrison R., 89
Walker, George Herbert, 164
Walker, George Herbert II, 164, 168
Walker, George Herbert III, 164
Walker, John, 164
Walker, Ray, 164, 179
Walker, Samuel Jr., 172, 187
wars:
    Civil War, 87, 134
    Vietnam War, 71, 165, 173, 178, 188–89
    World War I, 87, 108–09
    World War II, 87, 164, 166–67, 185
Washington Post, 72, 168
wealth, 4, 65
wedding ceremony, 154–57
Weisberg, Jacob, 112–13
Whiffenpoofs, 34, 187
White, Mabel, 183
White, William Gardner, 167

White House, 10, 171, 173–74, 181, 190
Whitehouse, Charles S., 174, 187
Whitney, Harry Payne, 187
Whitney, William X., 183
Wier, J. Alden, 86
Wilhelm, Kaiser, 201
Williams, Anthony, 72
Wirt, William, 81
Witter, Dean Jr., 127
Wolfe, Tom, 13
Wolf's Head, 38, 42, 60, 63, 67, 68, 69, 73, 74, 108–09, 149
women in Skull and Bones, 7, 73, 132, 134, 137, 151–59
Wooden Spoon, 29
Woodward, Bob, 65, 169, 172
Woolley, Knight, 166
Woolsey, Theodore Dwight, 37, 39, 99
World Bank, 186
Wrexham, Wales, 15, 20, 146–47
Wright, Henry Parks, 51

Yale admissions, 71, 175–76, 195
Yale Corporation, 42, 64
Yale, Elihu, 15, 19–20, 119, 121, 146–47
Yale Spirit, 16–18
Yarborough, Ralph, 169
Yorick, 120, 121

Zapata Oil, 168
Zeta Psi, 58, 59
Zorthian, Barry, 173